Jhumpa Lahiri: The Master Storyteller

A Critical Response to *Interpreter of Maladies*

Jhumpa Lahiri: The Master Storyteller

A Critical Response to *Interpreter of Maladies*

edited by

SUMAN BALA

K P H

Khosla Publishing House

Published by
Khosla Publishing House
New Delhi 110 002

in association with
Prestige Books International
New Delhi 110 060
email: prestigebooks@gmail.com

ISBN: 81-7551-125-7

Printed in India

Contents

Jhumpa Lahiri: The Master Storyteller

SUMAN BALA

The present essay is intended to highlight the contribution of the short story to literature and the position of Jhumpa Lahiri as a storyteller. Although the short prose narratives may be traced to ancient times, the short story as a distinct literary genre has existed for about two centuries now. American writer Edgar Allan Poe may be considered the father of the modern short story as it is he who evolved and formulated the technique of short story in English language. He strongly believed that literature is not a spontaneous overflow of emotions, but a deliberate and designed effort. He greatly stressed on the need of a total effect on the production of a short story, something that is possible through compression, immediacy, verisimilitude and authenticity of experience.

Indians have been using English for literary expression in prose for about 200 years. The earliest prose writing in the language by an Indian is C.V. Boriah's twenty-eight page tract "Account of the Jains" (1809). The short story however came to be written much later. But within a short period, it became a highly popular form of literature. Much before the publication of the novel as an art-form in the literary realm, it has been the staple of literary taste of the readers and has been the chief source of their entertainment. Literary periodicals, women's magazines, journals and numerous dailies thrive on the publication of eagerly sought-after stories. The readers' imagination and curiosity are easily fed by these, especially if they are detective stories, or tales of fear and wonder, or thrill and suspense.

Short story has evolved itself in a fine art in the modern times. As a broad generalisation, one may argue that story in the last few decades has moved from the individual to the social, from relatively simple narrative point of view to a more complex, and more significantly from the obvious to the subtle. On the basis of this, one can make a few tentative formulations and highlight the notable contributions of some of the contemporary short story writers.

One of the most prolific Indian English short story writers is Manjeri Isvaran who wrote as many as nine short story collections, beginning with *Naked Shingles* (1941). For two decades, the 1940s and 1950s, he immensely enriched the corpus of Indian literature by writing stories on varied subjects. Isvaran's own comments on the role of the short story writer and the nature of short story emphasize the preoccupations with the revelation of his mind and heart. In his preface to *A Madras Admiral*, he declares:

> The Storyteller cannot absolve himself of the role of the seer—'one who sees truth and inner harmony on which things are strung together.' He sees the short story writing winning the world—with a marvel of his intelligent heart, seeing other hearts write with sympathy, shared wonder and the joy of beauty.

Isvaran was born in a family which was deeply steeped in Hindu rituals and myths. No wonder he makes an abundant use of Hindu mythology in his stories. All his writings, poems and stories, are rich with philosophical insights. Apart from religion, most of his stories, about seventy in number, deal with domestic life and social relations. His stories, like Chaucer's *The Canterbury Tales*, project a picture-gallery of social and religious life of the times.

In the recent decades, a number of writers, including Mulk Raj Anand, R.K. Narayan, Raja Rao, Khushwant Singh, Ruskin Bond, Manoj Das and a host of other writers have used the short story as a vehicle of expression. It is however the women writers who score over their male counterparts in this regard. It is universally admitted that story-telling comes naturally to women. In almost all the languages, women novelists have taken a foremost position in the art of narrative. There is thus a spurt in the output of stories produced by women writers. Special stress is being laid on feminist literature. It is increasingly being believed that women are super storytellers as is evident from the stories written by Anita Desai, Kamala Markandaya, Ruth Jhabvala and Nayantara Sahgal. A major theme in the stories written by these writers and especially by Shashi Deshpande is man-woman relationship. The family in India and elsewhere in the world has been under a process of social change. There is a conspicuous change in the spheres of roles and values. From the sociological point of view, the role of husband-wife is the principal component in a family context and that has undergone a vital change due to growing enlightenment and the movement for emancipation of women. In this regard, literature has played a sterling role in raising the readers' consciousness. In her stories, Shashi Deshpande delineates the position of women, especially educated middle-class women, in Indian society.

Jhumpa Lahiri who took the literary world by storm by publication of her short story collection *Interpreter of Maladies* won her the Pulitzer Prize for Fiction 2000. As the blurb says: "Lahiri's elegant stories tell the lives of Indians in exile, of people navigating between the strict traditions they have inherited and the baffling New World they must encounter everyday." Indeed her range is very wide, in terms of peoples and lands. In this sense, she may be considered an international writer. She was born in London of Bengali parents and grew up in Rhode Island, U.S.A. Since she has an Indian origin and many of her stories have a typical Indian flavour, she may be considered an expatriate Indian writer. In this respect, she stands in the same category as that of V.S. Naipaul, whom Bharati Mukherjee calls an Indian expatriate writer.

It will be desirable to compare Jhumpa Lahiri with other Indian expatriate writers to judge her position as a writer of fiction. There are quite a few women short story tellers of Indian origin who have excelled in the art of story telling and in creating an aroma of Indian setting and environment. For instance, Bharati Mukherjee, an Indian-American writer, Uma Parameswaran, an Indian-Canadian writer, and Mena Abdullah, an Indian-Australian writer, are notable writers of Indian Diaspora.

Bharati Mukherjee, now settled in the USA, is a significant woman novelist and short story writer. Born in 1940, she went to the U.S.A. in 1961. Her popularity shot up when *The Middleman and Other Stories* bagged the 1998 National Book Critics Award in America. This collection seeks to dramatize the immigration experience in America. It consists of eleven short stories and depicts the problems of emigrating to America and the dream of a new life which tempts them to go there. The characters hail from the different countries of the world—India, Pakistan, China, Sri Lanka, Hungary and Afghanistan. What connects most of these characters in the stories is merely sex, which proves to be an ephemeral bond. In this work, Mukherjee is straightforward and the stories have great passion and energy. In many of these, she writes from a very authoritative third-person point of view and in some others, she adopts first-person point of view. The style of writing is in conformity with the themes and atmosphere in the stories.

Uma Parameswaran, an established academic and creative writer, is Professor of English at the University of Winnipeg. Her writing career spans three decades. Her early work appeared in newspapers in India, and she received her M.A. in Creative Writing from Indiana University with a thesis consisting of four short stories. Subsequently she published, in 1967, a story "The Door I Shut behind Me," which won her a literary prize. This indeed is an interesting story. The protagonist of the story is one Mr. Chander. He is an Indian from Madras who, having acquired his higher education, decides to go to the U.S.A. for 'greener pastures'. He meets a number of Indians during his journey and those settled in the U.S.A. and is amazed at their behaviour and way of life. He finds some of them highly nostalgic about India and Indian way of life. Some of them talk very highly of Indian culture and society. As one Mr. Behl says, "When we leave our country we shut many doors behind ourselves though we are not aware of it at the time." To this remark, Chander makes a cryptic reply, "There are many doors ahead of us." The author seeks to convey the message that there is both loss and gain in the act of migration. While renouncing one culture, we may regret its loss to us, but at the same time we are likely to gain something new in the country of our adoption and we may look forward to a bright future, without having any regret.

Yet another woman story writer who has made a mark as an immigrant writer is Indian-Australian writer, Mena Abdullah. Her short story collection *The Time of the Peacock* was published as a single volume in Australia by the renowned publishing house, Angus and Robertson in 1965. It became extremely popular and was reprinted in 1973, 1974 and 1989. The volume was well received in literary circles, both in Britain and Australia. Favourable reviews appeared in the *Times Literary Supplement* in Britain and the *Western Australian Review* in Australia. The Australians congratulated Abdullah on her sensitive depiction of a beautiful world in Australia and culturally-rich canvas of India.

Mena Abdullah comes from a Punjabi family. Her parental family migrated to Australia from Punjab in the nineteenth century. Her father arrived in Australia in the 1880s when he was only 15 years old. He spent his early days as a hawker and later on as a farmer. Mena was born in 1930. Her early days were spent in her father's farm, as a rather lonely child. These early experiences have a great bearing on the writings of Mena Abdullah.

The story "The Time of the Peacock" is truly representative of the two worlds of the writer—India and Australia. The story tells us about the childhood days of Nimmi when she, along with her sister Rashida and brother Lal, enjoyed the open fields of New England. It was a time when she was under the influence of her Hindu mother who used to tell her about the teachings of Lord Krishna and how Krishna could move even the hills.

Another important story in the volume is entitled "The Babu from Bengal", which is truly multicultural in character. As is obvious from the title, the central character in the story is a Babu from Bengal, now settled in Australia. His description by the author is interesting: "He is a Babu, a Hindu, can read and write, a clerk, a half-educated man." The Babu has a special relationship with the narrator who is a Hindu woman married to a Muslim in Australia. Very often, he nostalgically talks to her about the rich festivals of India like Diwali and Holi. Mena Abdullah is thus able to juxtapose the two societies—Indian and Australian—in her stories. But she does not take sides. She depicts human life and human condition that has a universal appeal.

Jhumpa Lahiri, like Bharati Mukherjee, Uma Parameswaran and Mena Abdullah, may be regarded as a significant short story writer of Indian Diaspora who has enriched the corpus of international writing in English. *Interpreter of Maladies*, a collection of short stories is her first creative work. It has received tremendous response and made a mark on the contemporary literary scene. The first edition of her book, published by HarperCollins, was sold out in a record time. It has received unqualified praise from readers and critics. According to *The New Yorker,* Jhumpa Lahiri is one of the best twenty young writers in America today. Her work exemplifies the role that Diaspora plays in shaping an artist's imagination. Her anthology has an interesting subtitle "Stories from Bengal, Boston and Beyond." Her range is really wide. Spanning three continents, moving effortlessly from Boston to London, to Calcutta, and even Dhaka, her stories tell us about the lives of Indian immigrants, of people navigating between the strict traditions they have inherited and the baffling New World they encounter everyday.

Here I take up for detailed discussion the titular story in the collection entitled "Interpreter of Maladies" which is the most representative and establishes Jhumpa Lahiri as an adept and master storyteller. The opening scene is very significant as it throws light on the main theme of the story: man-woman relationship. We are introduced to Mr. and Mrs. Das who are hotly arguing as to who would take Tina, their daughter, to the toilet. It is typical of western culture where husband and wife are equal partners and both are supposed to take care of the children. Very often, it leads to bickering about their respect duties, as in the case of Mr. and Mrs. Das.

The story is about the visit of an Indian-American family—Mr. and Mrs. Das—along with their three children—daughter Tina and sons Ronny and Bobby. They are in Orissa, visiting

Sun temple at Konark. The family is being escorted by the tourist guide, one Mr. Kapasi. The author gives a graphic picture of the touring family. Mr. Das, about thirty years of age, was dressed in shorts, sneakers and a T-shirt. The camera slung around his neck, with an impressive telephoto lens and numerous buttons. Similarly there are lively descriptions of Mrs. Das and the children.

They are all set to reach Sun temple which is eighteen miles north of Puri. As their car speeds to the destination, the children are excited as they see monkeys on both sides of the road. The car they were travelling in was not in good condition and they felt uncomfortable. Mrs. Das complained to her husband, "Isn't this an air-conditioned car?" Mr. Das however does not pay any heed to it. Soon afterwards, Kapasi stops the car as Mr. Das takes a picture of a barefoot man, his head wrapped in a dirty turban, seated on the top of a cart of grain. Mrs. Das meanwhile takes much interest in Mr. Kapasi's profession as an interpreter that he feels quite flattered.

Kapasi had been a devoted scholar of foreign languages and the owner of an impressive collection of dictionaries. He had dreamed of being an interpreter for diplomats and dignitaries, resolving conflicts between people and nations, settling disputes of which he alone could understand both sides. He had started working as an interpreter, in addition to his teaching job, in order to pay the increased medical bills of his family. Mr. Kapasi started reflecting at the situation. He started realising that Mr. and Mrs. Das were a bad match for each other, as were he and his wife.

Mrs. Kapasi is pleased that the Das family likes the temple. He feels tempted at the bare legs of Mrs. Das and wonders if she would propose to him. He looks forward to a happy married life with her in the years to come. In the course of discussions, Mrs. Das tells the secret that Bobby is not the son of Mr. Das as once during his absence she had sexual relations with a Punjabi visitor, a friend of Mr. Das. She is puzzled whether she should tell this to her husband or not. She has kept the secret for such a long time and now she seeks Mr. Kapasi's advice, some kind of a remedy.

At the end of the story, Mrs. Das is at the crossroads. Though she has made a confession, Albatross is still hanging around her neck. The author leaves the ending open to the readers' imagination. Would she share the secret with her husband? If yes, how would the husband respond? Would they stay together or go for a separation? The story is essentially based on marital discord, but the protagonist is an emancipated woman and is free to make a choice and shape her fortune. The entire story is revealed step by step and the reader holds his breath as the facts are unfolded to him. Jhumpa Lahiri lends fine touches to the details so as to keep the verisimilitude intact. The reader is so absorbed with the characters and the conversations that he just cannot withdraw from the fictional world of Jhumpa Lahiri.

Of Defining and Re-Defining the Asian-American Diaspora: A Case Study of Jhumpa Lahiri

SOMDATTA MANDAL

> We are no longer the America that I read about as a child, or that I saw in MGM musicals when I was in Calcutta.
>
> Bharati Mukherjee

Definition

Defined in the simplest terms, Asian American literature is written by persons of Asian descent in the United States, not necessarily citizens. While some writers are new arrivals, others have been residents for many years and sometimes their forbears for generations. Some have journeyed to the United States via Africa or the indentured laboring class from the West Indies. Today, new forms of colonization dictated by the geo-political and geo-economic realities of a capitalist "new world order" continue to necessitate migrations and relocations from South Asia into North America. Similarities of situations from the post-colonial trope abound in such Asian American writers—the "trishanku" image of being suspended between two worlds and belonging to none; the insider-outsider or "desh-pardesh" syndrome; the role of memory, nostalgia and assimilation in their works are often discovered with striking similarities. Moreover, Americans do not now talk of assimilation, the end product of the melting-pot process, but of multiculturalism.

This paper evaluates such a situation found in the writings of Asian American writers of Indian descent, with special reference to Jhumpa Lahiri, not only because the editor of *The New Yorker* had earlier proclaimed her to be one of the twenty most promising talents under forty in the American literary scene; nor because she is the first writer of Indian origin who is a recipient of the coveted Pulitzer award; but also because through her stories in *Interpreter of Maladies*, aptly subtitled "Stories from Bengal, Boston and Beyond," she manages to "erase nations" so to say and address nuances of outsideness. As a writer of uncommon elegance and poise and a wonderfully distinctive new voice, she chronicles dislocation and social unease in a fresh manner as did her predecessors like Bharati Mukherjee or Chitra Banerjee Divakaruni. Readers of contemporary Asian American and postcolonial fiction are, by now, so thoroughly conversant with the themes of migration, homelessness, exile, loss of identity, rootlessness, and final assimilation, that Lahiri's stories—dealing with the trials and tribulations of displaced people struggling to make sense in an unfamiliar world—initially seem to tread on a well traversed terrain. A closer look however reveals that even when she is immersed in the petty details of the disappointments and disenchantments of immigrant lives, she never lets her writing get bogged down by the morass of lost marriages and frustrated lives she is documenting. Her tone remains lucid and clear, shot through with a keen sense of humour.

Themes and Technique

All the nine stories in *Interpreter of Maladies*, set in America and India, are united by the motifs of exclusion, loneliness and the search for fulfillment. They do not restrict themselves only to the experiences of migrant and displaced individuals. Themes that interest Lahiri—love, fidelity, tradition, and alienation—crop up in the lives of Indians and non-Indians alike. Communicating the fact that exile and exclusion are not the privilege of any one group of society alone, Lahiri portrays the specific situations of individuals as symptomatic of the ubiquity of loneliness and alienation. The common theme is an inability to communicate. But this happens for many reasons—the dynamics of a relationship, cultural differences, immigration and adjustment—and sometimes these disjointed interactions change during the course of the story. She chronicles the attempts of married couples, adulterous lovers and immigrants to cross borders and, as E.M. Forster wrote, "only connect." The condition of exile and loneliness—which in "The Third and Final Continent" is expressed through an individual who ruminates on the distances he has travelled, both literally and metaphorically—is probably the "beyond" that connects Bengal and Boston. In story after story, Lahiri successfully achieves the same effect: of people hoping and searching for that elusive bit of magic in the lives they seem to lead almost despite themselves. What makes all the stories work is the fact that, irrespective of whether the protagonists fail or succeed in this quest, their experiences are never portrayed simplistically. We are offered no assurance that their lives would have been any more meaningful had they acted differently. While some of the characters are directly drawn from real life (cf. Bibi Haldar, a woman who lived in the same building as her aunt and uncle and with whom she "struck a friendship, not terribly deep and abiding, but a friendship nonetheless": Mrs. Sen based on her own mother who baby-sat in their home—"I saw her one way but imagined that an American child may see her differently, reacting with curiosity, fascination or fear to the things I took for granted") Lahiri emphatically states that most of her characters are "semi-real—most are composites—though the situations are invented." Though most of Lahiri's Indian characters are Bengalis, yet their situations are universal.

Unlike many (most?) authors, Jhumpa Lahiri writes in the voices of both genders. Moreover, the stories are narrated in a polyphony of voices. Whether it is the omniscient narrator of "A Temporary Matter" or "Sexy," the first person narrator (interestingly, we never find out who she is) of "The Treatment of Bibi Haldar" or the ten-year-old child's perspective in "When Mr. Pirzada Came to Dine," the eleven-year-old Eliot's observation of Mrs. Sen—the voice seems ideally chosen. To Arun Aguiar Jhumpa admits that the narrator in "Bibi Haldar" is "not anybody in particular. It's a group of women, so there's no particular identity to the narrative voice. A Faulkner story ["A Rose for Emily"] I admired used that voice and I wanted to try it out. That's why I wrote the story the way I did. It was an experiment for myself." In another story, "This Blessed House," the omniscient narrator captures meticulously how a young man reacts with faint disgust and dislike to his new wife's unsuspected fascination with kitsch Christian artifacts.

What makes the collection truly outstanding is Lahiri's understanding of her subject as well as of the craft of writing itself. The stories are narrated in a style that combines economy of expression with a charming lyricism, and one that conveys the complexities of situations and characters as much by the implied as by the stated. Sparing in words, yet extremely eloquent, she weaves visual images for the reader in a startlingly realistic manner. One important reason for the appeal of Lahiri's stories is of course the freshness of her language. Sometimes she plays around with words—for instance, the crux of the title story hinges on the ideas of what "interpreter" means. Mrs. Das, desperate for advice, confides in Mr. Kapasi, hoping that as an "interpreter of maladies," he will offer an explanation for her unhappiness. Mr. Kapasi, unaccustomed to such a request, is at a loss as to how he should "interpret" her secret. Finally, he asks a single question, "to get to the heart of the matter," and the truth unfolds from there. Further, an ear for dialogue, a feel for unusual metaphors and an astute descriptive ability imbue Lahiri's prose with a rare power and grace. The endings of her stories are so pregnant with possibilities—the true hallmark of the genre.

Her Own Point of View

In an interview given to Nicholas A Basbanes in 1997, Bharati Mukherjee defined her status as a writer thus: "I have chosen and achieved the right to be an American, and the concept of "America" is what fuels all of my writing. That is what makes me an American writer." Interestingly, she also included her Indian heritage while describing her niche in contemporary American literature: "I maintain that I am an American writer of Indian origin, not because I'm ashamed of my past, not because I'm betraying or distorting my past, but because my whole adult life has been lived here, and I write about the people who are immigrants going through the process of making a home here. . . . I write in the tradition of immigration experience rather than nostalgia and expatriation."

Chitra Banerjee Divakaruni is happy and impressed that "there is an outburst, and all of a sudden there are many Indian American writers saying in loud print what we have been wanting to say for a long time." Speaking about women who read books with multicultural themes, she states:

> We cannot ignore the crucial part played by the growing number of immigrants who read our books because they understand their own communities better since we write from a perspective that is not available to a writer who has lived in India or China for the most part. . . . But a growing number of American women—who are curious about the foreigners living in their middle—want to read their stories too. . . . Many of us articulate in our books the deepest fear and trauma faced by women in India and here—and show them emerge, at least in many cases, as stronger and self-reliant women. Some of our characters are good role models for women readers and women activists.

Echoing Divakaruni's thought, Marina Budhos adds that women writers of the diaspora "tell stories from a perspective that is fully explored. There is a kind of hunger for these stories." Like some African American writers like Toni Morrison, some writers of the diaspora tell their own stories and those in the larger ethnic community in a starkly different way from that of an American writer. Anjana Appachana is happy that apart from Indians living in America the mainstream readers have also appreciated her novel *Listening Now*, but she thought she is realistic about the appeal of books like hers stating: "I did not write a magic realism novel or a book about exotic women . . . nor did I write a book about poverty and destitution in India," most Western reviewers found it to be replete with Indianness.

Textual evidence bears out that none of these writers is out of place but more often occupies a space in between—that is, a liminal space, which is often a tense site with potential for both confrontation and harmony. Like all her sisters in the trade, Jhumpa Lahiri reiterates her Indianness too: "My parents never consciously sat down and told me things about India, they sort of correctly assumed that I would learn things just by virtue of being their child. I think it has always been important to them to maintain strong social ties with Indians living abroad and visiting India."

Clearly admitting that her relationship to India changed as she grew older ("As I grew older, going to India was frustrating, because growing up in America is different . . . in Calcutta, we had to respect the family's concerns"), in an interview to *Newsweek* she emphasized the role that Calcutta plays in her imagination:

> I spent much time in Calcutta as a child—idle but rich time—often at home with my grandmother. It enabled me to experience solitude—ironically, because there were so many people, I could seal myself off psychologically. It was a place where I began to think imaginatively. Calcutta nourished my interest in seeing things from different points of view. There's a tradition there that we just don't have here. The ink hasn't dried yet on our lives here.

Though Calcutta, the city that she "know[s] quite well," "is the place where my parents are from, a place I visited frequently for extended time and formed relationships with people and with my relatives and felt a tie over time," "it was also "a sort of parenthesis in my life to be there." Like Chitra Banerjee Divakaruni and Bharati Mukherjee, who make repeated references to the cultural tradition of Calcutta and their cherished moments of nostalgia or moments of bewilderment in encounters with the real Calcutta, Jhumpa also tries to relocate her cultural space and identity mediated by significant cross-cultural influences. She confessed to Radhika S. Shankar, "I went to Calcutta neither as a tourist nor a former resident—a valuable position, I think for a writer. I learned to observe things as an outsider, and yet I also knew that as different Calcutta is from Rhode Island, I belonged there in some fundamental way, in the ways I didn't seem to belong in the United States. The reason my first stories were set in Calcutta is due partly because of that perspective, that necessary combination of distance and intimacy with a place."

In several other interviews she states her inability to define "where she is from" and categorically states that "the problem for the children of immigrants, those with strong ties to their country of origin, is that they feel neither one thing nor the other. That has been my experience in any case." As a second-generation immigrant in the United States, which is "home" to her, she still feels "a bit of an outsider too." In her visit to Calcutta, the city tried to claim the famous "Bengali" as its own but Jhumpa insisted that she belonged to no one place in particular and that she inhabits a perplexing bicultural universe. "I'm very fond of Calcutta. I've been coming here since the age of two. I have been learning about the city where my parents were born and still have a vital connection with. It's been a wonderful part of my life. But it's not home." In the online essay "To Heaven without Dying," she categorically states:

> I have always lived under the pressure to be bilingual, bicultural, at ease on either side of the Lahiri family map. The first words I learned to utter and understand were in my parents' native tongue, Bengali . . . my ability to speak the language made me feel less foreign during visits to Calcutta every few years. It also made me feel less foreign in the expatriate Bengali community my parents socialize with in the United States and, on a more quotidian level, in my own home. While English was not technically my first language, it has become so. . . . When it came to my own writing, English was, from the beginning, my only language.

Looking at her stories as a whole, we feel that Jhumpa is aware that she is preoccupied with language, as if this concept, this fact of human life, were itself an element of drama. She seems especially preoccupied with the presence in any given character's life of two languages and sometimes more, in different sorts of equations. Almost all her characters are translators, insofar as they must make sense of the foreign in order to survive. The failed linguist in the title story literally makes his living off his knowledge of English and other languages. In "Sexy," Miranda's curiosity about Bengali is a way for her to gain access to her married and increasingly unavailable lover. In "The Third and Final Continent," the protagonist notes that when his wife arrives in Boston, he speaks Bengali in America for the first time. Yet there is no discernible change in the style of his dialogue, he speaks to his wife in the same manner that he speaks in English to Mrs. Croft. For the ancient Mrs. Croft, meanwhile, modern life has itself become a baffling foreign language, one she neither participates in nor understands. The protagonist in this story also fears that his son will no longer speak in Bengali after he and his wife die. This is displaced anxiety on Jhumpa Lahiri's part—her own fear of her parents' death. For if she is to survive them, it is she who will suffer that linguistic loss: "Whether I write as an American or an Indian, about things American or Indian or otherwise, one thing remains constant: I translate, therefore I am."

She admits that there is less of a divide between American culture and Indian because of the greater access and communication channels, "But I have observed a sense of emotional exile in my parents and in their friends that I feel can never go away." On the other hand, "the problem for children of immigrants, those with strong ties to their country of origin, is that they feel neither one thing nor the other." To another interviewer, she confesses:

> I've inherited my parents' preoccupations. It's hard to have parents who consider another place "home"—even after living abroad for thirty years, India is home for them. We were always looking back so I never felt fully at home here. There's nobody in this whole country that we're related to. India was different—our extended family offered real connections. To see my parents as children, as siblings, was rare.

In spite of such strong emotional nourishment, Lahiri at the same time also does not fail to mention the typical immigrant phenomenon of belonging nowhere and that even in India, she did not feel at home. "We visited often, but we didn't have a home. We were clutching at a world that was never fully with us." "The older I get," she continues, "the more aware I am that I have somehow inherited a sense of exile from my parents, even though in many ways—superficial ones, largely—I am so much more American than they are." When Gaiutra Bahadur interviewed her in *citypaper.net*, Lahiri was specifically asked why her stories are not preoccupied with issues of identity. Does identity interest her as a writer, or is it a cumbersome expectation to be "multicultural"? The response was interesting:

> It's always a bad thing to try to answer people's expectations. There hasn't been a lot of writing from the perspective of Indian-American writers and some people will look to my writing to answer some of those questions. But I never think of self-consciously trying to answer issues of identity. I work from a character and a conflict in a character's life.

She also stresses the dichotomy of growing up in two cultures—how it bothered her when she grew up that there was no single place to which she fully belonged. "Growing up in two countries, I see things in a way that not everyone around me can. I'd talk to my cousins about what life's like in America and still know that they'll never get it because they haven't been here. Talking to Americans about India is the same—it's always partial. As a story teller, I'm aware that there are limitations in communication."

In the essay, "To Heaven without Dying" again, Lahiri interprets herself and raises the question of the end of authorial freedom and beginning of identity politics. In order to exemplify the perplexing bicultural universe she inhabits and the expectations and assumptions that she has always shuttled between, she refers to an interesting anecdote:

> A letter came recently to my father's office from a Bengali gentleman in Calcutta. The author of the letter, unknown to my family, explained that he was a lifelong writer of fiction, adding that his "pen was never still." This prolific gentleman, impressed with the fact that I, with my recognizably Bengali name, had won the Pulitzer Prize, wanted to know how he himself might apply for the honor. On the phone from New York, I explained to my parents that it hadn't been a matter of applying, that it had actually been the single greatest surprise of my life, something like winning the lottery without ever having bought a ticket. When my father asked whether Indian nationals were eligible for the Pulitzer, I told him what I knew: that the book had to be by an American citizen, and deal, preferably with "American life." At this point my mother interjected that the judges had made an exception in my case. I might

> have been naturalized as an American citizen when I was eighteen (I was born in London), but in her eyes I am first and forever Indian. Furthermore, my book, in her opinion, wasn't about American life. It was about people like herself and myself—Indians. I suppose I should be grateful that my mother wasn't on the Pulitzer committee.

Her Place in the Asian-American Canon

Critics and scholars of Asian American writing have been debating endlessly whether there are colonized cultural spaces within the U.S. itself, especially when in a turn-of-the century global village, outsiderhood has become part of the human condition, and geographical dislocation is no requisite for temporary phases of exile. Phrases like "oriental alienation," "Asian abjection," "Diaspora," "difference," and "representation" have been used to define the canon, formulations in the discourse on race by James Baldwin, Zora Neal Hurston, Henry Louis Gates and Appiah have stimulated Asian American criticism. Sau Ling Cynthia Wong's post-structuralist *Reading Asian American Literature* associates fictions with their critical and attendant culture histories. Another critic, David Leiwei Li, believes that post-1960s exegesis by Asian Americans follows three phases: ethnic nationalism; women centered; and today's market multiculturalism, critical professionalization and Bakhtinian "heteroglossia." In Jhumpa Lahiri's case, though she lives in the United States, her work is imbued with Indian culture and sensibilities. Wherever they are set, she explores "Indianness" in some of her stories, while others deal with immigrants at different stages on the road to assimilation. Her confession that "it is still very hard to think of myself as an American" makes her predicament unique as well as typical too. Her books, instead of reeking with ethnocentricity, have a universal flavour and appeal that an immigrant from any corner of the world would be able to relate to.

Lahiri believes what first drove her to write fiction was to escape the pitfalls of being viewed as one thing or the other. As an author, she could embody any individual her imagination enabled her to, of any origin. This sense of freedom was, according to her, one of the greatest thrills of writing fiction, and for a person like her, who has never been confident of what to call herself or of where to say she is from, it is a solace. But what she has discovered upon publishing her book is that authorial freedom is limited to the process of writing itself, in the private sphere of creation. Once made public, both her book and herself were immediately and copiously categorized. Take for instance, the various ways she is described: as an American author, as an Indian-American author, as a British-born author, as an Anglo-Indian author, as a NRI (non-resident Indian) author, as an ABCD author (ABCD stands for American born confused "desi"—an acronym coined by Indian nationals to describe culturally challenged second-generation Indians raised in the United States). According to Indian academics, she's written something known as "Diaspora fiction"; in the United States, it's "immigrant fiction." In a way, all this amuses Jhumpa. She claims that the book is what it is and has been received in ways she had no desire or ability to control. The fact that she is described in two ways or twenty is of no consequence to her; as it turns out, each of those labels is accurate.

Reception and the Media

Whether we Indians can claim Jhumpa as ours remains a debatable question. The media hype that followed her Pulitzer award on April 10, 2000 was similar to that experienced after Arundhati Roy won the Booker prize. The publication scenario and the Cinderella syndrome were similar for any debut writer and in many ways a repetition of the Roy-phenomenon—initial rejections and the sudden rise to fame. Though the $5000 prize amount is much less than the Booker, the award given "for distinguished fiction by an American author, preferably dealing with American life" took the literary world by storm, especially when a debut writer was placed on the same pedestal with such American stalwarts as Edith Wharton, Pearl S. Buck, William Faulkner, and Ernest Hemingway. Five days after the Pulitzer declaration, Mira Nair, who was already in the news for other controversial issues, decided that "A Temporary Matter" would make a good film and the declaration to do so was published in *The Times of India* on April 16 ("Nair to film Lahiri story"). Last week, a cyber search on Jhumpa Lahiri resulted in 463 sites, all of them carrying the same picture and broadly telling the same story—her experiences at being initially rejected by the publisher; how she is a writer of uncommon elegance and poise; how most of her characters play out a simultaneous existence in two cultures; how being as American as a WASP, she changes cultural perspective as easily as a bilingual writer shifts from language to language; how she has minutely observed Calcutta and the middle-class Bengali milieu; how she has deftly depicted cultural disorientation.

Critical opinion about Lahiri's book also stands sharply divided. Those of Asian, particularly Indian descent find their own voice and predicament replicated through the young writer. The eulogy awarded by Amy Tan, which features on the back cover of the text is sincere: "Jhumpa Lahiri is the kind of writer who makes you want to grab the next person you see and say, 'Read this!' She's a dazzling storyteller with a distinctive voice, an eye for nuance, an ear for irony. She is one of the finest short story writers I've read." The response of the mainstream white Americans is also easily predictable. So, statements like "Lahiri's fiction transcends mere ethnic exoticism," "Someone finally gets all the tiny bargains that assimilation asks of us!" or "Lahiri writes about the Indian American experience from all angles in indelible, lifelike stories that are completely predictable—but only in retrospect" (David Kipen); "Lahiri doesn't write jeremiads about the loss of cultural identity; her characters are both relieved when they adjust to their new world and regretful at the separation from their original cultures." (Charles Taylor) Katherine Guckenberger, while emphasizing that it is a story collection that "decodes mysteries of culture" tells us that "For an American reader, these stories are at once subtle and informative, filling cultural gaps with the invisible ease granted only to writers of foreign heritage and exceptional skill." Though she is aware that "these are heady days for Indian writing, and they're only getting headier," she does not care for ethnic exoticism at all and is happy that Jhumpa does not fall in that category:

> Most of the Indian fiction we read is carefully manipulated to appeal to us—customs, history, and geography obvious to an Indian audience are explained in detail; national figures, such as Gandhi, are introduced like strangers; Hindi words, unless utterly clear in meaning, are defined. As an American, I appreciate such concessions, but the risk of over compensation, in many cases, overweighs the benefit. I know who Gandhi is.

An Asian American immigrant herself, Rani Sinha feels Jhumpa has lent voice to her own feelings and is eulogical in her review of the book:

> Jhumpa Lahiri is sensational because of her manner, which is anything but sensationalist in describing the psyche of Bengalis who have settled into North American cultures. Unlike the propensity of recent purveyors of "ethnic exotica," and I mean writers like Bharati Mukherjee or Chitra Divakaruni, to aspire to florid excess in describing acculturation's aches and pains, Lahiri writes with a depth and honesty which require no melodrama.
>
> Perhaps because I share her background in many ways, I am particularly mesmerized at finding for the first time in her *Interpreter of Maladies* glimpses and snatches of a world intimately familiar to me. I cannot praise Lahiri enough. . . .
>
> The scenes in "When Mr. Pirzada Comes to Dine" revolving around the preparation of dinner, which was to be eaten while watching the evening news (what a relic of the pre-CNN age!), with mother at the stove, father snacking on cashews as he leans against the fridge, and a young girl interacting with them—both were evocative of Indian American life in a way that only one who has lived that life would perceive.
>
> "Mrs. Sen's," the story of a young woman trying to adapt to the lonely life of a housewife married to an untenured and anxious math professor, who tries to expand her horizons by babysitting a neglected, young white boy in her apartment after school, brought back my memories of many women of my mother's generation. Their sincerity and anguish in coming to grips with the postscript of marriage to a stranger then moving to a strange new culture were captured precisely by Lahiri's sensitive portrayal of the title

character. I particularly enjoyed (and cried over) the subplot of Mrs. Sen's determination to find fresh, whole fish.

Lahiri is the first writer of Indian American experiences who has struck a chord within me. Read this book!

Interestingly, despite her "mainstream acceptance," the cosmopolitan Lahiri is still marketed as an "ethnic writer." Though one never gets the sense that she set her stories in India in order to give white suburban American women (who apparently are the biggest purveyors of ethnic fiction) an easy armchair tour of India, that her India is replete with quaint customs and rich traditions, this label seems difficult to be erased permanently. Instead one feels that her stories shuttle back and forth between India and the U.S. because those are the countries and cultures she is most at home in and can write about with the greatest confidence.

Critics were puzzled when Jhumpa, whose home is in the U.S.A. and who categorically stated that Kolkata was not her home, decided to get married in Kolkata in traditional Bengali style. Could it be to renew public interest (to say nothing of the much-maligned Bengali curiosity about other people's private lives) in a book published nearly two years back and sell a few hundred copies more? According to the writer of course. "It doesn't really signify anything." The more cynical ones suggest that the ethnic flavour adds a particular exoticism that western readers are very fond of. Lahiri has admitted that to play safe she will have to promise that she will never write about India or non-immigrant Indians again. But she says that her translation of India has evoked, for some readers and reviewers here and there, the illusion of cultural accuracy and resonance. She keeps on reiterating that her writing is less a response to her parents' cultural nostalgia and more an attempt to forge her own amalgamated domain.

To conclude, it can be said that till her first novel is released, we can go on basking in Lahiri's glory and feel proud that apart from the beauty queens who put India on the world map, we have appropriated a literary figure, who though born in England, brought up in Connecticut and now living in New York, can be claimed as a desi writer too, though her own idea of India is "of the mind" only. In the definition and re-definition of the Diaspora, for the time being at least, Jhumpa Lahiri is a writer who can hold her own in any grouping—among Indian writers in English, among short story specialists, and among American literary stars.

Bibliography

Aguiar, Arun. "One of One with Jhumpa Lahiri." *Pif Magazine*, July 28, 1999.

Basbanes, N.A. "Bharati Mukherjee Interview." *george jr. internet monthly*, Oct.-Nov. 1997.

Chacko, Susan. Online review, "Interpreter of Maladies."

Chopra, Rohit. "New Wine in Old Bottle." HYPERLINK "http://www.rediff.com" http://www.rediff.com

Guckenberger, K. "Translation: A Short story collection decodes mysteries of culture." *The Boston Phoenix*, June 10-17, 1999.

Hajari, Nishid. "The Promised Land: Indian American Jhumpa Lahiri's heralded debut only partly lives up to its advance hype," *Time*, September 13, 1999. Vol. 154.10

Kipen, David. "Interpreting Indian Culture with Stories." *San Francisco Chronicle*, June 24, 1999.

Kamath, A.P. "Women Writers of Indian Diaspora Create a Big Impact." *Rediff on the Net*, August 23, 1999.

Lahiri, Jhumpa. *The Interpreter of Maladies: Stories of Bengal, Boston, and Beyond*. New Delhi: Harper Collins India, 1999.

———. "To Heaven without Dying." Online essay.

Li, David Leiwei. *Imagining the Nation: Asian-American Literature and Cultural Context*. California: Stanford University Press, 1998.

McCurdy, Amy. Review. *IndiaStar Review of Books*, 2000.

Nayar, Aruti. "An Interpreter of Exile." *The Sunday Tribune*, May 28, 2000.

Pais, Arthur J. "Boston Brahmin." *India Today*, April 24, 2000, 89-90.

Patel, Vibhuti. Interview. "The Maladies of Belonging." *Newsweek International*, September 20, 1999, p. 80.

Roy-Chowdhury, S. "A Fresh Take on Immigrant Lives," *India Currents*, Oct. 1999. HYPERLINK "http://www.ncmonline.com/arts-and-culture/1999"

Sen, Ashok. "View from the Diaspora," *The Statesman*, May 15, 2000.

Sen, Aveek. "Enigmas of Distance," *The Telegraph*, April 30, 2000.

Shankar, Radhika R. "Lahiri's First Book Gets Raves." HYPERLINK "http://www.rediff.com/news/may/22/1999"

———. "*New Yorker* Chooses Lahiri as One of 20 Writers for 21st Century." HYPERLINK "http://www.rediff.com/news/jun/99"

———. "A Writer Free to Write All Day." http://www.rediff.com/news/1999/aug/23

Taylor, Charles. "Interpreter of Maladies." http://www.salon.com/books/review/1999/07/27/lahiri

Wallia, C.J.S. Review. *IndiaStar Review of Books*. 2000.

Wong, Sau-ling Cynthia. *Reading Asian American Literature*. The Hindu-Editorial: "The Bright New Breed." *The Hindu*, 14 April, 2000.

Lexis Nexis Online Academic Universe. University of Minnesota Library, Mpls. 24 may, 2000.

Other Interviews: Citypaper.net; Indiatimes.com; Indians in New York; Stir Magazine.

Other Reviews: *The Oregonian; Boston University Bridge; Parabaus* (Bangla).

Addenda

Jhumpa Lahiri's marriage with her Spanish-American boyfriend Alberto Vourvoulias ceremony in the traditional Bengali fashion in Kolkata cn January 15, 2001 took the local media people by storm, more so because they were officially barred from being present at the function. Tired, humiliated and having failed to get the story (except by piecing together information gleaned from bonafide invitees) the press shot back the next day, going into elaborate details of how papa Lahiri curtly told them to make way for the guests and the bride refused to admit the media because she was "too shy." As a reporter sarcastically commented: "But except for the bridegroom and the bride's accent, everything about the wedding will be Bengali with a vengeance." Thus Jhumpa Lahiri who came to Kolkata with a lot of hope to regain her Bengali roots, returned with an overdose of hype, adulation and bad press. Hailing her "exoticity" Sarbari Sinha thinks that it is probably only fitting that Jhumpa Lahiri's marriage should become a narrative event for her readers. Jhumpa, whose *Interpreter of Maladies* is an exploration of the married state, or the longing for it.

Broken Identities: A Comparative Study of Bharati Mukherjee's *Darkness* and Jhumpa Lahiri's *Interpreter of Maladies*

INDIRA NITYANANDAM

Indian-born Bharati Mukherjee is eager to be considered an American writer, to belong to the mainstream of the country of her adoption. She does not wish to be called an exile or an expatriate because to her "acculturation" is an important process which has the exuberance of acceptance or assimilation and not the pain of difference or exclusion or alienation. Her earlier writings reflect the pain of exclusion while her later ones portray the ability to forge an identity while being also accepted by the new cultural milieu. The collection of short stories *Darkness* portrays the splintered self and the coming to terms with the cultural and finding a meaning in life. On the other hand, Jhumpa Lahiri knows of India through her parents who make annual visits to the land of their birth as well as her own vacations in India. She believes that she has a "simultaneous existence" in two cultures for which she is indebted to her travels to India. Hers is a twice-removed relationship but her first collection of short stories is sub-titled: Stories of Bengal, Boston and Beyond. Both women writers explore the private world or the subjective self of their women characters which "women's domestic imprisonment have trained them to be so expert in."[1] This paper attempts to delineate the broken identities of the protagonists, which is one of the common factors linking all the stories in both the volumes.

A short story writer has to exhibit exceptional skill to create three-dimensional characters in spite of the fact that we see them for a very short while. She may have to employ shock tactics like a surprising twist of plot, a dramatic unveiling or an unexpected ending. These writers use these tactics and others too. Lahiri's protagonists are Indians living either in India or the U.S. Though the first story is set in Boston, we very soon move to Eastern India—Bengal and Orissa. Unusual characters make unusual stories seem to be her dictum for none of the characters are average, ordinary, common people. Instead, most of them are whimsical and eccentric except for Shoba and Shukumar. Two individuals trapped within themselves, refusing to communicate—Shoba "looking at thirty-three, like the type of woman she had once claimed she would never resemble"[2] and Shukumar who was a mediocre student:

> Until September he had been diligent if not dedicated, summarizing chapters, outlining arguments on pads of yellow lined paper. But now he would lie in their bed until he got bored, gazing at his side of the closet . . . at the row of the tweed jackets and corduroy trousers he would not have to choose from to teach his classes that semester. (4)

This same lack of ability to communicate compounded by the loss of identity one feels in an alien culture is portrayed by Mukherjee in "A Father." Mr. Bhowmick was in the U.S. at his wife's insistence. As a government engineer in Ranchi he had to go through "a long and humbling process" before he finally got his immigrant visa. However, "in Detroit he was a lonelier man."[3] When he realises that his unmarried daughter Babli is pregnant, he blames his wife who was responsible for their moving to the U.S. Though they lived a comfortable life in this new land, Mr. Bhowmick knows that "a dozen times a day, he made these small trade-offs between new-world reasonableness and old-world beliefs." (64) As Wandrekar says "Schizophrenia can be the ailment of aliens."[4] He could not give up many of his old beliefs but did not have the courage to admit it. His daughter too was equally confused: "girls like Babli were caught between rules, that's the point he wished to make. They were too smart, too impulsive for a backward place like Ranchi, but not tough nor smart for sex-crazy places like Detroit." (72) The story ends on a violent note unlike Lahiri's "A Temporary Matter" where the couple are able to bridge their chasm of silence.

In an alien land with constant cultural collisions, caused by cultural transplants and leading to cultural alienation, these protagonists find it difficult to adjust, to cope, and to come to terms with the reality around them. Moreover, they are always "mourning for the homeland left behind." They need to adjust socially, economically as well as culturally. In "Mrs. Sen," we see the psychological upheavals and reactions that an immigrant has to face: Baby-sitting for the 11-year old Eliot, Mrs. Sen is always thinking of home "everything is there." (113) Eliot is surprised to note that "when Mrs. Sen said home, she meant India, not the apartment where she sat chopping vegetables." (116) To her, everything about India is nostalgic—she remembers and keeps talking about the noise while here "I cannot sleep in so much silence" (115) and the weddings back home when "my mother sends out word in the evening for all the neighbourhood women to bring blades just like this one, and then they sit in an enormous circle on the roof of our building, laughing and gossiping and slicing fifty kilos of vegetables through the night." (115) She wonders whether she could drive to Calcutta, as soon as she got her driver's license. "Could I drive all the way to Calcutta? How long would that take, Eliot? Ten thousand miles, at fifty miles per hour?" (118) Very often we see Mrs. Sen through the eyes of 11-year old Eliot to whom she seems very different from his own mother. The story ends with Mrs. Sen going back to her earlier routine of only keeping house for Mr. Sen—thus failing to become a part of her new homeland.

The desire to move away from the past, to make a clean break with their own culture; to be given "a new and simple relationship" (34) in the new land impels some immigrants like the lady from Lucknow. Born into a traditional Muslim family in India, the narrator is a much-travelled mother of 2 who has "made homes in Lebanon, Brazil, Zambia and France" (24) and now lives in Atlanta, Georgia. IBM, for whom her husband Iqbal works, has been kind and generous to them and they live a decent life, quite different from the dingy cities of their childhood in India and Pakistan. Iqbal realizes that they are "a not-quite" (25) and so have to work harder. She remembers a childhood incident where a Muslim neighbour's daughter died after being beaten by her father for having fallen in love with a Hindu boy. "Americans are crazy for sex" (21) believes Iqbal not realizing that his Indian wife has a lover. The process of acculturation which Mukherjee considers immigrant includes such cultural differences as fidelity in marriage as contrasted to extra-marital affairs. The narrator does realize that "what had begun as an adventure had become shabby and complex." (33) She thinks of her neighbour Husseina and imagines the pain that can be inflicted—physically or mentally. Mukherjee here symbolically indicates the painful process that each immigrant has to undergo before becoming a part of this cultural landscape. As the writer Meena Alexander pertinently asks: "How long does one have to live somewhere to make it one's home anyway?"[5]

Extra-marital relationships form the theme for many of the stories in both the volumes. In Lahiri's "Sexy," nostalgia for one's homeland seems to be intrinsically linked to the affair of Miranda and Dev. Miranda's friend Laxmi is shocked and upset at the news that her cousin's husband has fallen in love with another woman: "It was a wife's worst nightmare." (83) Interestingly, at the same time Miranda is having a relationship with a married Indian—Dev. In all these stories, we notice that immigrants hardly ever come into real contact with the natives of their new land and are hence often misunderstood or not understood at all. Miranda thinks Bengali is a religion until Dev points out Bengal on a map of India. Miranda recollects her childhood experience when she went to a birthday party: "Miranda remembered a heavy aroma of incense and onions in the house, and a pile of shoes heaped by the front door. But most of all she remembered a piece of fabric, about the size of a pillowcase, which hung from a wooden dowel at the bottom of the stairs. It was a painting of a naked woman. . . . She had enormous white eyes that tilted towards her temples, and mere dots for pupils. . . . In one hand she brandished a dagger. With one foot she crushed a struggling man on the ground." (95-96)

The cultural differences are highlighted by such experiences. What seems to be mundane and normal, an everyday experience for an Indian may stun and shock people of another culture. Laxmi comes with her the Indian ideal of fidelity and could think of nothing else: "If I were her [the cousin], I'd fly straight to London and shoot them both" (97) she announced one day. Juxtaposed with Laxmi's reaction is Miranda's attempt to hold onto Dev even after his wife's return. Laxmi retains her native culture, Dev seems to be struggling to come to grips with the cultural conflict that he faces. The immigrant reacts to situations that are in conflict with his own upbringing in different ways—seeks to find an identity in the new homeland. "Confrontation with another society starts the process of destructing and reconstructing the self."[6]

In an attempt to find an identity, many immigrants find it necessary to change their names—names that sound less foreign, names that need not immediately call up images of some exotic, distant country. In *A Change of Skies*, Bharat becomes Barry, Navaranjani becomes Jean, in Bharati Mukherjee's *Jasmine*, Jyoti becomes Jane, etc. In consonance with the technique of short story writing, none of these stories have complex plots—instead they focus upon a particular episode or situation. The construction of identity and individuality has been of prime concern for both these short story writers. In an increasingly multicultural society that Canada boasts of—the melting pot image is gradually giving place to the concept of a mosaic though some have preferred the "pickle image" where with the passage of time absorption into mainstream takes place automatically. However, the question does remain as to what extent these writers or protagonists wish to totally submerge their identity in the new culture or alien land. The words "immigrant," "expatriate" and "diaspora," when used to refer to writing, are generally used as synonyms. It is essential to consider the original meaning of these words. In particular, the word "diaspora" has, because of its historical and religious connotations, underlying meanings which should not be ignored. The pain and anguish of an entire race or religion or community uprooted from its homeland, rendered homeless and then finally settling down in the new land (as in the case of Jews in Israel) cannot and should not be compared to that of what an immigrant writer feels. The same applies to the characters who are the protagonists of these short stories. Another important difference is that in the case of the original meaning of diaspora, the persons moving were forced to flee (sometimes on fear of death) while the expatriate writer today chooses—makes a choice—to move to a new land, usually for selfish/personal reasons like economic or academic or professional progress. The characters in these short stories have moved away from their homeland and attempt to create a new home. There is pain and anguish, loneliness and isolation, loss of identity and desire for assimilation but one which is certainly different from what the Blacks or the Jews who were forced to move must have felt. The process of acculturation however continues for many years before these characters begin to feel at home.

NOTES

1. Jeremy Hawthorn, *Studying the Novel* (London: Edward Arnold, 1985), p. 26.
2. Jhumpa Lahiri, *Interpreter of Maladies* (U.K.: HarperCollins, 1999), p. 1.
3. Bharati Mukherjee, *Darkness* (Canada: Penguin, 1985), p. 69.
4. Kalpana Wandrekar, "The Ailing Aliens," *Image of India in the Indian Novel in English*, ed. Sudhakar Pandey and R. Raj Rao (London: Sangam, 1993), p. 37.
5. Meena Alexander, "An Intimate Violence: Living in a Diasporic World" *The Muse and the Minorities*, Proceedings of the Seminar on Muse and the Minorities (New Delhi: The Steering Committee, 1998), p. 64.
6. Meena Alexander, p. 36.

Beyond the National Motifs: An Attempt to Re-Connect Peripherality to Universality Thematics of Tagore's Writings with Special Reference to Jhumpa Lahiri's *Interpreter of Maladies*

KEYA MAJUMDAR

The issues of Resistance and Protest among the indigenous, settlers and diasporic communities of the commonwealth had been investigated under political, historical, anthropological, social microscopes by hordes of eminent luminaries. This paper, on the other, would try to investigate some age old, basic structures as Nationality, Peripherality and Universality in a different perspective than the commonly used postcolonial definitions of the terms; and, by doing so would attempt to present a study of Reconciliation. Going beyond the continual preoccupation with colonizing forces and narcissism of racial awareness, within its short sphere, this paper will try to negotiate the territories of Human Soul viewed as Humanity looking back to pre-colonized cultural and aesthetic moorings of ancient and wise India represented in the writings of Tagore. When one talks of the urge to Re-connect people who are severed, separated, tortured unfairly and lost their lands, nothing can be more appropriate than this tug of Universal Brotherhood. As a representative literature of diasporic problems Jhumpa Lahiri's *Interpreter of Maladies* would be examined, that asks for remedies of its maladies.

When one cannot connect with the universal collective unconscious due to barriers in the corridors of nationality caused by colonialism or other schisms, people facing identity crisis float about in the periphery of existence. The word "Peripherality" in this article has been used in this context only. So, to bring these uncertain and confused people, viewed, for example, in Lahiri's characters, back to center, the "Universality" of artistic and humanistic vision is needed. The term "Universality" is used in this paper to emphasise the need for spiritual kinship of man with man in the entire world. For universality locates its language now within the national condition.

In the cross current of racial, political, cultural constructs, the concept metaphor of "Universality" flows on reshaping itself accordingly. So, when Keats says, "a things of beauty is a joy for ever," or Blake invites,

> To see a world in a grain of sand
> And a Heaven in wild flower
> Hold Infinity in the palm of your hand
> And Eternity in an hour.

we easily transcend the finitude of cultural differentialism, echoing Tagore:

> I have had roamed long enough
> Through endless days, nations, ways, means
> To see the wonders of the mountains and the seas
> And lo, the magic lies right here
> Where I'd least expected it
> In the dangling dewdrop on the blade of grass
> At my doorstep.

Looking back to the cultural moorings of ancient India which no amount of invasion or colonization could ever demolish or despoil, represented so vividly in Tagore's thematic exploration, is the enquiry of this paper. But more importantly, the ambition of the paper is to try to address the vital issues of Outer Form versus Inner Space, putting into contrast the narrowly Nationalistic against broad Humanity.

I

After deliberating on so many issues, born out of what he calls "decentred consciousness," this is what Edward Said had to offer in his essay "Orientalism Reconsidered," as the need of the hour, "A need for greater crossing of boundaries, for greater interventionism in cross-disciplinary activity, a concentrated awareness of the situation—political, methodological, social, historical—in which intellectual and cultural work is carried out."[1]

Literature, as one knows, is the best representation of culture that speaks across diverse cultural locations with positive authenticity. So its special power as a unique mode of discourse can be taken into account that helps to re-locate and re-create the space for human enterprises irrespective of class, creed and country.

Opposing polarities of cultural differentialism and cultural hybridity can be cemented by invoking the creative cross-cultural capacities. The stripping of all cultures of their individual historicity and single density thereof produces not a universal equality of all cultures, but their being reduced to a moral/psychological loneliness, that moves aimlessly in the forest of different masks like "hybridity," "contingency," "multiculturalism," "pluralism" etc. Doubtless, they are the functioning force in the representation of culture, but when aesthetically grasped and organized in a unique whole, the work of art emerges as the synthesizing creation. When cultures are examined as commodity-forms, we can be sure of the fact, that they are common or equal—only to the extent of their commodification, as Information Technology culture has done worldwide now. But that which looks into the one unique factor that binds all human beings, that resonates consistently against the tortures that have been propagated, the treaties that have been violated, is the enduring feature of the Universal brotherhood. Every human being is bound by this umbilical chord. And, this is the typical Indian vision that acknowledges the resilience of the human spirit that has called for one seamless human identity, outside the domain of discourse and pedagogy.

II

Tagore's enormous bulk of writings of which *Gitanjali* occupies a miniscule area, is the direct reflection of that universal longing to approach Truths of all kinds—truths that scorch, hurt, inspire, sensitize; but always is there like Dante's "Infoliate Rose," irradiating behind all experimental discourses. So, Tagore declares,

> Break up then
> Pile high the debris as you like
> The Bliss Incarnate still shines
> Bright
> Behind all the ruins.

The facts of universal brotherhood expounded by the Vedas and Upanishads are neither vaguely spiritual nor impracticably ideological. They are the modes of pragmatic, down-to-earth socio-cultural behavioural manuals to a great extent, formulated through its socio cultural context of the Vedic ages, nine thousand years back, that could boast of a very civilized, very enlightened civilization, when so-called Colonisers were not even civilized, Colonialism did bring about extensive ruins and tortures in the socio-economic and cultural fabric of this prosperous India called Jewel in the Crown. But while cutting off the thumbs of the weavers of Dhaka Gauze, it could not however deactivate the principal, spiritual moorings of the Indians which the archaic language of Sanskrit kept intact. Even as they superimposed their culture, language, "parody of education" as identified by Aime Ceasaire[2] on those of the Indians, they could not however drain out the essence of Indian spiritual power.

Because this has always been "universally valid," I may quote the words of Auerbach in *Mimesis*. Talking about "historical dynamics," he goes on to explain in this memorable treatise, where and how to look for it, "in art, economy, material and intellectual culture, in the depths of the workaday world and its men and women because it is there that one can grasp and what is unique and what is animated by inner forces, and what, in both a more concrete and a more profound sense, is universally valid."[3]

When the Upanishads address man as "Amrityasya Putra," or, children of Heavently Bliss, it is not mere rhetoric, it resonates with the assurance that the possibilities of Man are immense. He can yet build up picking up the bits and pieces of "broken images." Tagore's works sing hosannas to this Eternal man in various genres, in various applications, and stand as an antidote against the modern moral/spiritual malaise of rootlessness, alienation of ethnological differences and chaotic restlessness.

National Motifs, as diverse as they are, often have a blurring effect with shifting boundaries so much so that the historically clear terms like Colonial or Postcolonial do not hold good to identify distinctly the very complex parallel literary/intellectual theories. Aijaz Ahmad clarifies this problem in a very perceptive, conclusive manner: "These categories have no analytic value, nor any theoretical status, when they are mobilized to homogenize very complex structures of intellectual productions or the trajectories and subjectivities of individual writers and critics or broad intellectual strata. . . . For particular intellectuals or clusters of them, colonial cultural ambience can last far beyond the moment of decolonisation."[4]

This is how Tagore's creations, or ancient pre-colonial philosophical texts cannot be defined with any binding term of territorial, spatial or temporal motifs because they easily go beyond the particular national motif, in this case, Indian. Jhumpa Lahiri's Pulitzer prize winning *Interpreter of Maladies*, subtitled as "Stories of Bengal, Boston and Beyond," becomes so important a book in the present context, not merely because it located the "language" of the maladies of the people of cross cultural regions through its own interpretation; more significantly because as a solution to those typical diasporic problems, she looks "Beyond" the physical boundaries of mere national motifs. The title story itself suggests that the mere knowledge of language is not enough to pierce deep into the emotional-spiritual maladies of people concerned. Language is just the Periphery. Mr. Kapasi's daydream of being an Interpreter between two nations goes kaput as the wind sweeps off the written piece of paper. Lahiri touches the national motifs (superstitions, ways of life and such peripheral tropes) of India, Bangladesh, England and America to give out remarkable stories in "A Real Durwan," "When Mr. Pirzada Came to Dine," "Sexy," "The Third and Final Continent." We see the characters vacillating continuously in their given structure in search of stable values that would ultimately keep their houses in order. Important to note is their eager groping for something "beyond" their physical realities. Here, to locate this Beyond, we can apply the searchlight of Tagore's themes, to seek out the Fourth Dimension that the last story of the book, aptly titled, "The Third and Final Continent," hints at. Some critics have rightly suggested that despite Lahiri's skill in storytelling, a gaping sense of void can be felt while going through the stories. That void is the love and trust and the lack of the flow of humanity, which can be found only by going beyond the peripheral norms of claustrophobic nationality.

III

The difference between "stated" and "realized" is the difference between the texts of Lahiri and Tagore. With his astonishing poetic skill and compassionate humanistic outlook, Tagore knows how to bind the drifting souls together. While Lahiri adeptly negotiates the distance of the soul, Tagore's thematic explorations try to find out the roots of human relationships, where culturally specific determinants merge to become one with the universality of common human experience. Neither China Wall nor German Wall can pose any problem of alienation to him, as he opens out the horizon of Soul of the Beautiful,

> Thou art the sky and thou art also the nest,
> O Thou beautiful !
> Where thine infinite sky spreadeth for the
> Soul to take her flight,
> a stainless white radiance reigneth, wherein is
> neither day
> nor night, nor form nor colour, nor ever any word.[5]

From Indian identity to the universal identity is the motto and goal of Tagore's poetic journey. As and when he achieves that goal, he proves the redeeming value of his art that far more deeply interfuses the outer fringe with inner space, the peripheral ripples with the depth of the still point of the Centre, than any political, social, economical manifestos can ever do. One is immediately reminded of Yeats's comment on the panacea for all the maladies of misinterpretation, fragmentation, and parochialism, for the large chunk of suffering, confused and marginalized human race, floating ceaselessly in the empty space of topographical boundaries. So, when Mrs. Das peremptorily urges Mr. Kapasi in the title story of Lahiri's book, "I was hoping you could help me feel better, say the right thing. Suggest some kind of remedy," Mr. Kapasi has no answer for her. Unfortunately, the Interpreter is not supposed to suggest remedy. For that, one can turn back to Tagore, to Upanishads, to the ancient seat of learning of Indian philosophy that believes in the universal monolithic element of Trust, Love and Faith by which to reconnect Man with Man.

NOTES

1. Edward Said, "Orientalism Reconsidered," *Europe and its Others*, ed. Francis Baker et al (Colchester: University of Essex, 1985), Vol. 1, p. 27:
2. Aime Cesaire, "From Discourse on Colonialism," *Postcolonial Criticism* (1955; New York Monthly Review Press, 1972), p. 32.
3. Auerbach, *Mimesis*, trans. Willard R. Trask (Princeton, 1953), p. 444.
4. Aijaz Ahmad, *Theory: Classes, Nations, Literatures* (London: Verso, 1992), pp. 204-5.
5. One of the seven reprinted by Yeats in his *The Oxford Book of Modern Verse, 1992-1935.*

An abridged version of the paper was presented at the 12th ACLALS Conference held in Canberra, Australia, in July 2001.

The translations of Tagore are done by the writer except where otherwise stated.

Crossing Cultural Borders: New Voices in Indian American Literature

NILA DAS

The bridge gathers as the passage that crosses.

Heidegger

When I received an invitation to speak on "recent Indian American Literature" for a public event at the University of Connecticut, U.S.A., I was surprised. In Indian academia, Asian Indian American literature is yet to be recognized as a distinct genre. I did not know it has claimed such visibility in the U.S. universities as to organize interdisciplinary meets. While preparing for the event, the question that intrigued me most, as it always does, when I read Ved Mehta, Bharati Mukherjee, or Anjana Appachana, is who or what is a true Indian American? Who are the writers of Indian lineage, the American audience actually accept as contributors to American literature, however marginalized? The checklist of recent Indian American creative writers I received from the American library, Kolkata, was rather disappointing. Most of the writers enlisted were first generation migrants, educated in India, having a pre-history, so to say, whose professed American cultural identity is seriously suspect. I wanted to hear voices arising from the very soil of America, of writers of Indian descent, born and/or raised in the U.S., who speak American language, feel at home in American lifestyle, who are Americans by history and experience, not by mere United States citizenship, the "joyous Americanization" of self-chosen exiles, mostly economic refugees.

I did not have the old concepts of American "melting pot" or "symbiosis" in mind when I thought about the second generation Indian Americans. I do not think that some one hundred and forty ethnic groups in the U.S. can be or should be merged in a codified homogeneous American national culture, if such a phenomena exists at all or ever did for that matter. I do not believe that for all the postmodernist trumpeting of American multiculturalism and cultural "other"ness, any ethnic group in the U.S. exists exclusively in terms of "ethnically cleansed" cultural identity either. I have equal reservation in hoisting the new generation Indian Americans as "trans-national hybrids presenting an international culture."[1]

The anthology, *Our Feet Walk the Sky*,[2] that I came across at the university of Iowa, brought me close to the writers I had been looking for. I took up their poems, short stories, essays, as I did Pulitzer Prize winner Jhumpa Lahiri's *Interpreter of Maladies*,[3] expecting, perhaps too idealistically, that their literature is different from that of cultural and political diaspora, having a character and quality of its own, fostered by both Indian and American value systems and cultural presumptions, crossing borders at both ends, yet well within the borders. I searched for the "cultural bridge" that can widen and accommodate the creative mind to relocate culture in its own terms.

In Indian notion, culture has both individual and social connotations, especially when it propagates the terms *Kula* and *Shila. Kula* implicates biological and cultural heredity of both an individual and a group. It is a lifelong discipline, an intimate conviction, a commitment to and a mutual relationship with one's resource tradition. *Shila* is the behaviour pattern that individuals and groups develop for themselves. Since *Kula* is the received one and *Shila* the changing one, the two concepts stand for tradition and change respectively, and make culture an ongoing process. The concept is well illustrated in the image of a person walking. Unless the back foot is firm on the ground, the front foot moving forward loses balance. In India, culture is regarded as a dynamic, multidimensional ever onward movement. The *Aitreya Brahmana* dictum *Charaiveti* (ever move on) can be recalled in the context. A culture is enriched as it flows through the complex interweaving of history, crossing borders in some form or other in every phase, but without losing contact with what flows into it from the upstream. I had these ideas in mind. Much of my interest in the new generation Indian American writers centered on whether and how far they incorporate the "upstream" in their American experience and creative writing. I had been well aware that these writers seek space in American book market, that they write for an audience a large section of which are unfamiliar with, or are accustomed to viewing Indian cultural tradition, value systems, relationships through colonial images and versions. The expectation of American publishers and the publicity machinery can be a serious constraint on the writers.

The new writers, however, did respond to my search. A write-up on the London-born, U.S.-raised Jhumpa Lahiri highlighted that when she started writing seriously, she set her stories not in Rhode Island she grew up in, but in Kolkata, that existed elsewhere, at least for the majority of her Western readers. In an interview, Jhumpa Lahiri gave her reasons: "I went to Calcutta neither as a tourist nor a former resident—a valuable position I think for a writer. I learnt to observe things as an outsider, and I also knew, as different as Calcutta is from Rhode Island, I belonged there in some fundamental way I did not seem to belong to the U.S."[4] Setting stories in Kolkata, she argues, privileges her to a "double vision." "There was the necessary combination of distance and intimacy." It was interesting to read a Rhode Island writer refusing to identify herself as a Rhode Islander, withstanding "demography of internationalism," the recent fad, to negotiate intimacy to Kolkata, a locale and a culture manifestly alien to her. In her meeting with media persons on Kolkata turf in January 2001, however, Jhumpa Lahiri has shifted her stance in defining her relation to the city: "I have been learning about the city where my parents were born. . . . It's been a wonderful part of my life. But it's not home."[5] Jhumpa Lahiri set me pondering over what exactly is the "fundamental way" that makes one belong to a culture, and the inability to do so, turns one to an outsider, if not legally, at least in one's own mind?

In *Our Feet Walk the Sky*, the introductory notes on many of the U.S.-born and raised Indian American writers echoed

Jhumpa Lahiri's feelings in one way or other. Amita Vasudeva is quoted complaining to her parents that making her grow up in the U.S. "is a fate worse than death." Brookline-born, Ohio-raised Sumeeta Gwande makes public her "envy" of people, who can answer the question "where is your home in one word." In India, for all the ongoing changes, "home" implicates roots in a family, a community, a culture. It is unexpected of a second generation Indian American to miss home in the Indian sense of the term, if she has that in mind. Equally unexpected is the culture shock of Amita Vasudeva, an ethnic American of the postmodern nineties.

If not sheer cultural political stance to voice space for the marginalized, the thoughts and realizations of these writers call for a serious consideration of their relationship with and commitment to the cultural process that shape their life and outlook. Let us have a glimpse of some recent Indian American literature that mirrors the cultural imbroglio.

We begin with Radhika Sita Chari's short story "Different Small Town" in *Our Feet Walk the Sky*. "She and I met in a women's bar. 'You are from where?' we asked in amazement. So we both lived in that small town." The narrator is an Indian American woman, and "she" her white American schoolmate, long forgotten, though both live in the same small town. On finding each other, the white lady recollects the school days in first person plural: "Our memories at our school." The narrator does not. She has her own unshared story of growing up in constant humiliation as the "only brown kid" in the small town seemingly indifferent to her. She remembers her history teacher asking her about India, "Why do women wear red dot? Why is the cow sacred?," and her inability to explain the ideas that for ages have sustained Indian belief system and customs. A child, she could not contest the American teacher's very attitude in identifying a distant culture in terms of stereotypical images fostered in the West. "If she asked about my grandfather, maybe I could have answered her," she thought in self-defence, little aware that an Indian grandfather is not merely a person, he is an institution, an embodiment of a cultural tradition. The Indian granddaughters know it and tell about it.

The only memory the storyteller has of her present company at school is that of the routine run in which the white girl came out first, and herself almost last although she always started out strong. The gym teacher used to ask her cheerily what happened, but she would turn to the white girl who won to give her a hug. The discrimination, even if not racially intended by the teacher, had distanced the two girls, the memory of it distances the two ladies farther: "I looked at the white lady sitting across from me. What of my reality she understands?" The story ends with the white lady leaving with a grin: "It's great to have run into you. I can't believe, we are from the same town." If the town is the metaphor of a community and a culture, the two ladies certainly do not belong to the same town. Or perhaps they do, if a systematic separation of cultural identities, lack of negotiation in cross-cultural behaviour and relationships typify an American small town.

The narrator smiles back at the white lady, "confronted with the horrors of re-lived memories." Racial distance, discrimination, humiliation, integral to her American life, have made her what she is. Not really a cultural hybrid, she can neither own nor disown her Indian roots, as she cannot her American upbringing. Perhaps she embodies a culture in the making, emerging out of non-assimilation of two cultural traditions.

Amita Vasudeva's "The Journal Entry" (*Our Feet*) exhibits the agony and confusion in living with the tag of a cultural hybrid in the U.S.: "I guess I've always pretty much passed as white. Not in color, white in culture—outwardly only. . . . I never talked about my heritage when I was younger, there is always that ever present fear in children of not being accepted, or even being cast out, ignored, ridiculed." What beats the narrator subject most, however, is not racial discrimination as such, she has grown up through it, but the fact that her ethnic identity denies her, her individuality, the prime bid of U.S. culture. Used to thinking of her own self in the American way of individual "I" rather than collective "we," she registers her discontent: "When you are different, 'the other,' they strip you of your individuality." To her "they" of course refers to America, but "they" also implies India she has created in her mind from some mediazed images. "A girl at the amusement park asked me out of blue, why I did not wear a dot on my forehead." The dot as a mark of cultural inferiority makes her inwardly react to her resource tradition.

In course of the story, the narrator, rather unexpectedly, chooses to wear her cultural difference as a distinction. The exaggerated ferocity of the stance exposes a mind in turmoil. "I hate it when people, specially recent Indian immigrants, think of me as a totally assimilated American, because I am not." She does not feel at home with the immigrated Indians either. "There are certain situations where I am completely American, and feel natural, comfortable and good about it, because after all I was born and raised in the U.S. And there are of course times at home . . . when I can dress Indian, be around Indian people, and feel just as comfortable. . . . There is no denying the fact that I am both." Noticeably, the narrator has a love-hate relationship with both Indian and American cultures. She is yet to own her paradox. "The Journal Entry" raises a deeper issue. Is culture a phenomena one can construct in keeping with which is best to one's lifestyle or which one feels more "comfortable" with?

Meeta Gwande's poem, "My Bed has Big Warm Arms" (*Our Feet*) answers the question in a way that contradicts Amita Vasudeva's ideas. In the poem, Indian and American cultures are projected as two different if not opposite on-going life process an Indian American is caught in. The poet makes use of rather over-simplified images for the two cultural patterns, the prominent ones are that of the bed for the Indian and the computer for the American

> My bed has big warm arms. . . .
> Lie down baby. I would warm you,
> My swollen hand will press against
> The small of your back. I will press
> My face against your cheek. . . .

I will never hurt you. . . .
My desk is hard and icy.
The computer hums impatiently
The smiling face, the rectangle,
The flashing arrow
Parent, brother, paper, project, class, job
Application, resume, self
My hands grip the edges of the desk
My shoulder muscles tighten
My neck gives up, my hand will explode. . . .
I feel the blood leaving me.
My bed has big warm arms.

Instead of the familiar either/or choice of shedding the old and donning the new cultural cap, the persistent tension of living between two lifestyles and life views wears the young poet out. It is an agonizing threshold position, almost polar opposite to what Bharati Mukherjee says in the Indian American cultural context: "I see it now as a set of fluid identities to be celebrated."[6]

For an Indian American of the second generation, an Indian "home" in America, is not always a bed with big warm arms. Aarti Kohli's "Thrka" (*Our Feet*) highlights the cross-cultural intricacies in a middle-class Indian American family. The high school student Meera, too kin to shed her Asian Indian ethnic identity, finds herself opening up a dialogue with the migrated Indian student, Anil, though she had reacted sharply at the news of his arrival at the school: "Why does everyone think I'm going to like an Indian guy?" The difference in culture and experience draw the two students to and distance them from each other right from their first chit-chat. "Do you remember India?" Meera asks. "Of course, don't you?" Anil answers, evidently unaccustomed to socializing with second generation Indian Americans in spite of his five years of stay in the U.S.: "I was born here." Meera responds "shaking her head sadly." An Indian reader can wonder if Meera's sadness is a passing mood or a genuine ingrained feeling for all her gestures of disowning her Indian roots.

A month later, Meera is "convinced that they were lovers in previous life." The idea of previous life is unlikely to occur to Meera in her American situation. She lacks grooming in the Indian belief system. Perhaps it is the writer who imposes the idea on the character in order to build the story by stereotypes. The idea refuses to merge with the contemporary American context of the story. Meera's mother reacts sharply at the sight of her daughter holding Anil's hands. She points her finger at the youth she has never seen before and commands him: "you go home." The stereotypical docile Indian male obeys. Anil is an anticlimax to the widely marketed image of the self-contained powerful American man. The mother grabs Meera's arms, pulls her to the car, muttering "I can't believe this girl. . . . What a disgrace! What will people say?" The mother has her arguments to disapprove Anil as her daughter's friend: "he works in a liqueur store." His is a family of "illiterates." "They are not just our kind of people," "you can't ruin our good names." It is unlikely of an educated Indian American working woman of the stature of Meera's mother to conserve a set of redundant middle-class Indian prejudices, when her own periphery in America extends beyond home, and she herself is too keen to have her daughter roots in the "new world."

The story ends on a melodramatic note, with the mother pushing the daughter back within what she considers a conservative domestic barrier, virtually threatening to put Meera out on the street if she behaved otherwise. The self-sacrificial daughter chooses to stay back with her parents, instead of trying to make her own future in the American mode she is more familiar with. The entire projection of the Indian American home is geared to a distasteful thrill. Specially the uncouth image of the mother throws the status of the Indian mother at stake.

The last story on our agenda is Jhumpa Lahiri's "A Temporary Matter," the first story in *Interpreter of Maladies*. A young Indian American couple exchange confessions every night as they struggle to cope with the loss of their child at birth and their failing marriage. The story is actually a gender power game in a subtle form, filtered through the clash of two cultural perspectives. The narrator weaves the tale mostly over the husband's experience. Shukumar, the husband, is a thirty-five-year-old Indian American graduate student in process of living through ideas. Born and raised in the U.S. as an out and out American, he is unfamiliar with the land of his ancestors, and has hardly any interest in Indian life and culture. Still some stereotypical Indian notions and inhibitions colour his outlook. Unlike a white American husband of his age group, he suffers an anxiety that he is still a student at thirty-five, and has been playing an "irresponsible male" at the household run by his working wife. He cannot accept the collapse of the "ideology of domesticity" and the diminutive status of the male breadwinner in his own American home. Nor can he compromise with any other image of a wife than that of a caregiver. The husband wife distance broadens as Shukumar gives way to his inhibition that a dominant wife is a betrayer.

Shoba, the wife, herself a second generation Indian American, decides to move out and make a life for herself. In her American way, she feels she cannot do without having some space around her. Shukumar resents her subjectivism, as he does her strength of purpose. Gender relationship turns into a self/other combat zone. Jhumpa Lahiri's story ends in a touching sequence. Shukumar tells Shoba of the dead child he had held against him, and they weep together "for things they now knew." In India it is believed that individual as well as familial and social relationships are lived to the full when men and women inter-subjectively relate to one another in a shared socio-cultural space. And that is possible because they have a shared value base. The subjugation-confrontation formula in which Shukumar and Shoba live their relationship makes it doubtful if their shared moment of sorrow is indicative of a shared life in future. Shukumar does not involve himself in any dialogue with his prejudiced mind in this regard, nor does Shoba. The writer does not work much within the value levels of her characters. The clash of cultural practices, norms, assumptions, and the resulting agony and anxiety exhaust and destabilize the characters.

The new literary voices betray lack of confidence. The much needed analytic, comparative and interpretative explorations are largely sidestepped to generalizations, oversimplifications, insidious debunking, if not misconstruction of the Indian, and an uncritical appraisal of the American life ways and life views within some set sellable images and ideas. Many of the writers lack the larger perspective essential to deal with the idea system and life ways of the two distinct civilizations they bring to the fore. Each historic community has its own approach to life, each culture its own cast of ideas. A work of art is rooted in the history, philosophy and ethos of a culture. To write about a culture or to cross cultural borders without realizing the cast is to betray a gap in understanding. It is said that literature, or any art form for that matter, is both a cultural process and result. In *Aitreya Aranyaka* dictum, a skillful work of art improves one's own self by making life balanced and rhythmic. Maybe the new Indian American creative writers in process of learning cultural dynamics, if and when they do as they cross cultural borders, will find rhythm, balance and proportion in their own terms. Their literature is still at an amorphous, unsettled stage. It has miles to go to create its own space.

NOTES

1. Homi Bhabha, "The Location of Culture," *Literary Theory: An Anthology,* ed. Julie Rivekin and Michael Ryan (Blackwell, 1998).
2. *Our Feet Walk the Sky*: *Women of the South Asian Diaspora*, ed. The Women of the South Asian Descent Collective (San Francisco: Aunt Lute Books).
3. Jhumpa Lahiri, *Interpreter of Maladies* (New Delhi: HarperCollins, 1999).
4. *India Today*, 21 June 1999.
5. *The Statesman*, 11 January 2001, p. 3.
6. Roshni Rustomji-Kerns, "Expatriates, Immigrants, and Literature: Three South Asian Women Writers," *The Massachusetts Review* (1998), 29: 655-67.

Names as Symbols of Identity in Jhumpa Lahiri's Stories

SUDHIR DIXIT

Names as Symbols in Literature

What's in a name? As far as the functional role of a name is concerned, it hardly makes a difference whether we call a rose by its own name or by the name of jasmine. Nevertheless, symbolically, it makes all the difference. All names have meanings and that is what makes them meaningful and symbolic in life as well as in literature. Names are symbols of identity as well, because bastards, illegitimate children and slaves had no independent names as such; they were called by the fancies of their masters. Christians have first names or baptismal names, which is being followed by the surnames or ancestral patronymic. "Proper names have an odd and interesting status. . . . Our first names are usually given to us with semantic intent, having for our parents some pleasant or hopeful association which we may or may not live up to. Surnames however are generally perceived as arbitrary, whatever descriptive force they may once have had. We don't expect our neighbour Mr. Shepherd to look after sheep, or mentally associate him with that occupation. If he is a character in a novel, however, pastoral and perhaps biblical associations will inevitably come into play."[1]

A name has two or more parts, viz. first name or forename, surname, middle name, title etc. Surnames indicate the occupation of the bearer (Smith, Tailor), place of habitation (Lincoln, Washington), appearance (Black, Brown, Short), character (Fox, Goodfellow), or father's name (McDonald, Robertson). Surnames pass on within a family from one generation to another and they are a symbol by which ancestors are kept alive in their descendants. Surnames are received automatically at birth, but first names are received in the capacity of an individual.

However, in real life, names may or may not represent personality traits; after all names are given to persons in their infancy and their potential cannot be perceived or recognized by their parents. In past, clergymen decided names of children, while in modern age parents have become the deciding authority in this regard. In this way, we find that in real life a child's name can reveal much about the parents. Most of the names relate to the appearance of the child, name of a patron saint, name of a deity, good moral quality which he or she is hoped to attain, or natural world. However, this is not true of all cultures. "In the majority of cases, children are given 'good,' likable, and propitious names. In some cultures (e.g., in some parts of sub-Saharan Africa, formerly in China, and sporadically in ancient Greece), however, the children are (or were) sometimes given 'bad' names with meanings like 'ugly,' 'disagreeable,' or 'crippled.' The purpose of such names, which are called apotropaic names, is to make the child undesirable to demons."[2]

Names are considered to have magical qualities in some superstitious societies and to know the real name of a person is tantamount to have a complete hold on that person.

In literature, however, names become doubly important. In a fictional work, a name becomes the essence or embodiment of personality. The omniscient writer names the character, fully knowing his actions, thoughts and destiny. In real life, parents are ignorant about the future development of the personality or destiny of their children and this is why in life names are more a projection of the dreams of the parents rather than a reflection of the child's personality, unless they are named after physical appearances. Literary onomastics is a discipline in which the use of proper names is examined in literature. In the most precise terminology, a set of personal names is called anthroponymy and their study is called anthroponomastics. A set of place-names is called toponymy, and their study is called toponomastics. Literary onomastics or anthroponomastics often focuses on the names of characters in fiction, called characternyms. The special feature of the characternym is that it usually represents its bearer in some appropriate way.

Traditionally, a hero's name should sound dashing and aristocratic, revealing his exemplary bravery, sophisticated status or extraordinary personality (Solomon of the *Old Testament* derives his name from the Hebrew name Shlomo, "Peace"). A heroine's name should be romantic and delicate, epitomizing the beautiful and chaste personality of the woman (Viola in Shakespeare's *Twelfth Night* reminds us of violet as well as of violin). A villain ought to have a name, which should reveal the crudity and villainy of his character (Wickham in Austen's *Pride and Prejudice* has a "wicked" character as is evidenced in the initial syllable of his name). The comic characters should have funny names (This is why we find funny coinages of comic names in the Comedy of Manners, Comedy of Humour and Victorian novelists. For example, Lady Sneerwell in Sheridan's *The School for Scandal*).

"When Margaret Mitchell was drafting her novel *Gone with the Wind* (1936), she first named her female protagonist Pansy, only later changing the name to Scarlett O'Hara. Although Pansy O'Hara captures some of the personality of the character, especially her youthful naiveté, it does not suggest the unconventionality and resourcefulness that she eventually shows. Scarlett, with its connotations of brightness, explosiveness, vigour, strength, and disdain for conventional morality, better suits the character. The two central characters of Thackeray's *Vanity Fair*, Becky Sharp and Amelia Sedley could hardly have their names exchanged. Becky is the sharp dealer; Amelia is the better (ameliorated) of the two."[3]

In literature, names express several things about human beings, some of them are being discussed below:

1. Personality traits (Dheeraj signifies patience and Adheer the lack of it; Agatha means "good woman.")
2. Caste (in Indian context, the surname Sharma reveals that the person is a Brahmin, while the surname Rathore tells that the person is a Kshatriya.)
3. Class (prefixes before names such as Sir, Lord or Rai Bahadur.)

4. Gender (Pushpa Kumari is the name of a girl or woman not only because Pushpa is a feminine name but also because Kumari, Bai, Devi etc. function as feminine suffixes. A writer however can reverse the gender propriety to underline the gender shift in the character, for example by substituting the short male form "subhash" for "subhashini" or "suhas" for "suhasini.")
5. Physical appearance [a girl with Rose as her name must be beautiful in a literary work with a pinkish or reddish hue unless the name is ironically used. Moreover, we all have heard about Ashtavakra, the sage whose body was deformed at eight places: "Ashta" (eight), "Vakra" (not straight). In *He Who Rides a Tiger*, Bhabani Bhattacharya's protagonist is Kalo (black), whose complexion is pitch black. But in Arundhati Roy's *The God of Small Things* we find a similarly black character named Velutha, which means white in Malayalam; an ironical reversal of the physical appearance is achieved by the writer, symbolizing a colour revolt that black colour may not be so bad after all, dismissing the White superstition about the supremacy or the essential goodness of the white colour.]
6. Occupation (for example the prefix Doctor, Professor or Captain; the modern official titles. In past, surnames indicated the occupation much more effectively. A Swarnakar in India or a Goldsmith in England used to make gold ornaments and was not supposed to writer a novel called *Vicar of Wakefield.*)
7. Religion (a boy with Krishna as his name must be a Hindu and Abraham should be a Christian while Hanif ought to be a Muslim.)
8. Connotative Reference (In literature, a modern character named Hitler or Judas has to draw negative connotative references, while a modern character named Julius has to refer to Julius Caesar. The connotative reference is not limited to the real historical persons, but also to fictional characters.)

Women writers are particularly conscious while naming their characters. In particular, the names of their women characters are significant after their marriage. "A change of personal name can be a powerful symbolic statement. In Western society, a woman once automatically adopted her husband's surname as her own, and socially used his full name instead of names given to her at birth (as in *Mrs. William Smith née Heather Gibson*, where the French-derived *née* means 'born'). Current practice is variable. Generally, a compromise is achieved in the everyday form (*Mrs.) Heather Smith*, where the personal first name is kept but the personal surname is changed. . . . Some committed feminists have dropped their family surnames altogether, and do not take a new one if married, since all such names are from the male line; instead, they may use a middle given name as surname (so that Heather Rebecca Gibson becomes Heather Rebecca)."[4]

As identity becomes the core issue, the names become quite significant. They are conspicuous not only by their presence, but by their absence as well. From time immemorial, names have been used as identity symbols or significators. For example, Adam, the father of all human beings, has been named from the Hebrew word meaning "red earth." In Hebrew it is not used as a personal name, but is simply a generic term for "man." The Book of Genesis tells how Adam was created from the earth and as the colour of Adam's skin was red, hence the reference to red earth. In literature, a name can represent innocence and purity [In *David Copperfield*, the heroine's name Agnes means "chaste" from the Greek adjective *hagnos*. Proteus, the fickle lover of Shakespeare's *Two Gentlemen of Verona* gets his name from the word "Protean" (changing).] A name can also denote physical appearance in literature, for example Oedipus was named after his swollen or pierced feet and the name Plato signifies "broad (shouldered)" in Greek. A name is indicator of the native country, as in Romeo (of Rome). Sometimes a writer ironically uses the choice of names in a work of art as does Oscar Wilde in his play *The Importance of Being Ernest*, where the protagonist Ernest is a playful degenerate and the heroine is not in love with the man, but with his name. A writer can also create funny names for his comic characters, as does Charles Dickens in his wonderful debut novel *Pickwick Papers*, where the protagonist is a funny man called Pickwick with other funny men in his group including Snodgrass, Winkle, Tupman etc.

When we come to the question of immigrant identity, we find that names are particularly significant for the modern Black American and Commonwealth writers. In literature, especially in literature dealing with the clash of cultures, countries and races, names emerge as identity symbols. For example, in *The Tribal Hangover*, Sri Lankan writer James Goonewardene's immigrant hero undergoes an identity crisis. His Sri Lankan parents have given him a name "Harindra," but as he is adopted by German foster-parents living in Australia, he is renamed as Harry. This young boy, torn between his Asian genes and Australian, confronts an identity crisis. Ultimately he decides to forge his own identity by creating a new name for himself calling him "Harindranath X": "If he had no identity, Harindra claimed, then he had no claims to the myth of a surname. He was just Mr. X, the mathematical symbol which stands for any unknown quantity must stand for the surname he did not bear or have a valid claim to."[5]

In *He Who Rides a Tiger*, the protagonist's name undergoes several transformations. In the jail, he is called P-14, as a prisoner has no independent identity of his own. Later, he renames himself as Mangal Adhikari in order to dupe and avenge the Brahmins and thereafter this low-caste hero assumes the fake identity of a Brahmin. "Kalo, as Mangal Adhikari, had truly attained reincarnation."[6]

Names have a connotative and symbolic significance in literature as they can never have in life. As David Lodge asserts, "In a novel names are never neutral. . . . The naming of characters is always an important part of creating them." Literature has its manifestly artificial naming system, which affirms the arbitrariness of language.

Names have been related to identity because "people's names have been regarded as closely linked with their owners' inmost natures. . . . Monks and nuns give up worldly interests and assume new names to mark a new life. . . . A comparable reaction, especially in the U.S., is the dropping of traditional surnames by African-Americans who, seeing them as 'slave names' adopt instead African or Islamic names, as when the American boxer Cassius Clay became Muhammad Ali."[7]

A forename or the first name thus becomes a representative or reflection of personality or identity. A surname or the last name on the other hand is a part of inheritance, indicating ancestral lineage. Most writers invent characters and therefore personal names for them. Novelists choose names of their characters with care, to achieve the right connotative effect.

In Toni Morrison's novel *Song of Solomon*, a black American character Macon is given the surname "Dead" by the American clerk out of carelessness. This surname becomes popular in the name of "Macon Dead" and it becomes a potent symbol of white man's lethal and sinister intentions of black man's annihilation. Most of the other names in the novel are ironically and significantly named after Biblical characters.

Name Symbolism in Jhumpa Lahiri

The expressive function of a name varies from culture to culture, situation to situation. In Jhumpa Lahiri's stories, Indian names express the Indian identity of her characters. They become potent symbols and tools to highlight the immigrant identity.

Jhumpa Lahiri's stories are scattered with details of traditional Indian names, food items, cooking details and wardrobe list providing the Indian or the ethnic touch. For providing still more ethnic touch, she plants three of her stories on Indian soul. These are: "Interpreter of Maladies," "A Real Durwan" and "The Treatment of Bibi Haldar."

In Jhumpa Lahiri, names become significant even by their absence. Boori Ma does not have a name because she has lost her identity and has become just a functional durwan doing menial chores. The group of women sympathizing with Bibi Haldar has no names because these women form a collective group. Mrs. Sen does not have a name because she has no identity of her own, no individuality distinct from that of her husband. In Indian society, women usually adopt the surnames of the husband's families; and at times, even their names are changed after the marriage. This symbolically signifies the one-way merger of identity, in which the wife's personality ceases to exist except as a reflection of her husband's personality. In Indian society, a woman at birth takes the surname of her father and after marriage, the surname of her husband. This issue has attracted much feministic attention because, for a liberated woman, surname becomes a symbol of male dominance. The woman trying to free herself from male dominance has to get rid of her surname, as we find referred to in Arundhati Roy's novel *The God of Small Things*:

> For the Time Being they had no surname because Ammu was considering reverting to her maiden name, though she said that choosing between her husband's name and her father's name didn't give a woman much of a choice.[8]

In Jhumpa Lahiri's story, Mrs. Sen is powerless as an individual; she is living in an alien society and with a husband who is unable to understand her emotional needs and longings. Mrs. Sen pines for Calcutta but she is imprisoned as a bird in a golden cage because her husband cannot go, and she cannot think of going alone. Remarkably enough, in all the three stories set in India, we are not told the proper names of the protagonists. They are referred to by their surnames or titles of address, thus suggesting a representative characterization. The interpreter is called Mr. Kapasi in the short story "The Interpreter of Maladies," the spinster protagonist is called Bibi Haldar in "The Treatment of Bibi Haldar," and the old durwan is called Boori Ma in "A Real Durwan."

In "A Temporary Matter," Shukumar and Shoba exist on the level of individuals as they are in the process of adapting to the individualistic American society. Their ancestral inheritance has been more or less severed or forgotten by them and this is why surname is neither necessary nor appropriate to express their personality traits. The opposite happens to Mrs. Sen, who has lost all her individuality after her marriage. Mrs. Sen is perhaps the best example of the solitary life of an alienated immigrant living in America. Mrs. Sen's forename has not been mentioned and her actual surname before marriage is no longer hers. Her identity crisis is expressed by the use of her adopted surname (the surname of her husband) in the title of the story. The same happens with Bibi Haldar, whose lack of individuality is represented by her lack of forename. She has a common form of address "Bibi." Boori Ma also has no name because she has no personality or individuality. She only earns the nickname "Boori Ma" and this referent indicates the whole lot of old homeless women in similar condition.

In "This Blessed House" also, we find several interesting features of the symbolism of names. When Twinkle clips the name of her husband Sanjeev to Sanj, we find in it the symbol of the disintegration and dwarfing of the husband's personality at the hands of his wife. It is nicely paralleled with the explosive situation where the Christ-mania of Twinkle becomes a constant source of torture for her husband. Twinkle is in itself an interesting name or nickname. She prefers to be called Twinkle, a name originated from a nursery rhyme and associated with the little star. Her name and her personality are thus reshaped by herself and she in this sense forges her own identity. She has a childlike enthusiasm, playfulness and joy of life and the name from the nursery rhyme is an effective symbol in epitomizing it. Twinkle is not her name by birth; her name is actually Tanima but she prefers to be called Twinkle, much to the amusement of the Americans. Nevertheless, the connotations of the name viz. speed, music, shining quality fit in well with her character. Arundhati Roy also comments on this word, "Twinkle was a word with crinkled, happy, edges."

Lilia in "When Mr. Pirzada Came to Dine" is a mixed name having Indian name "Lila" in it but modified to fit in an American society. For Pirzada, his daughters are not individuals (All the seven daughters have names starting with letter A). Children cannot be treated as distinct individuals or little men of identity, when they exceed in number. This is why Mr. Pirzada cannot relate their names to their identity and fails to distinguish them by their names. In "The Third and Final Continent," the protagonist is not named, because he is the representative of the thousands of Indian immigrants and to name him would be to delimit his appeal. In the story entitled "Mrs. Sen's" names also serve as a tool of alienation. When Mrs. Sen is told that in the telephone directory, there is only one Sen, she feels alienated and dislocated, "The man said he looked up my name in the telephone book. He said there is only one Sen. Do you know how many Sens are in the Calcutta telephone book?"[9] By emphasizing her solitary surname in the telephone directory, she is stressing her solitary existence in Boston, whereas in Calcutta she is obviously in her group.

Incidentally, like Lilia, Miranda too has Indian "Mira" in it, as Dev recognizes in their first meeting: "Part of your name is Indian." (87) Dev's reaction brings out in sharp focus the Indian immigrant's quest for all things Indian in order to relate with their past and make their present a natural extension of the inherited past. This is also reflected in Mr. Dixit's refusal to jog in Western shorts, and much to the amusement of his neighbours he jogs fully-dressed as he would have done in the then India, for the bare body is considered to be below dignity in the high-class Indian society.

Names of the characters become symbolical, representative and significant in a novel, as they can never be in real life. By using Indian names, Jhumpa Lahiri has Indianised her stories even though they may be set in Boston. She employs the names very carefully and experiments with names in several ways:

1. No Names: In several stories, Jhumpa Lahiri does not give names of several significant persons. In two stories, viz. "The Third and Final Continent" and "The Treatment of Bibi Haldar," the narrator's name is not disclosed. In another story "When Mr. Pirzada Came to Dine," the parents of the narrator are not named. Elsewhere also, we find the absence of names. Sometimes only initials are given in place of names (though not in Jhumpa), as is the case with Dr. Kashyap of Arun Joshi's novel *The Last Labyrinth* who is referred to as Mr. K throughout the novel for he is not portrayed as a person, but as a functional character with a lim-

ited role in his official capacity. In Arun Joshi's another novel *The City and the River*, we find a character called "The Nameless-One," because he has not yet found his identity, mission, and vocation.

2. Only Names: In several of the stories, only names are given and no surnames are mentioned, for example, Lilia in "When Mr. Pirzada Came to Dine," Shukumar and Shoba in "A Temporary Matter," Twinkle and Sanjeev in "This Blessed House." This signifies that the characters have become or are fast becoming individuals, accepting a nuclear type of family, being cut off from their roots and joint family system (inheritance of culture, values and genes is through surnames).
3. Only Surnames: Characters with only surnames lack individuality and they are mostly characters representative of their class, caste or province. For example, Mrs. Sen is a representative of 50,000 and more immigrant Bengalis living in US pining for fresh fish. Bibi Haldar is a representative character of the epileptic and ageing unmarried women in India.
4. Complete Name: A complete name signifies the self-realization of a man. It is often used by writers at the end of the novel when a character realises his true vocation or mission in life and gains a true identity, insight or understanding about his role in his life. For example, Arun Joshi in his novel *The Foreigner* calls the central character Sindi throughout the novel. At the end of the novel, Sindi becomes Surrinder Oberoi, because now his self-realization is complete and now he is on his way to help others, to serve society and of being useful to his fellow-beings. The full name may be contradictory as in "Som Bhaskar" of Arun Joshi's novel *The Last Labyrinth* where the dual impulses within the protagonist are revealed in the dual implicit reference to moon and sun incorporated in the complete name itself. In Jhumpa Lahiri, we do not find the use of a complete name to depict the resolved identity crisis, because her characters are representatives or symbols of a fractured identity.

Thus, we find that Jhumpa Lahiri's handling of names in her stories is thoughtful and masterly. Names for her are closely interlinked to the art of characterization. Jhumpa Lahiri is well equipped in the technique and subtleties of fiction, thanks to the course in creative writing attended by her. Her technique is so unobtrusive, subtle and unimposing that at times the reader feels that she is not resorting to any technique at all. Jhumpa Lahiri in this regard becomes a living example of the adage, "Still waters run deep."

NOTES

1. David Lodge, *The Art of Fiction* (London: Penguin, 1992), p. 36.
2. http://www.britannica.com/bcom/eb/article/printable/1/0,5722,115611,00.html
3. Tom McArthur, *The Oxford Companion to the English Literature* (Oxford: Oxford University Press, 1996), p. 655.
4. *Ibid.*, p. 610.
5. James Goonewardene, *The Tribal Hangover* (India: Penguin, 1995), p. 7.
6. Bhabani Bhattacharya, *He Who Rides a Tiger* (Delhi: Arnold, 1993), p. 103.
7. McArthur, p. 610.
8. Arundhati Roy, *The God of Small Things* (Delhi: IndiaInk, 1997), pp. 36-37.
9. Jhumpa Lahiri, *Interpreter of Maladies* (New Delhi: HarperCollins, 2000), p. 124.

Bicultural Ethos and Conflicting Claims in *Interpreter of Maladies*

PASHUPATI JHA and T. RAVICHANDRAN

It [America] is home to me but [I] feel a bit of an outsider too.[1]

With *Interpreter of Maladies*, Jhumpa Lahiri bursts upon the literary scene out of nowhere just as Arundhati Roy did only two years back. The coveted acclaim from the Pulitzer Prize committee spurs rave reviews, many honourable but a few deplorable as well, on Lahiri and her *Maladies. The New Yorker* upholds her as "one of the 20 best writers under the age of 40."[2] *New York Times* finds in her "a wonderfully distinctive new voice" and "a writer of uncommon elegance and poise."[3] *Los Angeles Times Book Review* praises her for "delicate yet assured" touch, "leaving no room for flubbed notes or forced epiphanies."[4] Her story collection is called by *Newsday* as "a stunning literary debut."[5] Although published for the first time in this collected version, the stories seem "to have sprung full-grown, like Athena, from the head of its creator, with all the force and assurance of art."[6] Therefore, the collection is aptly called "a timeless treatise."[7]

But there is another side of the coin too; there is no dearth ever of a few carping critics. For instance, for Ragini Ramachandra, Lahiri's "experience is awfully limited and one is haunted by a sense of absence—the absence of *depth.*"[8] She is accusing the Pulitzer Prize Committee for selecting her for the prestigious award which "might have belonged elsewhere . . . . possibly to someone with years of toil, tears, sweat and blood."[9] In fact, she hardly has any praise for the artistic merits of Lahiri; rather, she finds neither "the idiom nor the experience"[10] in her. Further, she is appalled by her "utter artificiality," "over dramatization," "vicarious descriptions," "surface reality," and considers her "offensive and outrageous" dabbling in "uncanny theme and weird atmosphere."[11] The authors of this paper are reminded of similar negative criticism of C.D. Narashimaiah against V.S. Naipaul, calling the novelist's reputation "bizarre."[12] Or, for that matter, the same critic's rude shock and utter disbelief at the event of Arundhati Roy's winning the Booker Prize and hence his sharp criticism on her book as "a curse to creativity."[13]

It may be observed that while criticism from the West highly applauds the literary merits of Lahiri, those from the East share mixed responses. When the author herself is candid in admitting her bicultural ethos, we find, a prejudice against her ethnicity in the critical responses. However, untouched by these deprecatory remarks on Lahiri, we are attempting modestly to explain the central core of this collection, that is, how biculturalism and conflicting mind-sets contribute to searing strain, even if temporarily, in the lives of her major characters. These conflicts may be within the confines of a couple's life in their own house or may spread out to two different cultures that have not gone through the process of acculturation. Sometimes, it also spills over affecting a particular society inhabited by people with contrasting attitudes. Thus, all the stories in the collection finally boil down to the maladies of maladjustment.

The first story of the collection, "A Temporary Matter," depicts the disturbing early years in the conjugal life of Shoba and Shukumar, born of the Indian parents but settled down in the U.S.A. Shukumar is an academic who reluctantly has to go outside for a conference when Shoba is expecting a baby. When he returns back, he is stunned by the news of the birth of a stillborn baby, symbolically signifying the stillness that has crept in their own relationship. Now they live in the same house as strangers and have become "experts at avoiding each other in their three-bedroom house."[14] Shukumar wistfully thinks of those romantic days of the past: "He thought of how long it had been since she looked into his eyes and smiled, or whispered his name on those rare occasions they still reached for each other's bodies before sleeping." (5) He also wonders how Shoba has been keeping the house in disarray whereas earlier she used to put her coat on a hanger, her sneakers tidily in the closet, and pay all the bills on time. But after the trauma, she is treating the house as if it were a hotel.

In such a moribund relationship, it is the regular electrical blackouts in the evening, for a few days, which come to their rescue. Initially, they resent it because they have to hurry through all the chores of dinner and thereafter and rely on candlelights. Yet, it reminds them of India, the country of their parents which they used to visit but rarely. Shukumar fondly remembers his bygone days with his father who is no more. He wishes to know more about Indian history and geography and yearns for "his own childhood story of India" (12) whereas Shoba recollects a rice ceremony in India related to the birth of a baby there. But it serves a sharp reminder of their inability to perform the same at their home. Shukumar ruefully ruminates: "Their baby would never have a rice ceremony, even though Shoba had already made the guest list, and decided on which of her three brothers she was going to ask to feed the child its first taste of solid food, at six months if it was a boy, seven if it was a girl." (11)

This enveloping darkness for a few hours every night renders them unfit for going out or for any other work. Shoba, then, suddenly proposes a novel plan to relieve that boredom; they should tell each other something they have never told before. So, he tells her how he had cheated once during his examination of Oriental Civilisation some fifteen years back. Surprisingly enough, instead of shame, he feels cathartic relief. Gradually, he picks up enough courage to inform her that once he tore the picture of an attractive woman from her magazine and how he had felt an intense desire for that woman. It is the closest he has ever come to infidelity. Similarly, Shoba also confesses of her small pitfalls. Shukumar has an apprehension that Shoba may take this opportunity to inform him of some past affair. However, the only shameful event from her side is when she gave a lame excuse to avoid her mother-in-law during dinner by suggesting that she has to do a lot of work in her office but she had in fact gone out with her friend, Gillian, and had a martini. In due course, the couple welcomes this regular darkness at night because this results in stirring afresh their dormant relationship and subconscious desires:

> Something happened when the house was dark. They were able to talk to each other again. The third night after supper they'd sat together on the sofa, and once it was dark he began kissing her awkwardly on her forehead and her face, and though it was dark he closed his eyes, and knew what she did, too. The fourth night they walked carefully upstairs, to bed, feeling together for the final step with their feet before the landing, and making love with a desperation they had forgotten. She wept without sound, and whispered his name, and traced his eyebrows with her finger in the dark. As he made love to her he wondered what he would say to her the next night, and what she would say, the thought of it exciting him. "Hold me," he said, "hold me in your arms." By the time the lights came back on downstairs, they'd fallen asleep. (19-20)

As Sumana Roy rightly observes: "Shukumar and Shobha are exiles who are trying to locate space through time. It is only when the electric lights are off that the electricity of their closeness lights on them; their area of darkness is flooded by the flashlights of memory."[15] Unfortunately, for them, the repair work in that area is finished ahead of schedule, putting an end to their communion in the dark. Yet, they have survived the worst crisis of their life, at least, temporarily. In this respect, this is a highly psychological story in which light stands for the conscious reality that may be troublesome. This conscious reality is also the contrasting mindset of the couple asserting itself when there is light all around. Darkness, nonetheless, signifies the strong undercurrent of subconscious desire for love unconditioned by ego or will. So, even when the light comes, Shoba switches it off, and prefers to dine in the candlelight. Ultimately, this darkness has resulted into their self-knowledge, for the better or worse: "They wept together for the things they now knew." (22)

Is this patch-up between them just 'a temporary matter'? Or could it last forever? Because all the time Shoba had been looking for a separate apartment despite their novel but 'dark' way of communication, for she needs "some time alone." (21) In addition, she has been troubled by the final disclosure of Shukumar, so far unknown to her, that the stillborn baby was a boy and that the nurse had suggested Shukumar to hold the dead baby close to him for sometime which would enable him to bear his loss more easily. As this chance was denied to Shoba, who was not in her sense at that time, she now needs some more time to tide over her grief. Above all, loss of a baby is always more intense and unbearable for a mother than for a father. What Jhumpa Lahiri wants to suggest here is that it is always not so easy to reconcile the conflicting claims of two different mindsets suffering from 'the strange disease of modern life'; especially, when the only point of reconciliation in the form of a baby is lost.

Fortunately, the conflicting claims of different minds are easily reconciled in the next story, "When Mr. Pirzada Came to Dine." Here, the narrative voice is that of Lilia, a small girl living happily with her parents in New England. In their sedate family life, a lot of warmth is added when Mr. Pirzada, on a scholarship from Pakistan to USA for some Botanical research, visits them almost every night. Mr. Pirzada has an appealing personality; a lecturer in Botany at Dacca University, he has to leave behind his wife of twenty years and seven daughters ranging between six to sixteen with all of their names beginning with the letter A. The story throws light on the cultural difference between an Indian family settled in the USA and a Muslim academic who is temporarily there. The only link between Mr. Pirzada and this Bengali family where he comes for dinner is the common language. For 10-year-old Lilia, Mr. Pirzada is only an Indian, till her father informs her that after Partition of 1947, Mr. Pirzada is no more an Indian, which in any case is, beyond the grasp of innocent Lilia. In fact, it is rather difficult for her to make any sense out of it:

> It made no sense to me. Mr. Pirzada and my parents spoke the same language, laughed at the same jokes, looked more or less the same. They ate pickled mangoes with their meals, ate rice every night for supper with their hands. Like my parents, Mr. Pirzada

> took off his shoes before entering a room, chewed fennel seeds after meals as a digestive, drank no alcohol, for dessert dipped austere biscuits into successive cups of tea. (25)

The tension in the story builds up when in 1971, due to turmoil in East Pakistan, there is exodus of millions of refugees for asylum in West Bengal leading to war between India and Pakistan and the genesis of Bangladesh. Coming to Lilia's house becomes critical for Mr. Pirzada since he needs to know the latest development of the war situation by watching the television news at night. He is particularly worried about his family living in Dacca, and his anxiety is shared by the entire family of Lilia. Lilia now has the feeling that Mr. Pirzada has always been smartly dressed as if "in preparation to endure with dignity whatever news assailed him, perhaps even to attend a funeral at a moment's notice." (31) Lilia also waits for a surprising moment when Mr. Pirzada's seven daughters would suddenly appear on the television blowing kisses and waving hands to the father. After the news, there are long discussions between Mr. Pirzada and Lilia's parents "as if they were a single person, sharing a single meal, a single body, and a single silence, and a single fear." (41) This story, therefore, is unique in the sense that emphasis is here on fostering a cultural bond despite apparent differences of birth and breeding.

Perhaps, the only case of cultural conflict in this story is evident when Lilia is caught red-handed by her teacher in the library while browsing through the pages of Asian History, instead of doing a class assignment on American History. Otherwise, the focus is on an overwhelming cultural link between Mr. Pirzada and the Bengali family. Mr. Pirzada is the most welcomed guest and Lilia always waits for the candy that Mr. Pirzada brings for her: "I coveted each evening's treasure as I would a jewel, or a coin from a buried kingdom." (29) Moreover, all of Lilia's family feels the absence of Mr. Pirzada when he returns to his country, now Bangladesh. For months together, they eagerly wait for the news of his family, but nothing comes from that end—was their cultural bond so tenuous that it got snapped so easily? No, they finally get a card from him commemorating the Muslim

New Year along with a letter with the happy news that all of his daughters and his three-storey house are safe. He then writes in his letter that mere "thank you" would be meagre to express his feeling of gratitude for all the dinners, all the love and concern that he received from them. At this point, even young Lilia realises what it means to miss someone who is so many miles away and understands the agony of Mr. Pirzada when he had missed his wife and daughters for so many months.

However, culture clash becomes the crux of the matter in the title story, "Interpreter of Maladies." Lahiri brilliantly shows the conflict between the first generation Indian-American couple from New Jersey, Mr. and Mrs. Das and their children, Tina, Ronny and Bobby, who have never visited India, and Mr. Kapasi, an old-fashioned Indian tourist guide. "Lahiri piles them together into a bulky white Ambassador car on one hot day in Konark in Orissa and for a brief moment brings them tantalizingly close together before shattering their tenuous bonds into smithereens."[16] That the Das couple is mismatched is clear at the outset itself. Even the taxi driver, Mr. Kapasi, notes their casual attitude towards their children: "Mr. and Mrs. Das behaved like an older brother and sister, not parents. It seemed that they were in charge of the children only for the day; it was hard to believe they were regularly responsible for anything other than themselves." (49) In addition, while Mr. Das seems to be more attached to India, Mrs. Das is indifferent in her attitude towards this country. Her hostility arises mostly because of the hot climate here: "'I told you to get a car with air-conditioning,' Mrs. Das continued. 'Why do you do this, Raj, just to save a few stupid rupees. What are you saving us, fifty cents?" (49) In this manner, the mental conflict runs here on two levels—one, in the personal relationship of Mr. and Mrs. Das and the other, in the too brief embryonic emotional exchange between Mr. Kapasi and Mrs. Das.

> The self-absorbed Mrs. Das stops polishing her nails and removes her sun glasses the moment she hears Mr. Kapasi's part-time job as an 'interpreter of maladies.' He explains the symptoms of Gujarati patients to a local doctor who does not know that language. So far,

> none has taken his profession seriously. His own wife looks down upon this job and when other women ask her, she tells them that he is a doctor's assistant. Mr. Das too is quite unimpressed by Mr. Kapasi's profession; he rather likes his job of a guide since he himself has to bring his students periodically to museum and explain things to them. Only Mrs. Das finds this job of interpreting maladies so romantic: "She did not behave in a romantic way toward her husband, and yet she had used the word to describe him. . . . Her sudden interest in him, an interest she did not express in either her husband or her children, was mildly intoxicating." (53)

Mr. Kapasi, so far living a drab life, suddenly becomes lively and yields to the urge to look back at the rearview mirror to get a complete view of the charming face of Mrs. Das. Subsequently, Mrs. Das, so intrigued by his job of an interpreter, asks many questions related to that and finally concludes that such patients are very dependent on him and hence he is more important for them than the doctor himself. After all, the doctor's remedy depends on the accuracy of his interpretation. This is news for Mr. Kapasi himself:

> Mr. Kapasi had never thought of his job in such complimentary terms. To him it was a thankless occupation. He found nothing noble in interpreting people's maladies, assiduously translating the symptoms of so many swollen bones, countless cramps of bellies and bowels, spots on people's palms that changed color, shape, or size. (51)

He begins to read his importance in the eyes of Mrs. Das, further sustained by her invitation to come to the same dining table while having lunch. Not only that, he is invited to be present in the family snaps, there is rather one photograph of him with Mrs. Das alone. He starts fantasizing his future affair with her. He cherishes romantic ideas when he finds Mrs. Das carefully observing the erotic sculpture of the Sun Temple. When Mrs. Das wants his address from him on a piece of paper, torn from a magazine showing a movie hero and heroine passionately embracing each other, he imagines his future date with Mrs. Das. Thus highly encouraged, "In addition to glancing at her face he glanced at the strawberry between her breasts, and the golden brown hollow in her throat." (53-54) Later, when he gets a chance to be physically close to her, he is overwhelmed by the smell of "a scent on her skin, like a mixture of whiskey and rosewater." (55) In contrast, he becomes aware of the bad smell emanating from his own perspiration.

Mr. Kapasi does not want their romantic encounter to end so soon, so after the Sun Temple he brings the Das family to the hills of Udayagiri and Khandagiri. As Mrs. Das is too tired to climb the hills, she remains with Mr. Kapasi in the taxi. For Mr. Kapasi, it is a golden chance to enjoy the enchanting proximity of Mrs. Das; for her too, it is a god-sent chance but for a different reason. She suffers from a malady and feels that Mr. Kapasi can interpret the reason behind that. The story reaches its climax when Mrs. Das confides in him that one of her three children, Bobby, is not born of Mr. Das but of a Punjabi friend of her husband during his sojourn at her home. She has been suffering this agony for the last eight years because she has not told the truth to Mr. Das so far. Unknown to such maladies, Mr. Kapasi fails to offer her any satisfying remedy. He rather alienates her by asking her indiscreetly, "Is it really pain you feel, Mrs. Das, or is it guilt?" (66) Mrs. Das glares at this confronting question but her silence proclaims the imminent gap engulfing the two. Ironically, in order to rescue Bobby from the harassment caused by monkeys, and soothe him by her maternal care, Mrs. Das brings out a hairbrush from her straw-bag to comb his hair. But she, inadvertently, throws the address of Mr. Kapasi out, "it fluttered away in the wind. No one but Mr. Kapasi noticed. He watched as it rose, carried higher and higher by the breeze, into the trees where the monkeys now sat, solemnly observing the scene below. Mr. Kapasi observed it too, knowing that this was the picture of the Das family he would preserve forever in his mind." (69) Thus, Mr. Kapasi, who can interpret the maladies of hundreds of patients, first fails to diagnose his own malady and then to interpret the painful past of Mrs. Das and offer her an alleviating remedy.

In "Sexy," the only story narrated by a non-Indian character, the attitudinal conflict is apparent in the beginning itself in the extra-marital affair of Dev, a Bengal-born settled in the U.S.A.

now, with Miranda. First, he attempts to Indianise her name to Mira, but he has himself become more western in his outlook on extra-marital life than her. That is obvious in his desperate and repeated attempts to adjust her limbs during lovemaking and yet his resentment that "he couldn't get enough of her." (85) Miranda, nevertheless, is more curious to know about Bengal so that she can get emotionally close to her increasingly unavailable lover. Hence, after Dev leaves her apartment, she returns to her bed "still rumpled from their lovemaking and studied the borders of Bengal." (85) Subsequently, they have weeks of intense enjoyment when Dev's wife, who appears to be very much Indian in beauty and attitude, is away for a while in India. Even after her return, Dev comes to Miranda on Sundays pretending to his wife that he is going for a long jog. At the same time, Miranda gets to know of a harrowing tale of infidelity from her friend in the office, Laxmi. Laxmi reveals her of the sad plight of her cousin, even after nine years of her marriage, who is grieved to realise that her husband has been carrying on an affair with a European girl half his age. The turning point in the story comes when Miranda has to look after Rohin, the precocious son of that cousin, for a few hours.

The caption for the story comes from the use of the word, 'sexy' by Dev for Miranda in a highly romantic situation, and for her: "It was the first time a man had called her sexy, and when she closed her eyes she could still fell his whisper drifting through her body, under her skin." (93) Incidentally, there are so many 'firsts' in the story; Dev is the first man in her life with moustache, first to bring bouquets for her and first to whisper her name again and again while making love, and she is the first woman for Dev with such long legs. However, when the word "sexy" gets repeated in an unusual situation, revelation dawns upon the mind of Miranda. That innocent child Rohin calls her "sexy" after he sees her in a glamorous silver cocktail dress. When asked to explain what he meant by it, he says, "It means loving someone you don't know." (107) Then he explains that his father has used the same word for an unfamiliar white girl during his travel in the aeroplane causing the misery of his mother: "she cries, sometimes for hours. Sometimes straight through dinner. Sometimes she cries so hard her eyes puff up like bullfrogs." (104)

Touched by the poignant narration, the same expression 'sexy' has a somewhat different impact on Miranda: "Miranda felt Rohin's words under her skin the same way she'd felt Dev's. But instead of going *hot* she felt *nümb.*" (107-8, emphases added) Miranda is haunted by the image of Rohin's mother desperately shrieking at her husband, "tell me if she's sexy." (108) This results in an attitudinal change in Miranda, who now starts making lame excuses to avoid Dev. Determined not to become another home-breaker, one Sunday she ventures out alone but under "the clear-blue sky spread over the city" (110)—the open sky signifying her freedom from Dev with a clear and heightened perspective on man-woman relationship. In this way, the cultural conflict operates in a different way in this story; Dev, an Indian, acts more westernised than the western Miranda who comes closer to Indian values of compassion and self-sacrifice.

The story which follows "Sexy," has no sex at all. "Mrs. Sen," deals with the utter loneliness, disorientation, and despair of a Bengali lady in the U.S.A., who has to cope up "simultaneously with being foreign and being a wife."[17] Mrs. Sen, a woman of thirty and without child of her own so far, has to spend almost all her time in the university apartment, while Mr. Sen, Professor of Mathematics, is all the time busy in his academic engagements. Mr. Sen suggests his wife to learn driving and move out of the house when free. But, for a typical Indian housewife, driving does not come easily. Eventually, Mrs. Sen takes up the job of baby-sitting but at her own house. Eliot, a child of eleven, comes to her house everyday after his school, because his mother works fifty miles North and his father lives two thousand miles away. Eliot's mother is aloof; she hardly shows warmth even for her son. Even after her dinner at home, she leaves the left-over work for Eliot to finish. To the contrary, for Mrs. Sen, Eliot becomes a surrogate-son; she always gives him some thing to eat which is outside her official obligation. Eliot too enjoys and reciprocates her affection.

The cultural conflict here works on two levels—Mrs. Sen's sticking to Bengali culture without adjusting to the American one, and the conflicting attitude of her Indian habits with those of Eliot's mother. Mrs. Sen remembers every moment her Calcutta, her dear city, where fresh fishes of favourite types are available in plenty all the time. She tells Eliot: "in Calcutta people ate fish first thing in the morning, last thing before bed, as a snack after school if they were lucky. They ate the tail, the eggs, even the head. It was available in any market, at any hour, from dawn until midnight." (123-24) Other than relishing fish, the next important thing in her life is letters from home. Once when Eliot collects a letter and gives it to her, overjoyed, she embraces him, which in American way may be uncalled for. She is always waiting for those letters coming from her relatives because they contain the details of her past life in Calcutta. Yet, those letters are vexing too because her relatives have wrongly concluded that she is leading a heavenly life in America, while she is quite miserable in an alien culture amidst alien people. She bursts out in frustration: "'send pictures,' they write. 'send pictures of your new life.' What picture can I send? . . . "They think I live the life of a queen, Eliot." "They think I press buttons and the house is clean. They think I live in a palace." (125)

In the whole of this collection, Mrs. Sen is the most isolated character because she had been unwillingly plucked out from her own soil and planted in an alien country where her roots are drying out. The real crisis comes when the shopkeeper informs her on phone that the fish of her choice is available and she has to rush immediately to take its delivery. When she phones her husband in the University to drive her to the market, he delays it much, leaving Mrs. Sen fuming and fretting around her house. Mr. Sen finally comes, drives her and Eliot to the market but the damage had already been done. So the next time, Mrs. Sen does not wait for him and drives the car on her own with Eliot inside resulting into a minor accident. Intolerant of such irrational craving for fish, Eliot's mother takes her son back from Mrs. Sen. Throughout the story we find the juxtaposed and conflicting mindsets of the aloof and officious attitude of Eliot's mother with that of the deeply emotional attachment of Mrs. Sen; and both representing the uneasy mix of American and Indian values. However, the one who is really affected in this conflict is the unfortunate child Eliot, whose attempt to relate himself and belong comes to an abrupt end. Eliot has to live with that hangover, left to fend for himself, looking "out the kitchen window, at gray waves receding from the shore," with a forced self-denial and subsequent withdrawal. (135)

The caption of the next story, "This Blessed House," is highly ironical because there is constant bickering between Sanjeev and his wife, Twinkle. They have recently moved from Boston to Connecticut where Sanjeev is a high profile professional soon to become the vice-president of his company while he is still thirty-three only. Therefore, everything looks smooth in his life except the ever-conflicting mindset of the couple. When Sanjeev chooses to marry Twinkle she has already been abandoned by her American lover. However, Sanjeev has never had his taste of love and easily accepts the matchmaker's offer for the attractive Twinkle. While Sanjeev is all for Indian food and fondly recollects his student days when he used to go to an Indian restaurant for bellyful of Mughlai chicken with spinach, for Twinkle Indian food is a bother: "she detested chopping garlic, and peeling ginger, and could not operate a blender, and so it was Sanjeev who, on weekends, seasoned mustard oil with cinnamon sticks and cloves in order to produce a proper curry." (144)

The conflict arises when the couple starts discovering in the new house so many scattered pieces of Christian things left behind by the earlier tenant. While these items—a white porcelain effigy of Christ, a wooden cross key chain, a small plastic dome containing a miniature Nativity scene, a painting of unbearded Jesus, a plaster Virgin Mary statue—are treasured by Twinkle, Sanjeev is vexed to his last bone by these Christian paraphernalia. Each discovery irritates and unnerves Sanjeev and he secretly waits for a chance to throw everything in the garbage. Further, his ire gets aggravated when Twinkle succeeds in motivating the whole of Sanjeev's friends, who come for the party, to join in her hunt. And later, she emerges a stunning victor with a solid silver bust of Christ, weighing a good thirty pounds, from the attic. Moreover, even Sanjeev cannot but acknowledge "its undeniable value" and its "dignity, solemnity and beauty." (157) Yet, because of the widening mental gap between him and his wife, he dislikes even this creation of superb art, "he hated it because he knew that Twinkle loved it." (157) This brief quotation is enough to indicate that conflicting claims are at the core of their conjugal life; a house becomes really 'blessed,' not by outward decorative pieces, but by inner harmony between the inhabitants.

The adjustment with foreign culture again surfaces in "The Third and Final Continent." The narrator-protagonist of this story leaves his home in 1964 for England where he lives with 'penniless Bengali bachelors,' all struggling to educate and establish themselves abroad. He attends lecture at the London School of Economics and works at the same time in the University Library. In 1969, he gets an offer from MIT to join there as a librarian and he arrives by plane the day Americans land on moon. For full six-weeks, he has to become a tenant of Mrs. Croft, who like other Americans, is overwhelmed by the unfurling of American flag on the moon, and this strange lady makes him to call this event 'splendid.' There is a contrast between this wonderful moment of Americans and the sad and sordid plight of this Bengali librarian slogging his hours among the dusty shelves and sustaining himself on nothing more than cornflakes and milk. Even his newly wedded wife is still in India and she has to clear the formalities of visa to join her husband.

His wife gets the first taste of cultural clash even before she lands up in America. She does not take any meal from Calcutta to Boston because her appetite is killed by the mere thought that she is offered oxtail soup on plane. She is a traditional Bengali lady and, like Mrs. Sen of the earlier story, looks misfit here. When the narrator brings her to Mrs. Croft, for her approval, he has apprehension that this fastidious lady, aged 103 and living mentally in the previous century, may reject outright his wife Mala. However, after a searching scrutiny, she declares to his amazement, "She is a perfect lady!" (195) From this point onwards, love sprouts in his heart for his wife. In fact, Mrs. Croft becomes mother-surrogate for the protagonist; as he has lost his mother, so Mrs. Croft's acceptance of Mala does not only bridge the cultural gap but the emotional one too. Though initially he has not yet adjusted to his wife of arranged marriage, the old lady's acknowledgement of his wife's perfect elegance gives him an epiphanic vision and allows him to commence a long-lasting loving relationship.

There are two more stories in the collection, "A Real Durwan" and "The Treatment of Bibi Haldar." These two stories, unlike the previous ones are set in Bengal. Like her father, for Jhumpa Lahiri too visiting Calcutta periodically is not only a ritual but also an obsession. Her observant eyes have collected from there a few events and characters to pen these two stories. In "A Real Durwan," the cultural clash is replaced by the clash of changing fortunes. Boori Ma is a refugee from East Pakistan, now settled in Calcutta in a destitute plight. There is both fact and fiction ('believe me or don't believe me' is her constant refrain) of what she says about her past. She is now separated from her husband, four daughters, a two-storey house, her rosewood *almari,* and a number of coffer boxes. She always points to the better off of the apartments that she has also once "tasted life." (71) As per her story, her life in East Pakistan was simply a luxury and she used to bathe in scented water with petals and perfumes. Now, she has to work as an unofficial Durwan (guard) of those apartments, living on the charity of those inhabitants. Despite her honesty, she is finally fired off when the newly fitted washbasin gets stolen. The inhabitants accuse her of her negligence and start looking for 'the real Durwan.'

'GIRL, UNSTABLE, HEIGHT 152 CENTIMETRES, SEEKS HUSBAND'—these words in a newspaper matrimonial column would speak for the plight of a naïve misfit, who has epileptic fits in "The Treatment of Bibi Haldar." The attitudinal clash here is between her simplicity and the craftiness of her cousin and his wife. Orphaned since childhood, they take care of this simpleton, but they extract a lot of labour from her in running their shop.

> When it comes to her marriage, they make many excuses, because it will involve a lot of expenditure. They finally leave her in the lurch and she survives only on her prudent savings and the kindness of others. When she becomes a mother without marriage, delivers, and nurtures the baby, her fits are miraculously cured. This indicates that had her cousin taken some care of her, there would have been no malady in her life. Thus, this story comes down to the bare clash of simplicity and selfishness.

In conclusion, though most of the stories are of Bengali individuals, they touch on universal themes, making them both specific and broad in their appeal. The conflicts of these individuals are the maladies of the inhabitants of a bicultural universe. Talking about the bicultural universe, Jhumpa Lahiri herself admits that it perplexes her. Notwithstanding her skeptical critics, Lahiri is modest enough in acknowledging the fact that winning Pulitzer had actually been the single greatest surprise in her life, "something like winning the lottery without ever having bought a ticket."[18] Pulitzer being a Prize bestowed on an American author for distinguished fiction dealing with American life, Lahiri gives contingency to the doubts in the minds of her own parents too. Though at 18, she got American citizenship, yet for her mother, she is first and forever an Indian. For this reason, Lahiri surmises: "Furthermore, my book, in her opinion, wasn't about American life. It was about people like herself and myself—Indians. I suppose I should be grateful that my mother wasn't on the Pulitzer committee."[19] Lahiri is equally amused by the way she has been categorised:

> as an American author, as an Indian-American author, as a British-born author, as an Anglo-Indian author, as an NRI (non-resident Indian) author, as an ABCD author (ABCD stands for American born confused "desi"—"desi" meaning Indian—and is an acronym coined by Indian nationals to describe culturally challenged second-generation Indians raised in the U.S.). According to Indian academics, I've written something known as "Diaspora fiction"; in the U.S., it's "immigrant fiction." In a way, all of this amuses me. The book is what it is, and has been received in ways I have no desire or ability to control. The fact that I am described in two ways

or twenty is of no consequence; as it turns out, each of those labels is accurate.[20]

The above quote, straight from the author's mouth, sums up the central argument of this paper too and speaks of the bicultural ethos and conflicting claims which underline all her stories.

NOTES

1. Jhumpa Lahiri in an interview, http://www.rediff.com/news/2000/apr/11jhumpa. htm, p. 1.
2. As quoted in http://www.saja.org/lahiri.html, p.1.
3. Editorial Reviews, http://www.amazon.com/exec/pbidos/ASIN/039592720X/ref=ase_pifaliterajournaA/107-4587518-1373353, pp. 1-2.
4. *Ibid.*, p. 3.
5. *Ibid.*
6. *Ibid.*
7. Parmanand Jha, "Home and Abroad: Jhumpa Lahiri's *Interpreter of Maladies,*" *The Indian Journal of English Studies*, Vol. XXXVIII (2000-2001), p. 116.
8. "Jhumpa Lahiri's *Interpreter of Maladies*: A Temporary Matter?," *The Journal of Indian Writing in English*, Vol. 29, No. 1 (Jan. 2001), p.50
9. *Ibid.*
10. *Ibid.*, 51.
11. *Ibid.*
12. The Function of Criticism in India: Essays in Indian Response to Literature (Mysore: Central Institute of Indian Languages, 1986), p. 133.
13. C.D. Narasimhaiah, "The Booker Prize: A Curse to Creativity, Arundhati Roy, *The God of Small Things (*1997)" in *The Literary Criterion*, Vol. XXXII, No. 3, 1997.
14. Jhumpa Lahiri, *Interpreter of Maladies* (New Delhi: HarperCollins India, 1999), p. 4.
15. Sumana Roy, "Fusions of Horizons in Jhumpa Lahiri's *Interpreter of Maladies,*" *Critical Practice*, Vol. III, No. 1 (January 2001), p. 95.

16. Sandip Roy-Chowdhury, "*Interpreter of Maladies*: A Fresh Take on Immigrant Lives," *India Currents* (Oct. 1999), http://www.ncmonline.com/arts-and-culture/1999-10-08/books.html, p. 2.
17. "Maladies of Belonging: An Interview with Jhumpa Lahiri" by Vibhuti Patel, *Newsweek International*, 20.9.99, http://www.umiacs.umd.edu/users/sawweb/sawnet/books/patel_lahiri.html, p. 2.
18. Jhumpa Lahiri, "To Heaven without Dying," http://www.feedmag.com/book2/essay_lahiri.html, p. 1.
19. *Ibid.*
20. *Ibid.*

Acts of Migration and the Despondency of the Lonely Traveller: Reading across *Interpreter of Maladies*

ALESSANDRO MONTI

In the short story "Interpreter of Maladies" Jhumpa Lahiri evokes the act of translation in terms of a failed act of speech, a fantasy of fulfilment and desire that ends however in anxiety and defeat. A part-time tourist guide and interpreter for the patients of a medical man who does not speak Gujarati, a language common among his practice, the Indian protagonist of the short story tries to negotiate his interstitial position within a fragmented (that is polyglossic) society by slipping towards a sentimental gesture of migration. His furtive slippage is aptly couched in modes of voyeurism (represented by the perturbing view of the partially exposed body of the expatriate woman), surely a pun on his activity as a guide—one who makes the other(s) see, a promoter of gazes who in his turn submits the other(s) to his incessant gaze.

The situation of interwoven scrutiny constitutes with a revenge the spirit of the colonial travelogue in a nutshell, since it involves the explorer (in our case, the expatriate family back to India for a while) and the native. This paradigm of mutual gazing transforms the body of the female newcomer into a spectacle. This reversal in the economy of the act of viewing, one that implies a strategy of possession and simultaneously deconstructs the hierarchies of power, epitomises concealed options of migrancy, both in the refusal of the "archaic heritage" in which the unsatisfied guide is doomed to live (and whose closures are symbolically represented by the reference to the un-naked body of his wife, who does not undress even in the privacy of love-making) and the "available" body of the other woman. She, the

Indian woman from the States, is "imagined" through a view of bare legs and behaviour of haughty indifference. In other words, her image is "translated" into a passive object of sexual desire and silent hegemonic possession. Paradoxically, her half-anguished narration of the quick intercourse with a friend, an episode that represents the burning secret of her life, de-imagines her condition of "availability." She becomes "untranslatable" when she asks for an interpretation of her conjugal betrayal.

In answering the woman, the perplexed interpreter substitutes the full responsibility of the diagnostic for the uncommitting neutrality of the translator. By doing so, he constitutes the identity of the distanced woman in terms of fixity and, finally, of refused repeatability of circumstances. The rigid judgement that he pronounces on her ("Is it really pain you feel, Mrs. Das, or is it guilt?"[1]) shifts the meaning of their encounter from a fantasy of stereotyped desire to a calculating possibility of seduction. As a matter of fact, the economy of desire of which the guide is part does not tolerate any displacing confusion of roles and purposes in the distribution of responsibilities.

The interpreter cannot translate her words, that is, he cannot transfer her request for an explication into the responsibility of a full diagnosis. He is obliged to re-imagine his role, from interpreter of maladies to presiding mediator in the debate between the husband and the wife. His choice to keep to the borderlines of the story (now he cannot enact the imagined figure of the seducer any longer, since his act of betrayal has already been accomplished by someone else) should be turned into an erosive sign of pedagogy against the freedom of sexual exchange. Then, the truncated narrative of desire articulated by the guide moves cautiously to the edge of fear and withdrawal. This "cold" behaviour suggests a demonstrative shift towards fixity and simultaneously enunciates the disciplinary control of the too yielding woman. This "archaic" mixture of repression and stifled desire deploys a deep sign of disturbance, one that should be inscribed into a peculiar and ambivalent discourse. Such discursive opposition between the man and the woman does not recognise an explicit turning inside outside of the balance from the "affective" to the "effective." The "Romantic" aura to which the expatriate woman refers ("'But so romantic,' Mrs Das said dreamily, breaking her extended silence" [50]), when she hears of the interpreter's work and responsibility, percolates into the dull and almost dumb reaction of the man. He keeps quite stolidly to the literal limit of his profession,

> He was silent.
>
> "Mr. Kapasi, don't you have anything to say today? I thought that was your job."
>
> "My job is to give tours, Mrs. Das."
>
> "Not that. Your other job. As an interpreter."
>
> "But we do not face a language barrier. What need is there for an interpreter?"
>
> "That's not what I mean. I would never have told you otherwise. Don't you realize what it means for me to tell you?"
>
> "What does it mean?" (65)

His silence should be "interpreted" (sorry for the pun) as a surfeit of realism, since he defers discursively his contact with the woman to a narrative framework of supplementary and cumulative judgement against her. He shares, as it were by proxy, the insignia of male authority, but after discarding the more seducing identity of the lover,

> She did not resemble the patients in the doctor's office, those who came glassy-eyed and desperate, unable to sleep or breathe or urinate with ease, unable, above all, to give words to their pains. Still, Mr. Kapasi believed it was his duty to assist Mrs. Das. He ought to tell her to confess the truth to Mr. Das. He would explain that honesty was the best policy. Perhaps he would offer to preside over the discussion, as a mediator. (67)

The interpreter would assume the role of a "dry" go-between, of a messenger of guilt and then of pacified knowledge, rather than of domineering and tearing love. All passion seems to be spent in this story: here the act of migration ends in a sort of emotional and dumbish cul-de-sac, in a blind path to truth whose emotional stoppage and whose hints of authoritarian behaviour will come again to the surface in two other short stories of the volume, "Sexy" and "A Temporary Matter."

A similar kind of fixity is rehearsed in the short story "Sexy," in which the romance implying a possible small miscegenation is reduced to a tiring iteration of gestures ("the ends of the three cigarettes he always smoked in the course of his visits") and to a rigid surveillance of movements, "during the day he called every hour. . . . Once he learned Miranda's schedule he left her a message each evening at five-thirty. . . . Just so he said, she could hear him." (84) This artificial synchrony restores the obsession of the timetable and forces a consensual strategy of repeatability, one that ensures an everlasting act of control and consequently of possession. The disciplinary fetishism to which the woman Miranda is subject in the short story displays highly artificial sequences of "Romantic" time, whose rhetoric of passion deploys however the unmediated intensification of control. Instead of expressing the timeless "irrationality" of love, the situation represents the triumph of what Bhabha defines the "ghostly time of repetition."[2] We should associate the sequential structure of the single event that matters in the scheduling process of the narration (his repeated phone calls to the woman, according to a timetable grounded on the day's work) with a repressive notion of the act of gazing.

Such momentous reversal in the eulogy of contemplation (here the gaze of the lovesick seducer is surmounted by the domineering eye of the master, the Hiṇdu "pati") elicits uncertainty and finally produces a liminal and elusive state of being. The "ghostly time of repetition" (it is not a coincidence at all that the schedule of the clandestine and furtive meetings between the two lovers is regulated either by sequences of external domestic imposition or by a repetitive strategy of free time) appears to be more invasive than accumulative. Its recursive strategy *does* indicate an exorbitant transition from the relative safety of the "pedagogical" (such as termed by Bhabha, that is a coherent sign of reproductive temporality) to the "repetitious" dimension of the performative.[3] This framework generates a transgressive notion of "double-time," within which we should be able to detect the saucy movement that replaces for the freedom of love-making the "constitutional" pedagogy of jogging. However, this exchange of values requires an erasure of identity, one that exchanges a human being for a complex rhetoric of presence, but simultaneously obliges him/her to procedures of discursive silence. This un-mediated request interrupts the line of continuous development, given that it does not require necessarily the evolution of the past into the future. The couple have no real story of their own, except for the exterior paraphernalia of love and the crude shadow of passion.

However, this instance of sentimental alienation pushes to an interstitial importance the need for homogeneity and structured presence. In the midst of western order and duration the migrant, that is the male lover, questions the purposes of rationality and articulates ambivalence for himself and loss for the female other. This movement empties of whatever quality the space in which the female protagonist of the short story lives. The hegemonic migrant shifts impermanence and deprivation to the unsure self of the western woman, who is obliged to "imagine" herself through the medium of a cocktail dress. However, the time-honoured and slightly pathetic practice of seduction, adopted by the woman when "she dresses to kill," clashes against the cultural indifference of the male, who does not "authorise" a view of her body that can evade his scenario of surveillance,

> Miranda pictured the two of them at a restaurant in the South End they'd been to, where Dev had ordered foie gras and a soup made with champagne and raspberries. She pictured herself in the cocktail dress, and Dev in one of his suits, kissing her hands across the table. Only the next time Dev came to visit her, on a Sunday afternoon several days since the last time they'd seen each other, he was in gym clothes. After his wife came back, that was his excuse: on Sundays he drove into Boston and went running along the Charles. The first Sunday she opened the door in the knee-length robe, but Dev didn't even notice it, he carried her over to the bed, wearing sweatpants and sneakers, and entered her without a word. Later, she slipped on the robe when she walked across the room to get him a saucer for his cigarette ashes, but he complained that she was depriving him of the sight of her long legs, and demanded that she removed it. So the next Sunday she didn't bother. She wore jeans. She kept the lingerie at the back of a drawer, behind her

> socks and everyday underwear. The silver cocktail dress hung in her closet, the tag dangling from the seam. Often, in the morning the dress would be in a heap on the floor; the chain straps always slipped off the metal hanger. (93)

Here the cocktail dress represents the language of desire and select availability, whereas the male lover imposes a more essential economy of intercourse, whose norms of behaviour and tight time schedule are regulated so as to suit a prearranged organisation of meetings between the interstices of his week-ends. The man replaces the safety of routine for the pleasure of surprise and the progressive discovery of the other woman. He chooses to behave as a half-bored husband would do, rather than embodying the persona of the true passionate lover. The romance of seduction survives paradoxically in the incessant propensity that the cocktail dress has to slip off the metal hanger and fall in a heap on the floor. This gesture of disorder and undomesticated reaction constitutes in the text a substitutive vision of imagined nakedness. It stands for a pathetic reappraisal that reinstates the hurt movements of seduction contrived by the woman and simultaneously relegates the intimate play of desire to the "cold" secrecy of the closet. This uncanny splitting of powers and acts between the woman and the cocktail dress (since it does for her and instead of her what she is not allowed to accomplish) indicates a transferred view and a decentralised fulfilment of the female body.

We should outline a devaluation of her direct exposure and of her movements of seduction in such procedures of estranged displacement of the feminine body, whose visibility is submitted to a sign of authority that denies the unpredictability of its presence. The lazy gaze of the lover deconstructs the otherwise potentially nakedness of the woman into a broken and fetished sequence of separated items, whose unrecomposed fragments reduce her to the status of a walking icon, to a pair of bodiless legs. Of course we are dealing with a part-time love, a mundane act of migration "beyond the pale" and, I would like to add, across the transparency of desire. As a consequence, the act of recognition emerges into a repetitive exercise of discourse that substitutes for the real presence of the lover the distanced authority of an absent voice. The repetition of the word "sexy," first pronounced by her adult lover and subsequently echoed by the Indian boy, also constitutes in terms of distanced physical presence the act of viewing the other person,

> "Go ahead," he urged, walking backward to his end of the bridge. His voice dropped to a whisper. "Say something." She watched his lips forming the same words; at the same time she heard them so clearly that she felt them under her skin, under her winter coat, so near and full of warmth that she felt herself go hot.
>
> "Hi," she whispered, unsure of what else to say.
>
> "You're sexy" he whispered back. (91)

The voice of the male constitutes again an act of speech (similar to his obsessive and controlling telephone calls) that should be turned into a possessive sign of gendered power and authority. This movement invites safety rather than the true sting of passion—its stereotyped character is endorsed by the apparently naïve word "sexy," uttered by the boy gazing at Miranda in her cocktail dress,

> "Please put it on," Rohin asked, suddenly standing behind her. He pressed his face against her, clasping her waist with both his thin arms. "Please?" (105-6)
>
> Rohin fastened the zipper to the top, and then Miranda stood up and twirled. Rohin put down the almanac. "You're sexy." He declared.
>
> "What did you say?"
>
> "You're sexy."
>
> Miranda sat down again. Though she knew it meant nothing, her heart skipped a beat. Rohin probably referred to all women as sexy. He'd probably heard the word on television or seen it on the cover of a magazine. She remembered the day in the Mapparium standing across the bridge from Dev. At the time she thought she knew what his words meant. At the time they'd made sense. (106-7)

The iterated articulation of the word "sexy" confirms the reduced identity of the woman: she is just a body to be viewed and to be used. But the male gazer(s) construct(s) her identity through a peculiar repetition of utterance and explicative hints of possession. Both of them repeat a stance of cosmopolitan gaze that embraces the whole terrestrial globe, making it completely visible, "naked" as it were. These two "privileged" gazers, unified by the word "sexy," share for a while their powers with the woman. She is admitted to a full vision of the geographic and political globe when she visits with her Indian lover the Mapparium at the Christian Science centre. Again, the Indian boy Rohin plays with her the game of guessing the world's capitals. Both males share their knowledge with her, in a highly symbolic act of temporary transferred power, one that even includes diachronic summaries of colonial and postcolonial sequential duration, "He explained that many of the countries, like Siam and Italian Somaliland, no longer existed in the same way; the names had changed by now." (90)

A change of names is also suggested in the text by the implied pun "Miranda-Mira." The Shakespearean resonance of wonder and discovery, the aura of novelty and primeval freshness with which the name is imbued in *The Tempest*, are de facto domesticated by the half-concealed deconstruction of the original glamorous namesake into the slightly derogatory "Mira Masi" (or Auntie Mira),

> "Part of your name is Indian," the man said, pacing his steps with hers.
>
> She stopped, as did he, at a circular table piled with sweaters, flanked with pinecones and velvet bows. "Miranda?"
>
> "Mira. I have an aunt named Mira." (87-88)

Such cruel reduction to the inferior rank of "auntie" (as a rule, a marginal presence in the complex organisation of the Hindu extended family) signifies the desolation and solitude in which the American woman is obliged to live. She occupies an interstitial span of time in the full life of the eastern migrant, whose demand for her presence (or for the pleasure of her naked body) is regulated by the strict and unchangeable claims of another life and the pressures of distancing commitments. This contradiction, between his requests (the devouring hunger for her) and the barrage constituted against her intrusion into family life, could be represented by the antinomic meanings (or semantic clusters) that we find in the Sanskritised name "Mira." In fact, it can mean either "the ocean, the sea" or indicate "a limit, a boundary." Thus, we might as well pun on the name "Miranda," she who would roam at liberty but is limited by a boundary. This meticulous obsession for regularity (expressed in "Sexy" by the fixed ritual of the "sliced" dirty weekend) comes again to the surface in the first story of the collection, "A Temporary Matter." It narrates of a young married couple, who are drifting apart after the loss of a stillborn baby. The chronotype of the story moves initially backwards, to the initial time of their suffering: "Six months ago, in September, Shukumar was at an academic conference in Baltimore when Shoba went into labour, three weeks before her due date." (2) The radical stoppage of time here (one that reminds us of the "still" time in which Miss Havisham, the ghostly woman of *Great Expectations*, lives) should be argued in sheer terms of dualistic elision (or rupture) between the "past" represented by six months ago and the untimely "date" of three weeks before her due. This dissemination of analexes and prolepses reveals a purpose of displacement in the temporal construction of the text.

I could perhaps detect an intratextual quotation (or "inside" pun) in the concealed economy that shifts strategically the meanings across similarities. To me, the seemingly innocent notation "he was in Baltimore," supposedly at the crucial time of their loss, evokes the tearing juxtaposition of life and untimely death in the "romantic" Anglo-Indian short story by Rudyard Kipling "Without Benefit of Clergy." An English official lives in love with a Muslim "bibi" (or native wife), who is expecting his child. He returns on a short absence on duty to find that a son has been born. To express his joy, the father sings at the top of his voice, "In Baltimore a-walking, a lady I did meet!" However, the child will die untimely of a seasonal autumn fever, soon followed by his mother.[4] The very title "A Temporary Matter" seems to bring the echo and the forlorn pathos that are suggested by "Without Benefit of Clergy," not only because both stories lay high stress on the tearing theme of impermanence and final separation (albeit through the medium of different agencies of rapture), but also because of the subtle dialectic between knowledge and ignorance, shared happiness and its sad failure.[5] There, the Indian climate constitutes the external and deciding factor of disturb in the intimate life of the loving couple, an element that imposes conditions and stoppages in their doomed relationship. A more radical and intimate fixing of boundaries produces isolation and fear of living in "A Temporary Matter," through the disjunctive agency of death (from the Anglo-Indian "baba" to the migrated and westernised baby, I would say). These problematic boundaries in the time of everyday life are subsequently enhanced by a further imposition of disarrangement and the disavowal of a regular time-table. The stormy and icy winter of the North American subcontinent provokes a series of power failures, and introduces modified and sentimentally retroactive patterns of communicative behaviour in the private life of the estranged couple.

The new order imposed by the blackouts restores partially the time-table of food, a well-ordered symbol of organised regularity and undisturbed continuity in the once unfragmented lives of the protagonists,

> Each of the recipes was dated, telling the first time they had eaten the dish together. April 2, cauliflower with fennel. January 14, chicken with almonds and sultanas. He had no memory of eating those meals, and yet there they were recorded in her neat proofreader's hand. (7)

To store food away and to cook it might be seen as a metaphor of national identity and joint memory of the past. However, we should as well analyse the contention between a previous harmony and a split present in more sedate terms of personal and private experience. A well-stocked storeroom constructs the role of the migrant Indian wife in consonance with her "imagined" task of the "Laksmi-within-the-house." She is a purveyor of food, a force generative of life-to-be and wealth. With the loss of their son, the failed mother is reduced implicitly to the identity of a "masi," the drudging auntie in the house without a future of her own. The temporality of this story seems to be built around the latent contrast that opposes the "tik-tok" of the modernity to the archaic force of dharma. The title itself, "A Temporary Matter," seems to indicate that the permanence of a native ideology of life constitutes the deep motif in the story and that the shift to the "realist" time of the West has not been accomplished yet. Despite the emphasis on the importance of the romantic and sentimentalised attitudes nurtured by the couple in the dusky atmosphere induced by the power cuts, the question or the image of their restored homogeneity (even if temporary and partial) still depends on the communality of eating together. This site of mutuality (but also of hegemonic belonging and conformity to roles) is however distorted by the inversion of tasks between them; it is the man, not the woman, who goes around shopping and who does the cooking.

The sense of duration inside the story (beyond the emotional stoppage of which I have told) is measured by the progressive dwindling away of the food accumulated a bit maniacally by the wife,

> When she used to do the shopping, the pantry was always stocked with extra bottles of olive and corn oil, depending on whether they were cooking Italian or Indian. There were endless boxes of pasta in all shapes and colors, zippered sacks of basmati rice, whole sides of lambs and goats from the Muslim butchers at Haymarket, chopped up and frozen in endless plastic bags. (6)

> It never went to waste. When friends dropped by, Shoba would throw together meals that appeared to have taken half a day to prepare, from things she had frozen and bottled, not cheap things in tins but peppers she had marinated herself with rosemary, and chutneys that she cooked on Sundays, stirring boiling pots of tomatoes and prunes. Her labeled mason jars lined the shelves of the kitchen, in endless sealed pyramids, enough, they'd agreed, to last for their grandchildren to taste. They'd eaten it all by now. Shukumar had been going through their supplies steadily, preparing meals for the two of them, measuring out cupfuls of rice, defrosting bags of meat day after day. He combed though her cookbooks every afternoon, following her penciled instructions to use two tea-

> spoons of ground coriander seeds instead of one, or red lentils instead of yellow. (7)

As I have already indicated, the negative turning point in the situation is figured by the reversal of what I would like to term the "tik-tok" alternation: life and death, to live together and to drift into separation, the accumulation of food and its daily consumption. Finally, the man who tries to restore the broken balance (that is, the "archaic" normalisation) takes on himself the duties of a woman with respect to food.

The short story ends on a sad note of missed reconciliation ("they wept together, for the things they now knew" [22]), given the nature of the knowledge that has percolated through the interstices of time and reciprocal silence, a revelation that kills definitely the baby for the second time in his inchoative life and transfers the "unimagined" modernity of the migrant couple to a genealogical and gendered line of continuity: the father and the (lost) son, with the exclusion of the mother, a lack of "benefit" that separates them once for all,

> Now it was his turn to speak. There was something he'd sworn he would never tell her, and for six months he had done his best to block it from his mind. Before the ultrasound she had asked the doctor not to tell her the sex of her child, and Shukumar had agreed. She had wanted it to be a surprise.
>
> Later, those few times they talked about what had happened, she said at least they'd been spared that knowledge. In a way she almost took pride in her decision, for it enabled her to seek refuge in a mystery. He knew that she assumed it was a mystery for him, too. He'd arrived too late from Baltimore—when it was all over and she was lying on the hospital bed. But he hadn't. He'd arrived early enough to see their baby, and to hold him before they cremated him. (21-22)
>
> Shoba looked at him now, her face contorted with sorrow. He had cheated on a college exam, ripped a picture of a woman out of a magazine. He had returned a sweater and got drunk in the middle of the day instead. These were the things he had told her. He had held his son, who had known life only within her, against his chest in a darkened room in an unknown wing of the hospital. He had held him until a nurse knocked and took him away, and he prom-

ised himself that day that he would never tell Shoba, because he still loved her then, and it was the one thing in her life that she had wanted to be a surprise. (22)

The three short stories ("Interpreter of Maladies," "Sexy," "A Temporary Matter") that I have selected for my analysis are constructed agonistically on the dangerous border between a plea for reciprocated love and the maintaining of the "archaic" signs of authority, between silence and the dubious "benefit" of knowledge. In particular, "Sexy" globalises as it were the two major themes of the "mastery" and the act of "voyeurism" (maybe the "privatee" of which Chaucer speaks throughout "The Miller's Tale") in the man-woman relationship. In fact, the implied exposure of the female body in the short story evokes a postcolonial geography of the world, an acquired awareness of changed identities and a full list grounded on the exotic names of capital cities. These associations inscribe the body of the woman into a geography of shifting authorities and powers. Such procedures are mirrored in her shy and progressive "discovery" of the map of India (of Bengal, in particular), an act of inverted migration that extends the unseen boundaries of her life and makes a lonely traveller of the American young woman. A failed purpose of "imagined" migration through the half-viewed body of a woman is rehearsed in "Interpreter of Maladies," a short story that reconstructs truth in the wake of removed sexual tension and failed understanding. Similarly, in "A Temporary Matter," the difficult revelation of truth destroys whatever residual permanence of shared purpose is left in the estranged lives of a married couple: a "benefit" of solitude that this short story shares with "Sexy," whereas "Interpreter of Maladies" lays its emphasis on misunderstanding and emptiness of soul, on the famished desire for passion and on difference of tongues and aims.

NOTES

1. Jhumpa Lahiri, *Interpreter of Maladies* (Flamingo: London, 2000), p. 84.

2. Homi K. Bhabha, *The Location of Culture* (London and New York: Routledge, 1994), p. 143.
3. *Ibid.*, p. 145.
4. The short story has been collected in *Life's Handicap*, 1891, after a previous apparition (1890) in a literary magazine.
5. The title "Without Benefit of Clergy" should be primarily referred to the fact that in the Middle Ages persons that could be claimed to be clergy (that is, "clerks") might be tried by a Church court, which was considered less severe than a secular court. The test was ability to read Latin, and was applied with great laxity. Thus "Without Benefit of Clergy" indicates ignorance and means implicitly the condition of someone that is "doomed to die." The Latin verse that the claimant had to read was usually known as the "neckverse," the verse that he had to spell to save his life.

Nine Sketches Interpreting Human Maladies: An Assessment of Jhumpa Lahiri's Stories

RASHMI GAUR

> Being in a foreign country means walking a tightrope high above the ground without the net afforded a person by the country where he has his family, colleagues, and friends, and where he can easily say what he has to say in a language he has known from childhood.
>
> Milan Kundera, *The Unbearable Lightness of Being* (75)

This statement sums up the thematic dilemma of the stories included in Jhumpa Lahiri's Pulitzer-prize-winning collection *Interpreter of Maladies*, sub-titled "Stories of Bengal, Boston and Beyond." Out of the nine stories included in the collection, two stories present Indian characters exclusively against the Indian backdrop—locale, characters, superstitions and taboos; the other seven are based on the inner landscape and strafes of Indians who have settled—out of choice or compulsion—in Boston or beyond: "beyond" symbolizing the "emotional and spiritual reaching out." (*OP*, 91) Lahiri views herself as "an interpreter of emotional pain and affliction." (*LM*, 1) She boldly and brilliantly maps the shores of her protagonists' inner worlds, often blurring the lines between the concepts of optimism and pessimism, constantly underlying the fact that questions on which a meaningful happiness of life depends can be tackled in two ways—intellectually and existentially. Her characters intuitively understand that intellectual answers are superficial and lead to a banal existence, as the receptive and emotional absorption of experience is largely absent in such answers. At the same time, however, her stories suggest that questions related to life and its meaning, often do not even require precise solutions, as they are inherently incapable of refashioning the truth of the centre of being; and that when such questions are asked, they become different with the different moods in which they are asked.

Six stories of this collection are based on the predicaments and inner turmoils of Indian immigrants in the United States. These characters have been uprooted from the secure life-mode of a traditional set-up, and are struggling to cope with the new environment by learning new strategies and cope-up methods—but in order to provide an alternate life-mode, such learning has to be lived and experienced at first hand. Sometimes the process of adaptation is smooth, as in the case of the nameless narrator of "The Third and Final Continent," while sometimes it shatters the innermost defences of an individual who had no option but to surrender meekly to the brutality of circumstances, as in the case of the woman protagonist of "Mrs. Sen's." The other three stories are set in Bengal, though broadly speaking, the thematic approach to questions related to the fundamental purpose of life remains the same. Boori Ma in "A Real Durwan" underscores the impossibility of communicating emotional pain and loneliness to others while "The Treatment of Bibi Haldar" describes the trauma of a female victim of circumstances, who is trying desperately to carve out a breathing space for herself.

Lahiri's stories do not present any intrigue, mystery or formal denouement in the traditional sense. Her stories are the statements of human despair, felt particularly within the institution of marriage. Rooted in the time and locale when the old settled way of life is being radically challenged and refashioned, her characters often display shattered minds and frayed nerves, beneath which the nervous whisper of morbid passions is clearly audible. In some stories, though, we come across an inner resolve and determination to overcome the emotional imbalance and the indication that it is never too late to begin life afresh. The first story of the collection, "A Temporary Matter," illustrates on the one hand the fact that in New England marriage can be treated as a temporary matter, and on the other the reassertion of the validity of a new beginning in life. The style is simple, shorn of any superfluity which makes the underlying pathos and the dim hope of salvation towards the end all the more poignant. The story depicts Shukumar and Shoba trying to avoid each other, as after the death of their premature child they are facing an inner crisis and are not in a situation to communicate their feelings to each other. Shoba is not able to forget the absence of her husband at the time of the delivery of her still-born child. For her, the arrival of the child was a symbol of the fruition of her love for Shukumar, but its death marks the death of her love and sensitivity for life in general. Shukumar broods on how he and Shoba "had become experts at avoiding each other in their three-bedroom house, spending as much time on separate floors as possible. He thought of how he no longer looked forward to weekends, when she sat for hours on the sofa with her coloured pencils and her files, so that he feared that putting on a record in his own house might be rude. He thought of how long it had been since she looked into his eyes and smiled, or whispered his name on those rare occasions they still reached for each other's bodies before sleeping." (5) Shukumar's and Shoba's reactions to the personal tragedy of child-loss are different, though equally intense. Shukumar wants to stay in the house, seeking consolation in his inertia, putting off any movement to go out, "to get the mail, or to buy fruit or wine at the stores by the trolley stop." (2) He even seeks refuge in the room which was planned for the child, "partly because the room soothed him, and partly because it was a place Shoba avoided." (8) Shoba, on the other hand, forces a solitary aloofness on herself—her deliberate staying out, taking on additional projects, shirking from any emotional intimacy are part of a defense mechanism, which she has developed around her, to enable herself to bury the loss beneath the grave of her aloof silence.

To the Indian psyche, marriage is not primarily a sexual partnership; it is, as Bertrand Russell puts it, an "undertaking to cooperate in the procreation and rearing of children." (161) A child cements the bond of marriage—without a child, marriage is considered banal and incomplete. The loss of the child turns Shoba into a mechanized automaton. The systematic care and affection with which she had created a home for the two of them, cooking chutneys on Sundays, "stirring boiling pots of tomatoes and prunes," (7) writing meticulous instructions on her cookbooks and dating the recipes, has now dried within her. Engrossed in her misery, she overlooks the fact that Shukumar, too, has to tread through his own private hell—still he tries to create a semblance of home for Shoba by cooking food every evening almost religiously. Cooking is the only activity which links him to everyday normalcy and to Shoba, imparting him the satisfaction that he is doing something productive, because if "it weren't for him, he knew, Shoba would eat a bowl of cereal for her dinner." (8)

The situation changes when the electricity department announces a power cut for five-days, forcing the intimacy of darkness on them. During these power cuts, Shukumar and Shoba start telling each other something they had never shared before. Their confessions do not communicate their real emotion, but still break the ice. Shoba's revelation, on the last day of the power cut, of her plan for living separately shocks Shukumar. In order to hurt Shoba, he deliberately reveals the fact that their child was a male and he had held it close to his heart. Somehow this revelation brings them together in a flood of tears underlining the fact that cultural roots cannot be severed so easily. Their reunion is symbolized by the Bradford couple walking arm in arm on the road. Kindling of birthday candles is also symbolic, as it conveys the message of dispelling the darkness which sometimes surrounds us temporarily. The darkness of pessimistic situations can be dispelled by going back to those memories which have positive values and associations for us. The simple narrative technique of the story charms the reader.

By comparison, the second story of the collection, "When Mr. Pirzada Came to Dine" is rather stale. The tragedy of Mr. Pirzada does not convey any authentic poignancy, it remains rather superficial. The narrator of the story Lilia is a young girl of impressionable age, who is only vaguely aware of her cultural roots. Mr. Pirzada, a resident of Dacca, is forced to live through Bangla Desh's violent struggle for independence through the news bulletins, while working on a thesis in a distant land. He has no means to know the condition of his wife and seven daughters whom he had left behind in his native land. Perhaps for this reason, the child-narrator of the story becomes a special object of his affection, who, though a bit startled by the "theatricality of his attentions," (29) devoutly prays for the safety of Mr. Pirzada's family. Lilia is a keen observer too, and meticulously records all the details of his routine—hanging his gray and blue coat on the rack, offering lozenges and truffles to her, setting his pocket watch to the local time in Dacca and putting it in front of him during the meal. In Lahiri's other stories, the technique of simple narration is used very effectively, as it forcefully and tantalizingly suggests the tremendous play of human emotions underneath, but "Mr. Pirzada Came to Dine" somehow falls short—the presentation of the details of Mr. Pirzada's routine remains a mechanical and superficial detail, instead of giving us any glimpse of his inner turmoil. Mr. Pirzada, at his best, comes across as a wooden character. The only point of interest in the story is the description of the Halloween festival, which alleviates the monotony generated by the superficiality of handling.

The title story "Interpreter of Maladies," on the other hand, is a powerful sketch of the insuperable loneliness of human beings, done with superb strokes and without any maudlin sentimentality. Lahiri herself writes about it, "When I was putting the collection together, I knew from the beginning that this had to be the title story, for I think it best expresses, thematically the predicament at the heart of the book—the dilemma, the difficulty, and often the impossibility of communicating emotional pain and affliction to others, as well as expressing it to ourselves." (*LM*, 1) The title itself is suggestive of the need to communicate to others the pain of abnormal loneliness and imprisoned emotions. The thematic denouement is also clear—in order to overcome the maladies, one has to interpret them and seek refuge within one's own self.

Lahiri has carefully painted the details of the characters. Mr. Kapasi, the taxi-driver and guide, leads an empty life. In his youth he had "dreamed of being an interpreter for diplomats and dignitaries, resolving conflicts between people and nations." (52). Life thwarts his ambitions and the inchoate insipidity of his surroundings generates a sense of futility in him. Mrs. Das's interest in his profession and terming it as "romantic" (50) stirs his emotions and the dreams of his early youth are revived. Her interest intoxicates him and he looks for the signs of stale and monotonous marriage, "Perhaps they too, had little in common apart from three children and a decade of their lives. The signs he recognized from his own marriage were there—the bickering, the indifference, the protracted silences. Her sudden interest in him, an interest she did not express in either her husband or her children, was mildly intoxicating." (53)

The portrayal of Mr. and Mrs. Das is a testimony to Lahiri's maturity in handling the craft of fiction. Their alienation from their cultural roots and bondages to the conventions of a different society is presented with a strong under-current of irony. Their external glamour is contrasted with their inner claustrophobia and emptiness. This contrast, at times, becomes comic and the pathos of that comedy arises from their inability to grasp, in broader or profounder terms, what it is which significantly constitutes freedom and happiness in life. This contrast also coveys the gravity of the static, haunted loneliness which Mrs. Das had endured half-consciously. She is depicted as a woman, who at the age of thirty has "already fallen out of love with life." (66) She had been living with the secret guilt that her second son was born out of a momentary and purely sexual relationship with her husband's friend. Her lack of protest at the advances of the friend has to be understood in the context of her overwhelming tiredness and withdrawal. At a very tender age, she had been burdened with a child. Separated from her own family and friendless, she feels continually tired and cross. The sexual closeness to another individual could as well be a means to overcome this situation. But her Indian psyche transforms a single isolated event into a gigantic burden she is forced to carry throughout her life, "For eight years I haven't been able to express this to anybody, not to friends, certainly not to Raj . . . how terrible it makes me feel, I feel terrible looking at my children, and at Raj, always terrible. I have terrible urges, Mr. Kapasi to throw things away. One day I had the urge to throw everything I own out the window, the television, the children, everything. Don't you think it's unhealthy?" (65)

Mrs. Das has shared this secret with Mr. Kapasi in the hope that he, being an interpreter of maladies, should be able to suggest a remedy to her also. His inability to sympathize with her evokes, strangely, a confident reaction in her, "She opened her mouth to say something, but as she glared at Mr. Kapasi some certain knowledge seemed to pass before her eyes, and she stopped. It crushed him, he knew at that moment that he was not even important enough to be properly insulted." (66) Mrs. Das goes back to her children with a definite gesture which can be taken as a token of her new assertive self. She seems to have overcome her guilt in a revealing moment and understood that life still has to be lived with, if not exuberance, then vitality. Mr. Kapasi's romantic imagination is also portrayed with a certain sympathy. The deep anguish, which had been his fate in life, never leaves him. His flimsy hope ultimately evaporates when the small clip of the paper, on which he had written his address, flutters away. It symbolizes the ultimate despair of human condition. The story conveys definite psychic states through the presentation of minute routine details, along with an awareness of the basic inadequacy of each individual.

Another story which conveys similar chilliness of atmosphere and often-felt banality of human situation with equal emotional intensity and perfection of craft is "Mrs. Sen's." The story beautifully brings out the Laingian motif of the suppressed hostility between the world of the "self" and the world of "them." Mrs. Sen has been transported to the alien society of America by her marriage to a teacher of Mathematics. She finds herself totally misfit in that society—"home" for her means India. Externally she makes all the suitable gestures to get adjusted to her new surroundings—her driving lessons and baby-sittings are half-hearted attempts to adapt herself to a new society. But her sensitive soul seeks nourishment from the memories of the "home" which is reflected in every nuance of her behaviour—her dress, the dot of vermilion on her forehead and in the parting of her hair, her taste for fresh fish and constant inquiries about it, her traditional way of cooking and her hospitality which is invariably extended to everyone, including Eliot's reluctant mother. She has strong affection for everyone, which leaves its impression on the young boy. Lahiri's repetition of small daily habits and chores—removing the shoes in the doorway, chopping vegetables seated on newspapers, Mrs. Sen's constant worry about her driving skills—imparts an intensity to the narration. The repetition reinforces our perception of the loneliness and the hollowness of Mrs. Sen's life.

In "This Blessed House" the ghosts from the past constantly emerge in the form of figures, idols and posters which evoke different responses in Twinkle and Sanjeev. Sanjeev fails to understand Twinkle's obsession with the religious objects. Twinkle's bubbling enthusiasm changes the fact of finding certain objects in a new house into a journey of anticipating pleasure which she successfully communicates to her guests, who join her to explore the attic. Sanjeev's acquiescence gives us the message that one has to make adjustments in order to have a happy marriage.

"The Third and Final Continent" is the narration of the gradual adjustment of an anonymous male protagonist with an alien society. He is eager to learn and to adjust. The emotional side of his character is also beautifully sketched by Lahiri. He admires his 103-year old landlady Mrs. Croft for her pride in her country's achievement of sending a man on the moon, and remembers the last days of his mother with agonizing clarity. The story offers a statement of the difficulty and desirability of integrating the deepest needs of self-expression and self-realisation with the life one must lead as a social being. Using the flashback technique, Lahiri records his early impressions and delineates them suggestively till they form an individual pattern in which agonies and ecstasies are intricately woven. The story records minute details with precision—the details of daily routine, furniture, rooms and people. Unlike "When Mr. Pirzada Came to Dine," this story is able to delve deep into the psyche of its characters and project beautifully the staunchest strength of a human being which lies in the assurance of tie.

Home and Abroad: A Study of *Interpreter of Maladies*

PARMANAND JHA

A slim looking Jhumpa Lahiri has emerged as a literary heavyweight following the publication of her debut collection of short stories *Interpreter of Maladies* which won her the prestigious Pulitzer Prize, America's ultimate literary accolade, for the year 2000. Being the first South Asian to win an individual Pulitzer, Lahiri has joined the elite company of such illustrious winners of Pulitzer as Steinbeck, Norman Mailer, Saul Bellow, Ernest Hemingway, Pearl S. Buck and John Updike. With the stunning success of her very first literary venture, Lahiri has turned out to be the expatriate version of the one and only Arundhati Roy.

Born in 1967 in London to parents who emigrated from Calcutta, and raised in Rhode Island, America, Lahiri has been a precocious child, writing since the age of seven. "The very first stories I wrote, in the second grade during recess," reminisces Lahiri, "were imitations of what I'd learned to read in the classroom. Writing allowed me to observe and make sense of things without having to participate."[1] Her C.V. amply shows her insatiable thirst for academic distinctions—B.A. in English Literature from Barnard College, M.A. in English, M.A. in Creative Writing, M.A. in Comparative Studies and Ph.D. in Renaissance Studies—all from Boston University where she taught creative writing, apart from a short stint as a teacher in the Rhode Island School of Design. She has been a recipient of the Transatlantic Review Award in 1993 and a fiction prize from the Louiseville Review Award in 1997. In 1999 she was named by the *New Yorker* as "one of the 20 best writers under the age of 20" alongside Sherman Alexie, David Foster Wallace and Jurot Diaz.

Three of the stories in *Interpreter of Maladies* have already been published in the *New Yorker* and the title story has been selected both for the Henry Award and the award for the best American short stories.

Lahiri has been shuttling periodically between Boston and Calcutta. She views Calcutta as "a bustling, unruly city, so different from the small New England town where she was raised."[2] She has spent a lot of time in Calcutta with her grandmother, reading, writing and observing things and finding solitude in life amidst a crowd of people. Calcutta was the nursery where she learnt to think imaginatively. "Calcutta nourished my mind, my eye as a writer and my interest in seeing things from a different point of view,"[3] reminisces Lahiri.

Interpreter of Maladies, with the sub-title "Stories of Bengal, Boston and Beyond" deals with the problems of the immigrants in an alien land; the yearnings of exile, the emotional confusion, et. al. Being an immigrant herself, Lahiri deeply felt the importance of family bonds which tie people to their homelands. She has undergone the trauma of failing to find her identity in a world where she could never have a sense of belongingness and so tries to fall back upon the treasured memories of what Rushdie calls 'Imaginary Homeland' which with its vibrant colours and versatility gave life to her starving existence and stimulated her very being. "I went to Calcutta," Lahiri admits "neither as a tourist nor as a former resident—a valuable position, I think as a writer, I learned to observe things as an outsider and yet I also know that as different as Calcutta is from Rhode Island, I belong there in some fundamental way, in the ways I didn't seem to belong in the United States."[4] This is rather a problem faced by many others of Indian diaspora. In an interview with the *Newsweek,* just after winning the Pulitzer Prize, Lahiri said, "It's hard to have parents who consider another place 'home'—even after living abroad for 30 years, India is home for them. . . . We were always looking back so I never felt fully at home here. There's no body in the whole country that we're related to. India was different—our extended family offered real connections. To see my parents as children, as siblings was rare."[5] But the pangs of not growing up in India took its own toll. She further adds, "I wasn't a part of things. We visited often but we didn't have a home. We were clutching at a world that was never fully ours with encouragement."[6]

This dilemma, this sense of emotional exile and the excruciating pain it entails is at the core of the stories in *Interpreter of Maladies* which has not only gleaned rave reviews from countless critics but has also been sold in Germany, the U.K. and in several other countries. Six of the nine stories in the collection have their settings in America and deal with the lives of Indian immigrants "who hope to find a better life. But what they discover is often vastly different from what they imagined." The rest three are set in India and deal with the type of subaltern personalities and the conflicting encounters among them in a style that is highly accessible, absorbing and moving.

The opening story "A Temporary Matter" finely portrays the conjugal crisis of a young couple—Shoba and Shukumar—who don't know how to cope with the grief bequeathed by their stillborn child, and the gradual erosion of their intimate togetherness in Boston. The announcement of hour-long power-cuts in the evening—though a temporary matter—comes to their rescue. They begin to sit together again and communicate with each other during the black-outs, share some moments of intimacy, exchange confessions and appear to have moved closer to some understanding. Memories of India do play a vital role in their interludes of intimacy. "I remember during power failures at my grandmother's house, we all had to say something," Shoba continued, "Shukumar hadn't spent as much time in India as Shoba had. . . . He wished now that he had his own childhood story of India."[7]

"It was only then . . . that I knew what it meant to miss someone who was so many miles and hours away" (42) sets the tone of "When Mr. Pirzada Came to Dine," the second story in the collection. Set again in Boston, the story has Indo-Pak war of 1971 and the birth of Bangladesh as the backdrop. Mr. Pirzada, who has come to Boston on a grant from the government of Pakistan to study the foliage in New England, is a native of

Dacca, where he "had a three-storey home, a lecturership in Botany at the University, a wife of twenty years and seven daughters between the ages of six and sixteen whose names all began with the letter A." (23) Mr. Pirzada befriends an Indian Bengali family in Boston. Worried always about his own family in Dacca, he regularly visits the Bengali family to eat dinner and watch the evening news. The small daughter of the family, who knew India only through books, tries to make sense of events, through Pirzada's presence, taking place far from Boston and her history lessons in the American Revolution. The Indian family in Boston goes on playing the Good Samaritan until Mr. Pirzada is finally reunited with his family in Dacca. In this story, Lahiri attempts to "forge her own amalgamated domain" rather than respond to her parents's cultural nostalgia. In her own words, "My focus in this story wasn't the unilateral translation of a place or language. Instead it was a simultaneous translation in both directions, of characters who literally dwell into two different worlds."[8]

The title story "Interpreter of Maladies," the third and longest story in the collection, is set in Puri, India. The phrase 'interpreter of maladies' flashed across Lahiri's mind following an encounter with an acquaintance in Boston way back in 1991. "I asked him," recalls Lahiri "what he was doing and he said he was working as a translator for a doctor who had a number of Russian patients who had difficulty explaining their ailments in English. I had never heard of a job like this, but realized that it was a necessity in places where doctors and patients didn't have a common language."[9] It is a complex story about an Indian-American couple—Mr. Das, his wife Mina and their three children—Tina, Ronny and Bobby. They hire the services of one Mr. Kapasi as a tour-guide and chauffeur, to see the famous Sun Temple at Konark. During their conversation en route, the couple learn that Mr. Kapasi, besides his part-time job of a tour-guide, works as an interpreter in a doctor's clinic where he translates the Gujarati spoken by some of his patients. Mr. Kapasi who "found nothing noble in interpreting people's maladies" (51) is flattered to hear Mrs. Das describe it as "romantic." Unlike his wife, who "had little regard for his career as an interpreter," Mrs. Das had "reminded him of its intellectual challenges." (53) Mrs. Das, whose "shaved largely bare legs" had tickled Mr. Kapasi earlier, seemed to be interested in him, he thought, and he begins to imagine a romantic relationship with her. His fantasy is further fed when the couple invites him to be included in the photographs they take. Mrs. Das even asks him for his address so that she could send him copies from America. The real crisis, however, comes when Mrs. Das discloses to him, in the car, that one of her two sons, Bobby, was conceived from her husband's Punjabi-Indian friend in a mutually agreed sexual encounter in her own house. Mr. Kapasi, the interpreter of people's maladies, fails to offer any remedy to Mrs. Das's malady, which may be her falling marriage and falling out of love for life, which she had vainly hoped, he would offer. All he can utter is, "Is it really pain you feel, Mrs. Das, or is it guilt?" (66) Mrs. Das's scornful silence shatters the fantasy of Mr. Kapasi and thus puts an abrupt, early end to their strangely intimate relationship. "When I was putting the collection together," writes the author, "I knew from the beginning that this had to be the title story because I think it best expresses thematically the predicament at the heart of the book—the dilemma, the difficulty and often the impossibility of communicating emotional pain and affliction to others, as well as expressing it to ourselves. In some senses I view myself as a writer, insofar as I attempt to articulate these emotions as a sort of interpreter as well."[10]

The two other stories with their setting in India are "A Real Durwan" and "The Treatment of Bibi Haldar." In these two stories, Lahiri portrays the lives of servants and marginal figures. They are unlike their economically sound counterparts in other stories. Questioned as to why she made this choice, Lahiri answers:

> Both of these characters came out of observations of people when I was there (in Calcutta). What drew me to writing about them was partly a projection of my own feelings of being marginal when there, of not being a part of the culture, of feeling foreign even when this was a place my parents call home and refer to in their minds as home, even though they've been away for 30 years.[11]

"A Real Durwan" was written, recalls Lahiri, "soon after returning from a visit to India in 1992, in my bed room in my parents' house in Rhode Island." It is a pathetic but powerful pen-picture of an old lady, Boori Ma, a self-appointed sweeper of the stairwell of a multi-storeyed building. Her services "came to resemble those of a real durwan" (73) because in exchange for her lodging below the letterboxes, she kept the "crooked stairwell" spotlessly clean. Apart from this, "the residents liked that Boori Ma, who slept each night behind the collapsible gate, stood guard between them and the outside world." (73) But the same residents, accusing her of the theft of the basin, throw her out one day because they need a real durwan as Boori Ma has endangered the security of the building." (82) The vagaries of material possession plaguing human relationship forms the matrix of this story.

"The Treatment of Bibi Haldar" is yet another moving tale of a 29 year orphan, unmarried girl who suffers from a mysterious disease. Staying in a married cousin's house, she has to sleep, initially, on a camp cot downstairs but is, subsequently, forced to stay in the store-room for ever as her presence, the Haldar couple fear, will infect their new-born child. The women of the neighbourhood are sympathetic to her and try to persuade, unsuccessfully, the Haldar couple to get her married, as the doctor in charge of Bibi's case, after performing a series of blood tests "concluded that a marriage would cure her." (161) The Haldars, reluctant to waste their money on a wedding, finally move off to a new place leaving her in the store. She lapses into a prolonged isolation until one day when the women discover her "about four months pregnant." (172) Later one evening she delivers a son but would never "tell us who had done it." The women help her in raising the child and setting up a small shop in the store-room. The story ends on a positive note: "for years afterwards, we wondered who in our town had disgraced her. . . . But there was no point in carrying out an investigation. She was, to the best of our knowledge, cured." (172)

A brief but deeply intimate adulterous relationship constitutes the core of "Sexy," the fifth story in this collection.

Miranda, a young American, falls in love with Dev, a married Bengali investment banker, whose wife has left for India for a few weeks. They spend every night together, visit shops and theatres, drink sangria and eat pulled pork. One Saturday afternoon Dev takes Miranda to his favourite place in the city called Mapparium where, standing on a transparent bridge thirty feet apart, Dev wants Miranda to say something. Dev's whisper turns her on:

> she felt it under her skin, under her winter coat, so near and full of warmth that she felt herself go hot.
>
> "Hi," she whispered, unsure of what else to say.
>
> "You are sexy, he whispered back. (91)

Miranda's relationship with Dev begins to lose its passion and warmth after the arrival of Dev's wife. Dev's Sunday afternoon sessions of warming up Miranda do not help her recover from her gnawing loneliness. She offers to look after for a day, Rohin, the unhappy and precocious nephew of her friend Laxmi. Rohin asks Miranda to put on, for his entertainment, the slinky cocktail dress that she had once bought with Dev in mind. When she puts on the dress, Rohin, like Dev in Mapparium, remarks, you are sexy." (107) Miranda's heart skipped a beat. Later, forced physically by Miranda to explain the meaning of sexy, Rohin whispers, "It means loving someone you don't know." (107) "What the classicist and philosopher Martha Nussbaum has called 'Love's knowledge' is here eclipsed by a radical scepticism that is primarily sexual, but must also be implicitly philosophical."[12] The story ends with Miranda's deciding to end the relationship and returning to places where Dev had kissed her.

The poignant realization of the loss of the familiar is well treated in the next story "Mrs. Sen's." Mrs. Sen, the thirty-year-old wife of a mathematics professor, becomes the baby-sitter for the eleven-year-old Eliot, the son of a single mother who has her own problems to cope with. It is hinted early that Mr. Sen wants the job for an engagement to fill up her lonely afternoons. The more she tries to connect herself to the new environment, the more she finds herself cut off from her milieu. Eliot gradually becomes Mrs. Sen's companion and confidant and discovers that only two things make her happy—letters from home, that is, India and whole fresh fish from the sea. Unfortunately, she does not know how to drive and her husband has no time to drive her to the fish market. "It is very frustrating," says Mrs. Sen, "to live so close to the ocean and not to have so much fish." (123) She turns nostalgic and adds that "in Calcutta people ate fish first thing in the morning, last thing before bed, as a snack after school if they were lucky." (123) Mrs. Sen's acute sense of alienation reaches its climax when she turns philosophical in a conversation with Eliot:

> "Eliot," Mrs. Sen asked him while they were sitting on the bus. "Will you put your mother in a nursing home when she is old?"
>
> "May be," he said "but I would visit her every day."
>
> "You say that now, but you will see, when you are a man your life will be in places that you cannot know now."
>
> She counted on her fingers, "You will have a wife, and children of your own, and they will want to be driven to different places at the same time. No matter how kind they are, one day they will complain about visiting your mother and you will get tired of it too, Eliot." (131-32)

The story presents the difficulties faced by Indian wives in an alien culture, without friends or family, struggling to cope with the new surroundings they can't call their home. Also, it skilfully probes the mixed feelings of an American child—fear, astonishment, fascination and awe—toward an Indian living abroad. "In this beautifully observed story East meets West in the shared experience of loneliness and the poignancy of Mrs. Sen's situation is handled with utmost delicacy and control unsullied by any hint of mawkishness."[13] The story is partly autobiographical. Lahiri herself admits, "Mrs. Sen is based on my mother who baby sat in our home. I saw her one way but imagined that an American child may see her differently, reacting with curiosity, fascination or fear to things I took for granted."[14]

The reasons behind the emotional and spiritual distance between spouses trying to adopt the culture of their new home are excellently explored in the next story "This Blessed House."

Sanjeev, an ambitious corporate vice-president has recently married Twinkle, a 27-year-old girl. Their marriage is arranged through their parents who are old friends. They are only in the second month of their marriage and certain things begin to nettle Sanjeev: "the way she [Twinkle] sometimes spat a little when she spoke, or left her undergarments after removing them at night at the foot of their bed." (142) The discovery of a white porcelain Christ, St Francis postcards and Noah's arc-light switch plates left behind by the previous tenants proves deeply unsettling. While the wife seems fascinated by the discovery, the husband is scornful and dismissive. He under-estimates the tenacity of her whim and threatens to dispose of the found only to find her in tearful rage, who shouts at her, 'I hate you." (149) The story, like "A Temporary Matter," ends with a makeshift peace.

The last story "The Third and Final Continent" is, to quote Khushwant Singh, "perhaps the best in the collection." It tells us of an Indian immigrant who reminisces about his first few weeks in America thirty years ago. Having studied for four years in London, he makes a short trip to Calcutta for his arranged marriage with Mala. He moves to America only a week after his marriage, to work as a librarian at the M.I.T. His wife has to wait for her visa for six weeks before she can join her in America. On his arrival in Boston, he checks into the local YMCA. The year is 1969, the year of America's landing on the moon. "The timing is more metaphorical than coincidental; the new country the narrator stumbles upon is as foreign to him as the moon."[15] Sometime later, the narrator rents a room in the home of a 103-year-old crotchety widow, who lives by herself and is visited infrequently by her sixty-eight-year-old daughter. The widow is finicky about the class of the renter (he must either be from Harvard or MIT), about punctuality (both in matters of returning time and rent) and about the American Flag on the moon. When the narrator's wife joins him, the lady, Mrs. Croft, puts her through a series of scrutiny and interrogation and finally pronounces: "she is a perfect lady." (195) It is through this scrutiny that the narrator feels empathy for his bride as it reminds him of his own experiences as a confused and bewildered stranger in London. "I like to think," says the narrator "of the moment in Mrs. Croft's parlour as the moment when the distance between Mala and me began to lessen." (196) They later on shift to their new house and come to know one day of Mrs. Croft's death in an obituary column. The narrator grieves as if he had lost his own mother. The story comes to an end on a positive note as the narrator and his wife reconcile themselves to the new life on the third and final continent.

The nine stories in the collection offer a wonderful variety of experiences gathered from the cultural clashes rippling outward in many directions. The trauma of dislocation, an acute sense of loneliness and the pangs of estrangement suffered by the millions of "exiled Indians" who try unsuccessfully to balance themselves between 'home' and 'abroad' are the major maladies Lahiri attempts to interpret. Most of her characters keep hanging in limbo—between two identities—non-Indian and Indian, a fact that brings Jhumpa Lahiri fairly close to Bharati Mukherjee, another successful interpreter of 'immigrant angst.' In her attempt to diagnose the discrepancies that exist between 'home' and 'New home' abroad, Lahiri stands in close proximity with Shauna Singh Baldwin and even Amit Chaudhuri. In interpreting the 'meaning of distance' (as Miranda does in the story "Sexy") Lahiri reminds one of Amitav Ghosh in *The Shadow Lines.* In writing about the disturbed conjugality and its impact on the young couple ("A Temporary Matter") she reminds us of Carver. In portraying tour-guides, seduction and subsequent disillusionment ("The Interpreter of Maladies,") she comes close to Hemingway. She even draws obvious parallels with Isherwood when she writes about a landlady scrutinizing her young renter evoking contrary feelings of disgust and tenderness ("The Third and Final Continent"). The octogenarian young man Khushwant Singh likens her to Somerset Maugham: "Without striving to impress, without a witty turn of phrase, Jhumpa manages to hold the reader's interest. She reminded me of Somerset Maugham."[16] Like Bernard Malamud who dealt at length with the Jewish community in America, Lahiri has created a literature revolving around the Indian immigrants in America. Like James Joyce, she displays an insight and a penchant for documentation of details. Her keen awareness of the contours of her craft coupled with the use of direct, clear, elegant and sparkling prose makes *Interpreter of Maladies* a timeless treatise.

NOTES

1. Jhumpa Lahiri, "To Heaven without Dying," FEED (www.feedmag.com, copyright, 2000), 16.11.00, 17:2.
2. Lavina Melwani, "Interpreting Exile," *The Hindustan Times,* April 23, 2000.
3. Surabhi Khosla, "Beauty, Brains, Bounce and Bengal," *Swagat,* Nov. 2000, p. 155.
4. Lavina Melwani, "Interpreting Exile."
5. Surabhi Khosla, "Beauty, Brains, Bounce and Bengal"
6. *Ibid.*
7. Jhumpa Lahiri, *Interpreter of Maladies (*Delhi: HarperCollins, 1999), p. 12.
8. Jhumpa Lahiri, "To Heaven without Dying"
9. Naresh Fernandes, An Interview with Jhumpa Lahiri, *Literature,* 13 June, 1999, p. 18.
10. Lavina Melwani, "Interpreting Exile."
11. Gaiutra Bahadur, An Interview with Jhumpa Lahiri, Citypaper.net Sept. 16-23, 1999.
12. Aveek Sen, "Enigmas of Distance," *The Telegraph,* 1.5.2000.
13. Susan Ram, "Chronicle of the Cultural Interface," *Frontline,* Oct. 22, 1999, p. 71.
14. Vibhuti Patel, "Maladies of Belonging: An Interview with Jhumpa Lahiri," *Newsweek International,* 20.9.1999.
15. Greg Changn on *Interpreter of Maladies, The Atlantic Journal constitution,* ajc.com 1 of 2.
16. Khushwant Singh, "Between Two Continents," *The Telegraph,* 1.5.2000.

Crisis in Human Values as Reflected in *Interpreter of Maladies*

JYOTI MISHRA

Since the beginning of the civilization, every society had lived by certain human values and beliefs. These human values had gone into making the society more firm and solid. In olden times, people generally abided by these values at any cost. They had the fear of god. They believed in heaven and hell. But with the advent of science and technology, human mentality changed. The existence of Almighty was put to question and people now stopped looking to a life beyond the present one, So there developed a common tendency that, whatever is to be achieved, it is to be achieved only in this very life. "Dharma" and "Moksha" became futile and on the other hand "Kama" and "Artha" acquired prominence in human life. Subsequently, the human values changed and there arose crisis.

Under such state of affairs, what could the Indian writing in English today reflect other than the irony and the suffering of the common man caught in social contradiction. It made the writers sad but then they were exploring the present time in the perspective of Indian tradition and history.

Jhumpa Lahiri is one such writer, a dazzling storyteller with a distinctive voice, an eye for nuance and an ear for irony. She has very sublimely understated in her collection of short stories entitled, *Interpreter of Maladies,* the lives of Indians in exile, of people navigating between the strict tradition they have inherited and the baffling new world they must encounter every day. *Interpreter of Maladies* is her first published collection which bagged her the Pulitzer Prize for Fiction 2000. From the above collection the two stories under consideration for this paper are: "A Temporary Matter" and "Interpreter of Maladies."

"A Temporary Matter" is the story of Shoba and Shukumar, a young couple, who had lived in Boston for three years. Shoba worked in an office downtown where she searched for typographical errors. Shukumar was in the sixth year of his graduate school and was to enter the job market the following year. For some time, their life was not so happy as they had lost their baby who was born dead. Moreover, as Shukumar thought,

> how he and Shoba had been experts at avoiding each other in their three-bedroom house, spending as much time on separate floors as possible. He thought of how he no longer looked forward to weekends . . . and how long it had been since she looked into his eyes and smiled or whispered his names on those rare occasions they still reached for each other before sleeping.

So the more Shoba stayed out putting in extra hours at work, the more Shukumar wanted to stay in managing the household matters.

Under such state of affairs, crisis in their married life continued when a "temporary matter" in the form of a notice broke in. It informed them about the five-days's power cut off for one hour. This unexpected announcement provided them a chance to come closer to each other once again. Unable to think anything in particular about spending an hour in darkness, Shoba turned nostalgic and said, "I remember during power failures at my grandmother's house, we all had to say something. A little poem. A joke. A fact about the world." So, she suggested, "let us say something to each other in the dark. How about telling each other, something we've never told before."

Having thus decided, Shukumar and Shoba started revealing their untold facts to each other. Shoba told him about the times when they were newly acquainted and when she happened to steal a look into his address book to see if he had written her address there. Shukumar in his turn told her about how he had forgotten to tip the waiter when they went out to dinner for the first time and how the next morning he went all the way back just to tip the waiter.

Somehow the whole affair had turned into an exchange of confessions—the little ways they had hurt or disappointed each other. The following nights Shukumar told her about how he once ripped out a photo of a woman in one of the fashion magazines and carried it in his books for a week. He revealed to her how he hadn't lost the sweater vest Shoba bought him for their third wedding anniversary but had exchanged it for cash at Filene's and that he had got drunk in the middle of the day at a hotel bar.

Confession of each other's guilts was not all that the couple did but they also engaged themselves in some amount of love-making they had forgotten. Eventually, Shukumar started looking forward to the lights going out so much so that he was really disappointed when he came to know that the fault was repaired one day ahead of schedule.

The process of confession which started in the dark continued even in the light, for they had now developed the courage to face each other, and they no more required the veil of darkness. As a result, a startling revelation came from the side of Shoba when she said that she had signed a lease for a separate accommodation which she had been looking for for some time. Shukumar was sickened to realize that the game of confession was purposely designed by Shoba only to make her matters easy. He then took his turn and disclosed something he had sworn he would never tell his wife. It was about the sex of their child that Shoba herself had wanted to be a surprise until it was born. The final confession from either side was thus made. Shoba, who had initiated all this, burst into tears and Shukumar also joined her.

The crisis in the life of Shoba and Shukumar that simmered in the form of lack of love as faith in their interpersonal relationship and Shoba's efforts for isolated living came out through confession. But then these confessions proved a bliss in disguise—a bliss that cleared their hearts and brought them together once again

"Interpreter of Maladies" is the title story where Mr. Kapasi, a driver-cum-interpreter guided an American family of Mr. Das, accompanied by his wife and three children to the Sun Temple,

Konark. On his way to the temple, Mr. Kapasi told them about his other job, the job of an interpreter in a doctor's clinic. He said that he interpreted peoples's maladies, translated the symptoms of the Gujarati patients to the non-Gujarati doctor. Mr. Das had never heard of anything like that and Mrs. Das in particular remarked that it was a romantic one, a big responsibility, as the patients were totally dependent on him. Mr. Kapasi had never thought of his job in such complimentary terms. To him it was a sign of his failings as he had dreamed of being an interpreter for diplomats and dignitaries, resolving conflicts between people and nations.

Apart from everything else, Mr. Kapasi was a keen observer. He saw that Mrs. Das did not behave in a romantic way towards her husband and was not much concerned about her children as well. He wondered if Mr. and Mrs. Das were a bad match. Flattered by her praises, Mr. Kapasi started taking interest in Mrs. Das. He was anxious to be alone with her and indulge in some private conversation. He began to dread the thought of dropping the family off to the hotel from were he had picked them. So, on their way back, he suggested visiting the hills at Udayagiri and Khandagiri to which they agreed. When they got to the hills, Mrs. Das refused to get out of the car, whereas Mr. Das left the place along with the children. When left alone in the car with Mr. Kapasi, Mrs. Das made an astonishing revelation that one of her boys named Bobby was not her husband's son but his friend's son. She said that she had kept it a secret for eight years and had not even let her husband know about it. But concealing it from everyone was not easy for her as she constantly felt terrible. She developed an unhealthy state of mind and had a strange urge of throwing things away.

Moving in such a state of mind, Mrs. Das found Mr. Kapasi's role of interpreter promising enough to lighten the burden of her heart. She hoped that he would help her feel better by saying the right thing or suggesting some kind of remedy. Mr. Kapasi, on his part, could make out that it was not her pain pouring out but it was her confession of guilt. Not used to such kind of maladies, the interpreter "still believed that it was his duty to assist Mrs. Das. Perhaps he ought to tell her to confess the truth to Mr. Das. He would explain that honesty was the best policy, which would surely help her feel better." His thoughts remained locked in his mind, as he didn't find a chance to convey his remedy to Mrs. Das. But the solution to the crisis *was* successfully conveyed through the "interpreter of maladies" to the readers.

Interpreting Human Values in *Interpreter of Maladies:*

MADHOO KAMARA

Tasmac Chastrain Pramanam
Kary akrya—Vyavasthitau
Thatva Sastra—Vidhan Oktain
Karma Kartum inharhasi (*Bhagvad Gita,* XV: 24)

(Let the scriptures be your norm in determining what should be done and what not. Understand the injunction of the scriptures first and then set yourself to work.)

Is modem Indian English novel a variegated phenomenon which tries to catch reflection of what Sri Aurobindo has called, "the orange skies of the Mystic Mind"? Is it true that the modern Indian English novelists through fear and frenzy have bungled and brought this darkness called the "Shunya" upon us? Should we—the recipients—diet on negation of traditional socio-cultural values and live still in the dark before the right movement and affirmation may be possible. The horror-terror-pity evocating thought that there is "crisis in human values in Indian writing in English is to me mathematically unplausible." We should remember the time-tested pronouncement: "An author is literature: not scripture."

Certainly the spirit of India is dominated by ruthless technology; the simple human nature is tossed between the fire of greed and the ice of "hate" but the tremendous equation "tatwamasi" does establish a correspondence between the world "within" and the world "outside." Our modern Indian English writers came very near the Aurobindonian ideal of a theme creator of art:

> the true poet shows us truth in its Power of beauty in its symbol of image or reveals ft to us in the workings of life, and when he has done that his whole work is done he need not be an explicit spokesman.

William Meredith's tribute to Frost's poetic craftsmanship fitly describes the new form of the Indian English writing: "It has grown like a tree of new species, the layer of live wood is a perennial miracle of new life, but the tree itself is what is altogether astonishing—'a new tree.'"

Certainly, it strives to affirm in fierce imaginative terms that man will yet redeem himself and his fellows in spite of the present perversions and egoisms and that the world will endure the present social ills.

Transition is not decay. The "Sat" the permanently existent values like the truthfulness, tranquillity, aversion to slander, freedom from sensuality, gentleness, modesty, steadfastness, vigour, patience and fortitude are "centrifugal" although the "Asat"—the unreal fleeting environs—has become centripetal. The Asat has become trendy and relates to "Existentialism" "The Absurd," "The Surrealism" and the like. Here lies the clue, no matter what the resources are, the sadhana of the Great Taskmaster's eye continues to uphold; "Thou was not born for death, O immortal bird!"

The present study is a product of my exploration of *Interpreter of Maladies* by Jhumpa Lahiri, one of the few flagbearers of Indian English fiction whose genius as a story-teller has been appreciated by all. She has brought a strikingly fresh sensibility to Indian English literature, broadening impressively the thematic and stylistic contours of art. The present paper explores her as a new consciousness articulating and emphasizing the impermanence of values, inherent emotions and philosophical echoes. Therefore, her contribution to the genre of Indian short story is truly impressive.

Interpreter of Maladies is a collection of nine stories of which "A Temporary Matter" is the opening one. It records the process of restoration of faith after a long dividing doldrum—a threat to the otherwise gloomy conjugality of unwanted interdependency between Shukumar and Shoba. Shukumar with his elusive nature and Shoba with her professional specificity create discord that prevails for a moderate length of time and finally devours all unhappiness, leaving fertile bond to revive the long lost hope and reassemble conjugal bliss. Consequently, all mental doubts and apprehensions that cloud their life's guideposts are unweeded and the aesthetics of good compensates for the temporary loss of happiness.

"When Mr. Pirzada Came to Dine" epitomizes universal oneness—Vishwabandhutva—the elixir of peaceful and perfect living. Here, moralistic orientation forms the basis of constructive living, along with secular rationality and social solidarity. These human values infuse "Positivism" in a wretched father of seven daughters left all to their fate along with their mother, in Dacca—a country "invaded, torched and shelled by the Pakistani army." The elements of Paramartha surface on every page vibrating the reader with the throbs of a heart in destitute, but earnest in the process of well-wishing. Reunion of Mr. Pirzada with his family proclaims the novelist's belief in collective mental and moral energies—the core meaning of "Loka Samskar Sukhino Bhavantu."

"A Real Durwan" is a beautiful synthesis of thought and character. A note of despair prevails all through the length of the story to be resolved at the end by a marked optimism. The protagonist named Boori Ma is an emaciated old woman who voluntarily serves as a watchman in a multi-storeyed building in Calcutta. Her present is rooted in dead past as memoirs of lost royalty and grandeur. Jhumpa Lahiri projects a meaningful integrity functional in bettering existence as vital and potent in combating survival odds. The "Chaos" is henceforth saved by virtue of "Cosmos" and the ideal integrity envelops the purposive individual supported by harmonic "dharma" in the living forms of Mrs. and Mr. Dalal. Jointly they stand against the destructive practical selfishness of the inmates of the big building.

Transformation of the "force within" through the purgatorial trials and tribulations is the theme of the story "Sexy." Miranda realizes the mean, the animal and the irrational within her and soon mends her way to rise up to the heights of nobility which again is a moral medal. The story also emphasizes that awareness of righteousness is an achievement of a conscientious soul. This is the necessary deep-structure theme.

"The Blessed Home" voices the idea that man's never-ending task is to discover his limitations and to atone for the deficiencies of human life and surroundings. The story also elaborates the idea that success lies in our willingness to construct an adaptive and assimilative living, further to reconstruct "what has fallen apart." Here Twinkle and Sanjeev violate their convictions but are soon convinced that the joy of togetherness can only be consistent when proper room is shaped to accommodate mutual desires and demands. The advantage and necessity of interpersonal dependence is also focussed to express necessary participation in marital life, otherwise estrangement is the unavoidable catastrophe.

"The Treatment of Bibi Haldar" clinically examines the world of meaningless interpersonal relations "within a family" but meaningful affirmation "within a society" that aids the sublimations of a wretched soul of "a convulsing girl" to the state of blessedness. The group sensitivity is contrasted to domestic emotional numbness destructive enough to dismantle the airy pleasure dome of Bibi Haldar. Her single solitary living, her mawkish soliloquies and her maudlin sentiments are an endless worry to the reciprocative neighbourhood. "Vasudha ev Kutumbakam" is the rescuing force and the potential of the feeling of a neighbourhood is the fore-grounded element.

The title story "Interpreter of Maladies" is an in-depth study of socio-human relationships. The story registers the common-day-to-day bickering between a couple on the issue of attending upon yet-to-grow kids. Mr. and Mrs. Das along with their children—Tina, Ronny and Bobby—are on their visit to the Sun Temple at Konark. Mr. Kapasi, their escort to the Sun Temple, finds them quaint in their dress and interpersonal relationship. Against the shade of excellent imagery, the story reads hurriedly as curiosity mounts with the advancement of narration by the omniscient narrator. The long tedious journey is made pleasant by the experiences of the Interpreter and by his recollections of his past marital life against his observation of the cordiality between Mr. and Mrs. Das. Here Lahiri pinpoints the large-heartedness of Indians in encompassing even foreigners within their socio-cultural realm of interaction.

Further, under the effect of "universal love" and "universal energy," Mrs. Das confides in Mr. Kapasi that Bobby is not Mr. Das's son but of his friend to whom she surrendered in a swirl of passion when her husband was out on his daily work. The loom of "pativratadharma" nags her and she longs for "atmasamarpna"—of merging one's personality in another's—an account of "Aatmaglani." She says: "About my secret, and about how terrible it makes me feel. I feel terrible looking at my children and at Raj, always terrible." She adds, "It means that I'm tired of feeling so terrible all the time. Eight years, Mr. Kapasi, I've been in pain." This is how, trapped in the sterility of custom and tradition, the individuals struggle for their comprehension of the destiny, some discovery of interpersonal ties, some metaphor of meaningful selfhood and withering charm of one's being in a socio-cultural context. Her primary interest lies in the nature and quality of the human consciousness along with substantial emphasis on stories, on the steady flow of outward landscape and on the changing reality. We are made aware of the process of change, how it affects "living," viewed both from an internal and external focus:

> Shoba looked at him now, her face contorted with sorrow. He had cheated on a college exam, ripped a picture of a woman out of a magazine. He had returned a sweater and got drunk in the middle of the day instead. These were the things he had told her. He had held her son who had known life only within her against his chest in a darkened room in an unknown wing of the hospital . . . he still loved her then and it was the one thing in her life that she wanted to be a surprise. (22)

For this, Lahiri abstracts the temporal canvas of the Indian as well as emigrant life into an elaborate picture made luminous in the consciousness of a single person who either happens to be the narrator as in "When Mr. Pirzada Came to Dine" or the lives narrated as in "Sexy," "Mrs. Sen's" and "A Temporary Matter," endowed with special gifts of lyric insight, image and encompassing sympathy. Through this narrative emphasis on the individual's inner psyche, we are launched into the existentialistic wilderness where we find the images and glimpses of our true nature. Her stories do not reflect upon the cumulative sequences of life. Rather, they offer indiscreet moments of truth as they affect individual lives and build up a fairly consistent view of man and his world. Using short stories as epiphanies, Jhumpa Lahiri reveals the social and cultural turmoil with the being as the theme in focus.

Interpreter of Maladies also reveals Jhumpa Lahiri's capacity to transmute commonplace objects and ordinary experiences derived from the natural and human worlds into symbols of deeper speculative meaning. For example, the image of Boori Ma in "A Real Durwan" stands for eternal endurance and patience of India, baffling unending threats to its metaphysical richness. With her gentleness, compassion and exuberant love, she is a matriarchal figure, an apotheosis of Indian history and culture. Similarly, Mrs. Croft in "The Third and Final Continent" stands for the superior and the mysterious; the noble exalted to the love of the sacred.

Jhumpa Lahiri's stories are the impressive explorations of the human conditions as it shapes and is shaped by the varying textuality of the human personality and offer testimony to her interest in creating an organic evolvement of both "the content" and the "form." For example, "Sexy" voices existential despair. More painful than the physical hardships is the emotional trauma of separation. Her tragic lot lies in her willingness to fail as a beloved of a married man. The story is a powerful rebuttal to the commonly held notion that youthful girls are nasty "familial home wreckers."

The backdrop adds to the charm. India, America, Boston and Dacca are the changing landscapes but the tumultuous happening within the human and social worlds creates a universal story of love and unhappiness. The book also contains the drama with many of our key traits—self-assertion, self-negation, self-awareness, family ties, vanity and hatred which makes us feel that an imperfect human brain breeds dissonance in living pattern. The principle of causation and illustration highlights the necessity of introspection and improvement. The greatness of the book lies in the style, structure and accuracy in making the tale of human idiosyncrasies thought-provoking and soul-searching. Jhumpa Lahiri does not explicitly point out the remedy. She has presented people as they are, but it teaches the lesson of humility, equality and motivates us to retain the good of past in the face of the challenges of life with the head held high. Almost all stories end on a positive note, with the hope of a "tomorrow" which suggests that with little effort we can discard our shallow pretensions and move towards a society where the traditional and the modern world meet in their inherent goodness, asserting the worth of a human life.

The rise of a new sensibility accompanied by the growth of a peripheral mind is interpreted as "loss of moral perception," eroding thoughts of nobility. On the contrary, "the growth of the ideal" now "exemplifies the Indian mind transferred by knowledge, not of good and evil, but of a world that has for the first time photographed, measured, explored, analyzed and counted to relate a consciousness incredibly widened and deepened and justified for man's view of the world. In the evolution of this consciousness after Tagore and Aurobindo, R.K. Narayan, M.R. Anand, Kamala Markandaya. Anita Desai, Bharati Mukherjee, Arundhati Roy and Jhumpa Lahiri are the friends and the makers, certainly "The Paradise" is not lost. In the labyrinths of past rather it has evolved as "cosmic weather," a reflection of some glorious to which the modern writers are discoverers.

The body of literature to which these writers have devoted to give permanent form remain history of our age and provide means, for the next age, to transcend the nightmarish crisis in human values to the idyllic past in the present. Hence modern Indian English literature is profoundly moral. Its real aim is to redeem reality through art without being preachy or pious. It is a way through "Shunya" to "Ghayna." Ihab Hassan writes: "In great literature, there is no past, and no built-in obsolescence.

There is radical continuity. We cannot afford to live in the perishable present without knowledge, deep passionate knowledge of the continuous present. Men like Yeats, Lawrence, Kafka and Faulkner are still prophets of the continuous present. They tell us who we are and how we could live." (*The American Review*, October 1967)

Multicultural Commitment: A Study of *Interpreter of Maladies*

BHAGABAT NAYAK

India has a reason to be proud of the latest recipient of the Pulitzer Prize for fiction, Jhumpa Lahiri, the first ever writer of Indian origin (a writer of Indian diaspora) in 2000. Born of Bengali parents, this young writer of short fiction is the first creative writer of Asian origin to win the highest American Literary Award for fiction of the year 2000 for her slim collection of nine superbly crafted short stories, *Interpreter of Maladies*. In the closing decades of the twentieth century, some Indian English writers like Amitav Ghosh, Shashi Deshpande, Shashi Tharoor and Upamanyu Chatterjee created waves at home and others like Arundhati Roy, Vikram Chandra and Vikram Seth made inroads into the Anglo-American countries in particular and west in general by winning coveted prizes at the national and international level. Likewise, writers of Indian diaspora such as Salman Rushdie, Bharati Mukherjee and Jhumpa Lahiri have created waves in the west and made their impact on Indian literary scene. Jhumpa Lahiri created history by winning the highest American Literary Award (i.e., Pulitzer Prize for 2000) for a collection of stories the roots of which lie in India. For this literary achievement, she has bagged number of awards which include O'Henry Award for the title story, Transatlantic Review Award for best fiction, Louisville Review Fiction Prize, Fellowship of Princetown's Fine Arts Work Centre and *The New Yorker*'s nomination among 20 best writers under 40 for the twenty-first century.

Lahiri was born in London of Bengali parents, her father a librarian and mother a teacher. She grew up in Rhode Island, U.S. and has visited her parents' home city Calcutta several times during which she had felt "every visit was an emotional see-saw across continents and cultures." As an elegant outsider and shy immigrant Cinderella, she had her talents and beauty from her early age modeled for "Keo Karpin" at four for which her maternal aunt Anusua rightly comments: "Jhumpa is so beautiful that she could have easily entered the Miss World Contest."[1] She began her writing with a classmate during school recess harking back to the past—a nostalgic longing instilled in her heart by her mother. In course of her terminal visits to Calcutta, she had become bilingual and bicultural in her linguistic acquisition and cultural assimilation. On being asked about her Calcutta roots, she explains her perplexing bicultural universe which she inhabits, the expectations and assumptions between which she always shuttles. She says, "My mother has lived outside India for nearly 35 years; my father nearly 40. Since 1969 they've made their home in the United States. But there were invisible walls erected around our home, walls intended to keep American influence at bay. Growing up, I was admonished not to "behave" like an American, or, worse to 'think' of myself as one. Actually 'being' an American was not an option."[2] She also admits:

> When I began writing fiction seriously, my first attempts were for some reason always set in Calcutta . . . a vast, unruly fascinating city so different from the small New England from where I was raised shaped my perceptions for the world and . . . I learnt to observe things as an outsider and yet I knew that as different Calcutta is from Rhode Island, I belonged there in some fundamental way, in the way, I didn't seem to belong in the U.S.[3]

After her Ph.D. in Renaissance Studies from Boston University, she had planned to write her roots and origin as a struggling writer came into being after her completion of a creative writing graduate programme of Boston University. Being "homesick" in her literary sensation and diasporic in her immigration, she thinks of the question of her identity as a difficult one and yet feels that she belongs to the vast fascinating metropolis called Calcutta. A sense of isolation and state of immigration make her identity a baffling question. It appears:

> She is much more American than her parents. Yet it is never easy for those with her background to completely feel American either. She explains that for older generation of immigrants the challenges of exile, loneliness, sense, of alienation are more acute than they are for their children. For the latter, especially those who have strong ties to their country of origin, like her, is that they feel neither one thing or the other. And in her stories, her characters move constantly between two worlds grappling bravely with this cultural displacement.[4]

Her stories in this collection are set in India and America and establish a certain Indo-American cultural link, in the postcolonial context. She has chronicled her characters' lives with both objectivity and compassion while charting the emotional temper of their lives with tactile precision. She has made a search for identity with an emotional empathy through her protagonists in most of her stories who are busy like her doing research and completing their dissertations. Therefore, the jury on the Pulitzer Committee have chosen the book for the prize for her transcontinental cultural consciousness and her diasporic identity.

Lahiri had an interesting story to tell about the title of *Interpreter of Maladies*. She recalls the time when, as a graduate student of Boston University, she ran into a "friend's friend" who explained that he was "interpreting" ailments for a doctor who had numerous Russian patients. By the time she reached home, she admits, she had the phrase "Interpreter of Maladies" planted in her head and decided to write a story with that title. None of her stories in the book is "apprentice work." Sumit Mitra and Arthur S. Pais write how a quite "prolific range of narrative technique help her get at the inner weave of characters with unexpected twists in plots and situations."[5]

In the Lahiri family map, the immigrants are a four member family where Jhumpa and her younger sister Simanti have no brothers for which perhaps some of her stories have been written with a longing for male members. It appears more "liberating" to write for her from such a studied view—she enjoyed the experience so much that she wrote three stories in a row from the male point of view. This enhances the probability whether it will be a continuation of the theme of her short stories interspersed with different cultures and human conditions that have universal resonance. She agrees that there is less of a cultural divide between America and India due to greater communication and access, although she has observed a "sense of emotional exile" in her parents. In American tradition, the word "universal" has had a limited connotation. Collision between Europe and America, as in Henry James' novels is universal enough but in American social landscape Lahiri enjoys her life without a safety net of community support and individual relationships that turns freedom into a mockery. Unwittingly, Lahiri traces this tragedy in which all immigrants play their part in their Pan-American situation.

Lahiri is an Indian by ancestry, British by birth, American by immigration and targets the western audience by deliberately portraying the Indian-American life. This sense of freedom is one of the greatest thrills of writing fiction for her and she discovered her authorial freedom by publishing her debut book. By discussing her private sphere of creative power, one may copiously categorize her as an American author, as an Indian-American author, as a British born author, as an immigrant author, and as an ABCD author (ABCD stands for American born confused "desi" which describes culturally challenged second generation Indians raised in the U.S.). To Indian academics she has written something known as "diaspora fiction" and to the US academics "immigrant fiction" and this kind of demarcation amuses her. The book depicts the ordinary people and is written in simple, unpretentious manner, often evocative of the stories written in Bengal in the forties and fifties. All the nine stories in the book do not have any psychedelic passage or purple prose and no mists of magic realism.

Lahiri was influenced by William Trevor, Mavis Gallant, Joyce and Chekhov who had initiated her literary baptism but it changed her perceptions during her frequent visits to Calcutta. The earliest story in her book, "A Real Durwan" was written soon after her return from India in 1992, in her bedroom in her parents' house in Rhode Island. This story with another, "The Treatment of Bibi Haldar" has the setting in India. To the Indian readers, it appears as if both the stories express a "tunnel vision" of India which she defends: "My own experience of India was largely that of a tunnel imposed by the single city we ever visited, by the handful of homes we stayed in, by the fact that I was not allowed to explore this city on my own. Still within these narrow confines, I felt that I had seen enough of life, enough details and drama, to set stories on Indian soil."[6] In "Real Durwan," it is felt that she has "misrepresented the plumbing technologies" of Calcutta and narrating the life and experiences of Boori Ma, a sweeper. She is under the impression that "all houses in Calcutta have sinks." Lahiri narrates the life story of an East Bengal refugee, Boori Ma who, in spite of her proud and prestigious past, serves in a flat, satisfies the residents who are over jealous of one another's success and glory. She gains their favour by her sincere duty and faithfulness but becomes a victim of their anger with the theft of a basin from the flat and loses her job and the residents go for searching a real durwan. But in "The Treatment of Bibi Haldar" she presents the hysteric suffering of a thirty-year-old lower middle class woman. Bibi has an unknown cause of suffering. When Bibi has not been cured by the friends, priests, palmists, gem therapists, prophets, fools, allopaths, ayurvedics, hypnotists and holy water from seven holy rivers it is felt "Bibi's life was an encounter with one fruitless antidote after another."[7] (159) "Bibi has caused enough worry, added enough to expenses, sullied enough the family name." (163) It was "apparent that Bibi wanted a man. She wanted to be spoken for, protected, placed on her path in life." (160) The thought of a husband and marriage would cure her but her family thought her "a liability and a loss." But her problem is solved when she becomes a mother without marriage. Bibi never reveals the identity of the man with whom she perhaps had one night tryst but this cured her deliriousness. Thus, both the stories remind one of Amit Chaudhuri's writings which deal with the Calcutta commoner's life.

Lahiri's tryst in the transcontinental cultural matrix has made her conscious of her Indian diasporic identity which she admits, "I . . . lack the cultural ambidexterity to write about Indian life and characters in an authentic way. I have been accused of setting stories in India as a device in order to woo western audiences with exotica."[8] Reviewers and critics are of the view that she has only written about Bengalis in India which is "an unwise decision." But some of her stories are set in Orissa and Jaipur in Rajasthan which clearly disprove the critics' allegation. In her story "When Mr. Pirzada Came to Dine" she shows Mr. Pirzada's cultural identity with India though he is a Bangladeshi. The very important issue in the story is that man can divide the country, state and land surface but not culture. The complications of Indo-Pak diplomacy have given birth to Bangla Desh but Indo-Bangla cultural relation is not severed for which Mr. Pirzada, a Daccan, expresses his happiness over Indian official's announcement, "unless the world helped to relieve the burden of East Pakistani refugees, India would have to go to war against Pakistan." (36) The story is a turning point in Lahiri's career because for the first time she made her protagonist an Indian-American who lives in New England. The story seems to be a moving account of a family guest, Mr. Pirzada, who has returned to Dacca after his research work and Bangladesh's limping back to parliamentary democracy.

"A Temporary Matter" and "This Blessed House" have Indian and American background. In the former story, a young couple have fallen out of love and are playing hide and seek with each other. Shukumar, the protagonist prepares his dissertation and goes to attend a conference in Baltimore, Sobha gives birth to a still born child, again it has to be a caesarian. Both of them have avoided each other and though Sobha had become pregnant they had never photographed, stopped attending parties, went nowhere together, not confessed their feeling and disappointments, not exchanged ideas since their marriage day till the birth of their son—their relationship continued to be a formal. In "Blessed House," Lahiri has become bit nostalgic about Indian names of her characters like Twinkle and Sanjeev who express their valuable opinion on education that "it's an attempt to convert people." (138) Her frequent referring of the names of Bollywood actress and some romantic moments which her "Twinkle confessed that she was charmed by the way Sanjeev had dutifully refilled her tea cup during their conversation" (143) in a restaurant. The story presents beauty, solemnity and dignity in the blessed house which seems to be contrary to "A Temporary Matter."

In "Sexy," Miranda's infatuation with a Bengali, Devajit Mitra, a married and unavoidable lover, is expressed in no uncertain terms. Miranda was interested in Devajit with a mixed parentage; who came from Bengal, a state in India, "a bay below and mountains above" (85) and Dev was attracted towards her for she was "the first woman I've known with legs this long." (89) In their weeklong relationship, they have kissed, praised and met each other remembering the Tajmahal, "the most romantic spot on earth," "an everlasting monument to love." (92) Miranda got elated in ecstasy of their union when Dev whispered her "you're sexy" (91) though he had admitted before her that his wife resembled a Bollywood actress, Madhuri Dixit.

Lahiri's "Mrs. Sen" presents a heart-tugging story of an immigrant who works like a baby-sitter. Mrs. Sen is an Indian but Lahiri describes her American position who faces a lot of problems in adjustment. Mrs. Sen is a housewife and the wife of a university professor, looks after an office-going American woman's child at home and tries to learn how to drive. She has her typically Bengali likeness for fish. She likes to cut it with a blade, "curved like the prow of a Viking ship, sailing to battle in distant sea" (114) which she had brought from India. She becomes ecstatic when a blue aerogram with "stamps showing a bald man of a spinning wheel and blackened by postmarks" arrives from Calcutta. She has been living in America for several years but never likes to leave her cultural inheritance—wears a sari, coral gloss, golden bangles, vermilion paste in her parting of hair, chops vegetables and fish with a typical Indian household blade, has love for different types of fishes and uses "a green and black bed cover printed with rows of elephants bearing Palanquins on their backs." (115) Even when she tells home it means India and her apartment room looks "that's all . . . in India" (113) for which the little boy Eliot was thinking of her violating some unspoken rule. Expressing Mrs. Sen's likeness for fish, Lahiri writes: "She had grown up eating fish twice a day. She added that in Calcutta people ate fish first thing in the morning, last thing before bed, as a snack after school if they were lucky. They ate the tail, the eggs, even the head. It was available in any market, at any hour, from dawn until midnight." (123-24)

But her thoughts and attempts at self-Americanization end in tears and silence during her driving when "she was so startled by the horn that she lost control of the wheel and hit a telephone pole on the opposite corner." (134) It appears that Mrs. Sen is modeled on author's mother who had accompanied her husband abroad "in search of fish, fresh and whole in the alien markets of the west."

In her title story, "Interpreter of Maladies," Lahiri narrates the "pain" and "guilt" of a woman and sketches the character of Mr. Kapasi in a realistic and convincing way. Mr. Kapasi is an interpreter assistant to a doctor by occupation and tourist guide by profession. Being a "doctor's assistant," he translates and interprets the symptoms, pains and suffering of Gujarati patients to a local doctor. Mr. Kapasi had a long desire to be an interpreter thinking of its wider prospect of "being an interpreter for diplomats and dignitaries, resolving conflicts between people and nations, settling disputes of which he alone could understand both sides." (52) While he guides a Bengali-American couple to visit the Konark Temple his sensuous infatuation with Mrs. Das intoxicated him by the sight of her bare legs and short skirts. This is further condensed when he interprets Surya's beauty and power in different postures in the niches of the temple facades. On the other hand, Mrs. Das has become hopeful enough that Mr. Kapasi's revealing of his professional acumenship will help enough to bring a relief to her secret pain which she has been silently suffering for last eight years.

While visiting Khandagiri, Mr. Das was worried about the safety of her children because of the menace of the monkeys. She was less concerned about Bobby as he was not her husband's son. Bobby was the son of her husband's friend, a Punjabi gentleman who had come to stay with them for a week and he had made love to her one afternoon when he learnt that a London based pharmaceutical company had tired him. This guilt consciousness has made her to suffer for last eight years and this has made her sick. She says, "for eight years I haven't been able to express this to anybody, not to friends, certainly not to Raj. He doesn't even suspect it. He thinks I'm still in love with him." (65) She estimates Mr. Kapasi in belief and confidence and tells him, "I told you because of your talents." (65) She thinks that Mr. Kapasi would be able enough to bring a remedy for this terrible silent suffering by interpreting her malady. But for Mr. Kapasi it is a novel kind of case study to interpret and he becomes very serious about how to resolve this common, trivial and secret matter. Mrs. Das's seeking of Mr. Kapasi's help is a kind of searching for expiation of her soul from guilt. She has realised anything secret in sex other than her husband is unhealthy. He knows that it is his noble and honest self to interpret and assist her in bringing out a malady. So he desires to mediate between them to cure her "guilt" and "pain." But when Bobby is attacked by a host of monkeys on their return to the car, he is rescued by Mr. Kapasi. Mr. Kapasi has expressed his honesty and nobility and has expressed compassion for Mr. Das's suffering.

"The Third and Final Continent" is Lahiri's last story in the collection. It presents a Bengali gentleman's search for identity in three continents. The protagonist has sailed to London from Calcutta by an Italian Cargo Vessel, *S.S. Roma*, for higher study. He struggles hard for his study and for a job and finally joins in Dewey Library of M.I.T., Boston. The Indian has crossed the seas alone to make his fortune in Europe and America. He says: "still, there are times I am bewildered by each mile I have travelled, each meal I have eaten, each person I have known, each room in which I slept. As ordinary as it all appears, there are times when it is beyond my imagination." (198) He speaks Bengali with his wife when she arrives there in the same manner he speaks English with Mrs. Croft, his one time landlady in America who was always liking to listen from him "Splendid" success of the Americans that "there is an American Flag on the Moon!" (179) His searching for maladies in America with Mrs. Croft, his wife and son are many but he fears that his son will no longer speak Bengali after he and his wife die and it will be a "linguistics loss." Yet he encourages his son "if I can survive on three continents, then there is no obstacle he cannot conquer," (197-98) and "while the astronauts, heroes forever, spent mere hours on the moon, I have remained in this new world for nearly thirty years." (198)

The perennial question is put to Lahiri, "where are you from?" If she says she is from Rhode Island "people are seldom satisfied," since they want to know more about her name and appearance. If she says she's from India, that is not entirely accurate either because she was not born here nor has she lived here. Her search for identity is difficult and that is why she makes a multi cultural commitment. Her characters' search for self-recognition has a kind of autobiographical element (or authorial intention) which interests the readers.

Lahiri is profusely praised for her nine well-knit stories in which she portrays the characters drawn from all over the world—i.e. from India, U.S.A., U.K. and other commonwealth countries in their own situation. These immigrant characters are mostly psychedelic and they struggle for identity and commitment to life in the multicultural milieu of Bengal, Boston and the beyond. I would like to close with Amy Tan's remark from the blurb of the book: "Jhumpa Lahiri is the kind of writer who makes you want to grab the next person you see and say . . . she's a dazzling story teller with distinctive voice, an eye for nuance, an ear for irony."

NOTES

1. *The Times of India*, 21 April, 2000.
2. *Outlook*, Collector's Edition, 2000, 116.
3. *The Times of India*, 13 April, 2000.
4. *The Times of India*, 17 April, 2000.
5. *India Today*, Vol. XXV, 17 Nov. 2000, p. 74.

6. *Outlook*, Collector's Edition, 2000, p. 117.
7. Jhumpa Lahiri, *Interpreter of Maladies* (New Delhi: Harper Collier, 1999).
8. *Outlook*, Collector's Edition, 2000, p. 118.
9. Sumit Mitra and Arthur J. Pais. "Boston Brahmin," *India Today*, Vol. XXV (17 Nov. 2000).
10. *Outlook*, Collector's Edition, 2000, p. 117.

Between the Two Worlds: A Critique of *Interpreter of Maladies*

G. DOMINIC SAVIO

Jhumpa Lahiri's *Interpreter of Maladies* gives one the satisfaction of being an interpreter of melodies as one takes into account the graceful cadence with which the flow of narration gently glides, the thread of gentle suspense never cut. Her characters are rooted in middle class ethos: they are neither too low not to have any tradition of their own, nor are they too westernized so that assimilation with the New World becomes as easy as the shifting of gears. There is a trace of tender sorrow surfacing from their rather vague sense of loneliness, which provides these stories a gossamer thin nostalgic feeling. These stories of Bengal, Boston and beyond transcend the physical geographies of Continents and map the contours of mental geographies. The insulated hearts of Shukumar and Shoba, the trepidation in the mind of Mr. Pirzada for the safety of his family in the war-inflicted East Pakistan, the strain-easing confession of Mrs. Das that one of her song is not her husband's, the boomeranging of the tall tales of Boori Ma, Miranda's mysterious longings for the married Dev, Mrs. Sen's eagerness to learn driving so as to retain the baby sitting of Eliot, the Christian-motif discovering blessed house Hindu inmates, Sanjeev and Tanima alias Twinkle. Bibi Haldar's worries and the librarian narrator's preparation for life perhaps as lonely and as long, as that of Mrs. Croft are all the gentle twist of the kaleidoscopic imagination of the Pulitzer Prize winning Jhumpa Lahiri.

Each story is like a twist of the kaleidoscopic imagination of Lahiri. "A Temporary Mater" deals with the thirty-five-year-old Shukumar and his thirty-three-year-old Shoba. The proofreader Shoba is almost the breadwinner while the student husband is a bread maker. What begins as a curse, the one hour power shut down beginning at 8.00 p.m. for five days, helps them see each other in a newer light. The confession each one makes attains significance. When the normal power supply is restored ahead of schedule they feel cheated. In the artificially created darkness, Shukumar confesses that he had held their stillborn son in his hands before it was cremated. However it was Shoba who freeze-framed him with her confession that she was leaving him. In "When Mr. Pirzada Came to Dine" Lahiri introduces a visiting scholar from Pakistan on a meagre fellowship to study about the foliage of New England during summer and winter. The agony of separation with his family of wife and seven daughters is further hued with the news of the war breaking out between Pakistan and East Pakistan. The narrator, Lilia was ignorant of Asian geography and she referred to Mr. Pirzada as an Indian. Her father asked her what type of Geography she studied at school. With the help of a map, he instructs his daughter that a person like Mr. Pirzada was not an Indian as he came from Pakistan's Eastern wing. As an Indian what she should have known is outside the purview of the syllabus requirements of the American educational system. Lahiri portrays the emotional make-up of the mind of Lilia as she furtively looks up for the geographical positions of India and Pakistan. She has the guilt feeling of a culprit when cornered by her teacher Mrs. Kenyon. Lilia's participation in the Halloween dressed up as a witch adds a new ethnic colour to the American celebration.

The title story in the collection, "Interpreter of Maladies" deals with the experience of Mr. Kapasi as he takes one Indian American family on a tour of Konark. What prompts Mrs. Das to make a confession to this total stranger whom she would never ever meet in life is the reference he had made about another profession, which he handled. The Gujarati Kapasi acted as an interpreter to the Gujaratis in Bengal who came to a Bengali doctor for consultation. Mrs. Das wanted him to say something about her action. It was an unusual situation for Kapasi because he was not facing any language barrier in this context. She further told him "For eight years I haven't been able to express this to anybody, not to friends, certainly not to Raj. He doesn't even suspect it. He thinks that I am still in love with him."[1] Kapasi knows that she really did not give any importance to him as he found the slip of paper fluttering away in the wind.

In "A Real Durwan," Lahiri presents the sixty-four-year-old Boori Ma living as something of a janitor in a flat. She always spoke of her plight and the losses suffered by her since her deportation to Calcutta after partition. She was separated from her husband, four daughters, a two storied brick house, a rosewood shelf and a number of boxes. Her third daughter was married to a school principal. The rice was cooked in rose water. Distinguished guests were invited. There were men who came to pick dates and guavas. It was almost the burden of her speech, "Believe me one, and don't believe, such comforts you cannot even dream them." (71) The tenants, from Mr. Dalal who lived on the third floor to Mrs. Mishra the second floor-widow, were compassionate to her. Boori Ma receives a real jolt when they throw her out because the basin on the stairwell had been stolen. They felt that Boori Ma has endangered the security of the building. They all decreed, "What a building like this needs is a real Durwan." (82)

Lahiri focuses her attention on an American girl Miranda's love for a married Bengali, Dev. When she heard that he was Bengali, at first she thought it was a religion. Later Dev pointed out to her with the help of an issue of *The Economist* that Bengal was a place in India. As long as Dev's wife was in India, their relationship continued uninterrupted. Miranda had gone to the Indian store to find out how Madhuri Dixit looked like because Dev had told her that his wife resembled that Bombay actress. As days passed by, Miranda's deep felt longings for Devajith Mithra also evaporate.

In "Mrs. Sen's," Lahiri comments on the customary Nanny role the coloured women play in America. Mrs. Linden, the mother of the eleven-year-old Eliot was badly in need of someone to look after her son before she would return home. Mrs. Sen, the wife of a Mathematics Professor agreed to look after Eliot. It was expected that the child would be dropped in her house from school, as she did not know driving. Things went on smoothly with a harmless Eliot dutifully reading comics or watching Mrs. Sen as she chopped vegetables for the evening dinner. It was the little accident, which put an end to her whole plan. Unescorted by Mr. Sen, she drove off the road. When Eliot's mother arrived at quarter to six, Mr. Sen told her the details of the accident. She couldn't risk entrusting her son to the care of Mrs. Sen. The mother decided to give him a key with the instruction to call the neighbours in case of an emergency. "One of the most moving stories in the collection, 'Mrs. Sen's' is the archetypal story of the cultural outsider but even her plight is offset by the loneliness of little Eliot, her faithful ward for a few hours every day."[2]

"The Third and Final Continent" focuses on the librarian-narrator who reaches America from Calcutta via London. His first home in America was the house of Mrs. Croft, the hundred and three-year old widow. He had stayed there only for a few weeks paying eight dollars every week. It was from her that he learnt how proud she was as an American about the landing on the Moon in the magnificent desolation of the sea of tranquillity. She made him say that it was a splendid act. As he got his accommodation near the University he moved out. His stay in America, short though, had taught him not to expect any emotional farewell from Mrs. Croft. There was a streak of sentimentality when he brought Mala, his wife to Mrs. Croft. It was a happy and eventless life he had with Mala. It was the news of Mrs. Croft's death that brought him to think of life. To their son it was a matter of great astonishment that his father paid very little amount by way of rent. Concluding, the narrator says, "I know that my achievement is quite ordinary. I am not the only man to seek his fortune far from home, and certainly I am not the first. Still there are times I am bewildered by each mile I have traveled, each meal I have eaten, each person I have known, each room in which I have slept. As ordinary as it all appears there are times when it is beyond my imagination." (198) And that is the success of Jhumpa Lahiri.

The skill of Lahiri lies in her ability to weave a pattern through these apparently divergent stories. Deep down in them we find that each character feels that he or she is alone, misunderstood or at best only partially understood, drifting along the current of life like a flotsam. It is the subtlety of Lahiri's vision that she uses only suggestions and not statements in her observations. Her Indian American characters live in the New World surrounded by all forms of luxury, which is still an envy of their counterpart in India. Mr. Kapasi's admiration for the family of Mr. Das because of their superior lifestyle makes him feel despondent about his own ordinary living with a nearly illiterate wife. But Mrs. Das's revelation sounds like a knell to his reverence mixed admiration for Mrs. Das. Shukumar and Shoba live in the dark world of apathy for each other. That which could have cemented their relationship proves a disruptive element, their stillborn child. It is a strange mystery that they have been able to see each other's soul in the darkness of the one-hour power cut. It is Shoba who has the last laugh when she leaves Shukumar. The sacrosanct bonds of matrimony do not hold these Indians together in the New World. Dev doesn't experience any qualms cheating his wife when he carries on his relationship with the twenty-two-year-old Miranda. Lahiri presents both Mrs. Sen and Mala as dutiful Indian wives in the New Continent cooking food for their husbands and feeling immensely happy over their role.

Like Sheherzade Lahiri arrests our attention leading us from one emotion to the other but all streaked with a trace of loneliness. "She is a writer's writer: her prose is elegant and economical, her observations well craft, her characters perfectly believable. The smallest of details fail to escape her as she relies on subtle descriptions chronicling the landscapes of minutiae that make up her characters every day."[4]

NOTES

1. Jhumpa Lahiri, *Interpreter of Maladies* (New Delhi: HarperCollins, 1999), p. 65.

2. Shoma Chaudhury, "Debutante of the Year," *Biblio: A Review of Books*, Vol. IV, Nos. 7 and 8 (July-Aug. 1999), p. 19.
3. Nayantara Patel, "Near Perfect Rendition," *The Book Review*, Vol. XXIII, No. 12 (Dec. 1999).
4. Anurima Banerji, Rev. of *Interpreter of Maladies*, *Manasi*, 114 (Sept.-Oct. 1999), pp. 36-37.

Lahiri's Portrayal of Life in Exile

ARUNODAY MUKHERJEE

Jhumpa Lahiri, a voice of Indo-American origin, makes us aware of the psychological aspect of the Indian expatriates who have settled in America for their livelihood and higher studies in her outstanding collection of short stories entitled *Interpreter of Maladies*,[1] which brought her fame and the Pulitzer Award. Once she remarks in course of an interview that America is home to her but she feels a bit of an outsider too and so she finds herself at ease in dealing with the theme of exile, in her writing. Born of Indian parents in London, Jhumpa grew up in Rhode Island, U.S.A. and so she is still engaged in finding her centre. Like many writers of the commonwealth fiction, Lahiri, a writer of the Indian diaspora, also deals with the problems of rootlessness, insecurity, uncertainty and the cultural isolation of the Indian emigrants in America and thus, her short stories assume a universal character. In *Interpreter of Maladies*, the writer mostly deals with the lives of Indians or, to be precise, Bengalis in exile. The characters of Jhumpa's short stories are always navigating between the strict traditions they have inherited and the baffling New World they must encounter everyday. The two short stories of Lahiri are based in Calcutta where the characters find themselves in exile in their own native milieu. One of the short stories, "Interpreter of Maladies," is set in Konarak in Orissa, though the characters belong to a family of Indians settled in America, now holidaying in India. In the short stories of Lahiri, we see that it is not only the geographical displacement, but also the emotional exile which constitutes the main theme. Jhumpa Lahiri reveals the ingenuity of plots, sense of humour and a keen interest in the psychology of her characters in course of portraying life in exile.

A number of short stories of Lahiri are about marriages that are under great strain. In India the institution of marriage is given much importance, but in America the conception of marriage and family is losing importance day by day. The first short story of Jhumpa Lahiri's collection throws light on this kind of crisis. In the short story entitled "A Temporary Matter," the writer presents the Indian couple namely Shukumar and Shoba whose marriage is on the rocks following a still-born child. Shukumar and Shoba regard India as the land of their parents and ancestors and have the faint memory of this country. It is but natural for an exile to remember the native country off and on. Hence Shoba compares the load-shedding of America with that of India in the following lines: "It is like India. Sometimes the current disappears for hours at a stretch." (11)

Shukumar remains engaged in teaching his classes and doing research. In the course of his academic pursuits, Shukumar has to go to Baltimore to attend a conference and meanwhile Shoba gives birth to a dead child. The birth of dead child disturbs their domestic harmony and Shoba decides finally to separate herself from Shukumar forever. Although the short story centres round the temporary matter of power-cut for one hour, the writer suggests something else. The hour of darkness brings the couple close to each other and they spend the hour sharing their secret feelings. This renewed conjugal relationship does not last long as the line is repaired ahead of schedule. So marriage itself turns into a temporary matter in case of Shukumar and Shoba who are influenced by the American society in which the conjugal relationship depends on the whims of the couple. The insecurity and uncertainty in the relationship of the Indian couple living in America reflects exactly the unstable life in exile. In another short story entitled "This Blessed House" we again come across marriage under strain. Like Shukumar and Shoba, Sanjeev and Twinkle have also their links with India and so we find here another couple in exile. Sanjeev, an engineer working in a firm, moves to a new house at Connecticut with his wife named Twinkle. Twinkle discovers different objects related to Christianity like the porcelain effigy of Christ and a dishtowel printed with

Ten Commandments in this blessed house. Her childish infatuation with these objects has enraged Sanjeev, who is very conscious of his religion. Like an exile, desperate to save his cultural identity in the foreign land, Sanjeev asserts again and again that "We're not Christian." (157)

It is an irony that the domestic atmosphere becomes tense in the blessed house because Twinkle is in love with the silver bust of Christ. Hence the lines occur: "Most of all he hated it because he knew that Twinkle loved it." (157)

The tragedy of an exile becomes prominent in the short story entitled "Mrs. Sen's." Mrs. Sen represents the tragedy of a woman who has to live in exile with her husband after marriage. Mrs. Sen, a Bengali housewife, cannot change her taste and reveals an unusual craze for fish even in America. The writer's own confession makes it clear that Mrs. Sen, a typical Indian housewife, is modeled on her mother. Her forehead marked with vermilion reveals her effort to keep up her identity as a Hindu woman in the alien land. Her passion for fish highlights the nostalgic feeling of an exile. Her husband, a professor of mathematics, has no time to drive her to market daily for buying fish and a conflict arises for this reason. In fact, she tries to drive herself to go to market for fish out of annoyance and meets with an accident. Like every emigrant, Mrs. Sen also feels isolated in the alien society and so she expresses doubt in the following line: "Could I drive all the way to Calcutta?" (119) Mrs. Sen's desperate effort to keep an English little boy always close to her highlights her isolation.

Another remarkable short story in Jhumpa Lahiri's collection is "Sexy." Here we see how a person from a third world country is lost in the glamour of a Western country and robbed of his character in exile. A young Bengali executive in a bank named Devjit Mitra builds up an extramarital relationship with a Midwestern woman named Miranda when his wife goes to India. We also come to know another Indian who develops a relationship with a woman living in London and leaves his wife and son. Dev and the husband of Laxmi's cousin remind one of Ralph Singh, the protagonist of Naipaul's *Mimic Men*. As the husband of

Laxmi's cousin got off with another woman at Heathrow, Ralph Singh was also stripped of his character in London where he had come to obtain his degree and discover his individuality. Dev and the husband of Laxmi's cousin cannot refute the following confession of Ralph Singh:

> Coming to London, the great city. . . . I had tried to give myself a personality. . . . But now I no longer knew what I was. . . . I found myself longing for the certainties of my life on the island of Isabella.[2]

There is also a resemblance between Miranda and Ralph's wife named Sandra. Both of them are lonely women and seek sexual pleasure to remove the boredom of isolation. The loneliness of an exile is emphasized here in the following remark of Dev: "I know what it's like to be lonely." (89) A great triumph is achieved by Lahiri as a writer in writing the remarkable short story entitled "Interpreter of Maladies." Here the writer deals with the theme of exile in a different manner. A rich couple settled in America comes to India to find the traditional grandeur. Mr. Kapasi, a tourist guide, assists the couple to find the root on the way to the Sun Temple at Konarak. The influence of the two different kinds of world on the visiting couple is evident: "The family looked Indian, but dressed as foreigners did." (43)

We also come across a kind of emotional exile in this short story. Referring to the behaviour of Mr. and Mrs. Das, the writer remarks: "It seemed that they were in charge of the children only for the day, it was hard to believe they were regularly responsible for anything other than themselves." (49)

The aforementioned lines suggest the isolation of Mrs. Das. Her feeling of loneliness makes Mrs. Das fall a prey to the lust of her husband's friend. Like other short stories of Lahiri, here the marriage of Mr. and Mrs. Das is also in the doldrums and so an impromptu friendship grows between Mrs. Das and Mr. Kapasi, who works with a doctor as his interpreter. Mrs. Das confesses that the father of one of her children is a friend of her husband and her attempt to keep it a secret makes her restless and fall out of love with life. This short story has a suggestive end where

Mrs. Das urges Mr. Kapasi to interpret her malady which makes her sick in exile.

The nostalgic feeling of an exile is brilliantly highlighted in the short story entitled "When Mr. Pirzada Came to Dine." The behaviour of Pirzada, a lecturer, who has came from Dacca to study the foliage of New England in America on a grant of the Government of Pakistan, becomes ridiculous at times. He keeps a watch set to the local time in Dacca. The psychology of an exile living in home and abroad at the same time is brilliantly reflected in the following lines: "Life, I realized, was being lived in Dacca first . . . our meals, our actions, were only a shadow of what had already happened there, a lagging ghost of where Mr. Pirzada really belonged." (30-31)

Mr. Pirzada always seems to be anxious for the safety of his family in Dacca during the Bangladesh War of liberation and so he comes to the narrator's parental house every evening to watch the television and gather news of his native land. This short story ends with the return of Mr. Pirzada to Dacca where he feels much relieved after being reunited with his wife and children in his three-storey home. Mr. Pirzada's love for Bangladesh reminds us of the following lines of Wordsworth who is infatuated with his native land, England: "I travelled among unknown men/In lands beyond the sea,/Nor, England did I know till then/ what love I bore to thee."[3] In short, Mr. Pirzada epitomizes the universal feeling of an exile and his nostalgia.

The two short stories entitled "A Real Durwan" and "The Treatment of Bibi Haldar" have a different flavour but they also throw light on the agony of an exile. The protagonists of these short stories find themselves in exile even in their native milieu. Both these short stories are set in Calcutta. In "A Real Durwan" Boori Ma, an old woman, who came from East Bengal as a refugee, has been living in the stairwell of a block of flats for many years. She does the job of a charwoman and virtually guards the whole building without any payment of course. Boori Ma's services resemble those of a real durwan and the residents of flats are thankful to her because she patrols activities in the alley, keeps away suspicious men and summons a rickshaw at a moment's calling. Sometimes the residents welcome her to their flats and offer her tea. The following lines highlight Boori Ma's state of exile in a brilliant manner: "Knowing not to sit on the furniture, she crouched, instead, in doorways and hallways, and observed gestures and manners in the same way a person tends to watch traffic in a foreign city." (76)

The condition of Boori Ma becomes miserable when Mr. Dalal, a benevolent resident of the building, goes to Simla for an outing. One day she goes out for a walk and finds a basin fitted on the stairwell missing when she returns to the building. The blame falls on Boori Ma and she is thrown out of the house for neglecting her duty. In the beginning of the short story, Boori Ma is introduced as a refugee and at the end of the story we see her again as a homeless exile. Perhaps the writer wants to prove here that the geographical displacement is not the only condition for an exile, a person may lose his identity even in his native land in this selfish and materialistic world.

"The Treatment of Bibi Haldar" is another short story with a native flavour in which an ailing woman finds herself forlorn even among her relatives. Bibi Haldar stays with her cousin in an apartment of a four-storey building and spends her days recording inventory for the cosmetic shop of her cousin in a small room in exchange of her shelter, food and clothes. Her permanent illness confines her world to the four-storey building and she lives in isolation even among her own people. The following sentence reveals her pangs of loneliness: "She wanted to be spoken for, protected, placed on her path in life." (160)

Although she is desperate to find a husband, her marriage is impossible as she suffers from epilepsy. Meanwhile, her cousin winds up his business and moves away, leaving Bibi alone at the mercy of fate. The following words of Bibi signify the desperate efforts of an exile to conceal her sorrow and keep a smiling face: "Now I am free to discover life as I please." (170)

The short story entitled "The Third and Final Continent" is a biographical sketch of a person who travels through three continents in course of his struggle for existence. The narrator leaves India in order to establish himself in England and he has to move further to America later on for his betterment. The theme of rootlessness pervades the short story. The following lines reflect the fate and struggle of an exile in a brilliant manner: "I lived in North London, in Finsbury Park, in a house occupied entirely by penniless Bengali bachelors like myself, at least a dozen and sometimes more, all struggling to educate and establish ourselves abroad." (175) The narrator's journey to England for a glamorous life reminds one of the Journey of Ralph Singh, the protagonist of Naipaul's *The Mimic Men,* to England with the same purpose.

Jhumpa Lahiri describes in detail the difficulty of narrator in finding a home away from home in America in this short story. Although the narrator has settled in America with a full-time job and lived there for thirty years, he cannot forget his hard struggle for survival as an exile. The following lines emphasize the eternal struggle of an exile in a New World: "Whenever he is discouraged, I tell him that if I can survive on three continents, then there is no obstacle he cannot conquer." (197)

In the analysis made above it becomes evident that the aspiration, perspiration and frustration of an exile form the basic tenet of Lahiri's collection of short stories entitled *Interpreter of Maladies*. In short, the writer has succeeded greatly in presenting the problems and maladies of emigrants with her artistic observation and skill.

NOTES

1. Jhumpa Lahiri, *Interpreter of Maladies (*Harper Collins India).
2. V.S. Naipaul, *The Mimic Men* (Penguin), p.14.
3. William Wordsworth, "I Travelled among Unknown Men," *The Golden Treasury*, p. 180.

Jhumpa Lahiri's Quest for Identity through *Interpreter of Maladies*

SUNEETA PATNAYAK

> *We are like "chiffon saris"—a sort of crossbreed attempting to adjust to the pressures of a new world, while actually being from another old one.*
>
> Feroza Jussawalla[1]

Michiko Kakutani, book critic and Pulitzer Prize winner has called Jhumpa Lahiri's entry into the arena of immigrant writing a "precocious debut." One feels compelled to shed stereotypes that age is a necessary consort to wisdom because Lahiri's stories display maturity and wisdom much beyond her years. Her work reverberates with a precision and clarity, which ensures immediate and uncomplicated comprehension of the message that she has tried to convey. This message has been unanimously interpreted as one that voices the trials and tribulations faced by exiles in an alien country. Yet, how far does Lahiri identify with the fragmented self of the "chiffon sari" category as declared by Feroza Jussawalla?

Lahiri is a second-generation immigrant whose parents continue to look back upon India as home. One would not expect her to suffer from the problems of unsuccessful assimilation having lived in an alien country all her life. Yet, she confesses frequently to a certain sense of being an outsider in the USA. All the stories in *Interpreter of Maladies* do not deal with the trauma of immigrant life though the underlying theme of at least four of her stories is about somewhat misplaced conceptions of idyllic America. She claims to have inherited her parents' preoccupations with the past.[2] Thus India reigns supreme in all her stories. "In my dictionary, the biblical definition of *translate* is 'to convey to heaven without death.' I am struck by the extent to which this decidedly Western, non-secular definition sheds light on my own personal background of Eastern origin. For in my observation, translation is not only a finite linguistic act but an ongoing cultural one. It is the continuous struggle, on my parents' behalf, to preserve what it means to them to be first and forever Indian, to keep afloat certain familial and communal traditions in a foreign and at times indifferent world."[3]

The question of identity has always been a difficult one but it is more so for culturally displaced persons, people who transgress the boundaries of familiar surroundings in search of fresher pastures in a foreign land. In Bharati Mukherjee's words, they trade "top-dog status in the homeland for the loss-of-face meltdown of immigration."[4] This statement rings hollow when we read Feroza Jussawalla's opinion of Bharati Mukherjee which says: "Bharati Mukherjee definitely seems to have found her 'haven' in the United States, but with this comes an obsequiousness, a pleading to be mainstreamed."[5] Bharati Mukherjee has advocated for total assimilation of an individual to the American culture and society to bring about cohesive existence. Chitra Banerjee Divakaruni, another first generation writer admits to have felt exhilarated at everything American when she first arrived in America and felt a relief at having found mind-blowing liberalism as compared to the debilitating patriarchal society back home. Yet nostalgia exists, in spite of the denials, in the form of metaphors and symbols, which represent the world left behind. This nostalgia is particularly touching when Uma Parameswaran says,

And I shall bring Ganga
As Bhagirathi did of old
To our land
Our Assiniboine,
And the flute player
Dark as kaya blossom
Shall dance on the waters of La Salle [6]

Jhumpa Lahiri's maturity lies in the fact that her collection of short stories *Interpreter of Maladies* is bereft of any of the above eccentricities or distortions, which sometimes typify immigrant literature. Though she must be a completely assimilated immigrant she does admit in "Heaven without Dying" that what "drove her to fiction was the need to escape the pitfalls of being viewed as one thing or the other." But she also admits that her writing is less a response to her parents' cultural nostalgia and more an attempt to forge her amalgamated domain. Her portrayal of Indians in America seems tinged with a note of disapproval, a censuring attitude to protagonists who have accoutered themselves in the misleading American garb of liberalism. That probably explains her wish to be married in Kolkata amidst proper ceremonial rites when she could have chosen otherwise especially when she was tying the knot with a non-Indian.

The above observation makes one think that her predecessors have taken America a little too enthusiastically without actually having severed the umbilical cord. Lahiri has her umbilical cord with India intact but she has come to terms with reality quickly in spite of her young years and has accepted the discrepancies gracefully. None of her stories have in them bizarre and incredible conclusions that might reflect an impulsive temperament. Sandip Roy Chowdhury says about her: "I have to admit what I found the most startling about Lahiri's characters was the fact that to all appearances her Das-es and Sens are the happy contented Bengalis one meets at social functions. They are instantly recognizable, even likeable—the friendly polite people who have long leisurely meals and dip biscuits in their teas. Lahiri's achievement is in being able to get beneath that surface calmness and expose for one brief startling moment the real people underneath."[7]

Lahiri's quest for identity is a quiet one, which takes into account the obsessions of her parents with India and the fact that it might have been passed on to her as a legacy. She has loved being in Calcutta but has realized that she did not belong there just as she did not belong in America. Identity is the recognition of one's self. Lahiri in seven of her stories in *Interpreter of Maladies* speaks of her protagonists who face communication problems.

Bharati Mukherjee sums up her sentiments regarding the necessity to cohere and be part of the melting pot to survive in America: "In this age of Diasporas, one's biological identity may not be one's only identity. Erosions and accretions come with the act of emigration. The experience of cutting myself off from a biological homeland and settling in an adopted homeland that is not always welcoming to its dark-complexioned citizens has tested me as a person, and made me the writer I am today."[8] Her second novel *Wife* is about the psychological transformation wrought in an Indian woman by immigration. She says: "When an Asian man comes to America he comes for economic transformation, and he brings a wife who winds up being psychologically changed."[9] Dimple Dasgupta in *Wife* kills her husband in a "misguided act of self-assertion" and Mukherjee proves that confusion over identity causes traumatic consequences. "Mrs. Sen's" in Lahiri's collection and *Wife* by Bharati Mukherjee are two disparate sketches of the trauma of Indian women immigrants. One in her desperation to be part of the mainstream ends up killing her husband the other tries painfully to give up the past and fails. Jhumpa Lahiri gives a touching and honest commentary on the inability of the women of the Indian Diaspora to adapt to the new life. This story is about Mrs. Sen, the wife of an Indian professor, whose character is based on Lahiri's mother. She baby-sits an eleven-year-old boy called Eliot whose mother works late hours and is unable to give the attention to her son that an Indian child takes for granted. Mrs. Sen and Eliot have been poised against each other in the story to draw out the pathetic loneliness each suffers from. She is homesick, listens to the recorded chatter of her family on the tape and the only time she displays excitement is when she makes a routine trip to the seaside to pick up fresh fish. Eliot, on the other hand, is withdrawn and has no complaints about being fed a pizza every night by his mother because she is too tired. As for his father, he lived two thousand miles west according to the last information she had of him. He accepts this as normal while Mrs. Sen needs to convince herself that he does not miss his mother. She asks, "Do you miss your mother, Eliot, these afternoons with me?" He says, "I see her at night" to which she responds, "When I was your age I was not knowing that one day I would be so far. You are wiser than that, Eliot. You already taste the way things must be."[10] Mrs. Sen's inability to shake off the past and Eliot's placid acceptance of his style of life are juxtaposed against each other and in Lahiri's portrayal of Eliot's character lies her own approval of reticence in human emotions. He liked the short spell of family life he was exposed to while with the Sens' but accepts without question when he is given a key to his house, as he was a big boy. The last line speaks volumes when his mother asks him on the phone: "'You okay?' Eliot looked out the kitchen window, at gray waves receding from the shore, and said he was fine." Here the fact that Mrs. Sen and Eliot are more than accidental companions is confirmed. Eliot is the result of a very different culture and Mrs. Sen is encountering the difference for the first time.

Of the nine stories in *Interpreter of Maladies*, none actually seems to be the expression of a tortured immigrant soul. The fact that she places India as a backdrop is not necessarily an indication of torn sentiments being pulled to either side. Her stories seem to be the product of a keenly observant mind that has absorbed tiny details of exiles without allowing itself to be mired by insecurities. But her discomfort is sometimes evident through the veneer of apparent nonchalance. The small incident in the story "When Mr. Pirzada Came to Dine" when the pumpkin that the narrator had helped carve is shattered and the pieces are strewn all over the lawns on Halloween is an expression of the deeply embedded hurt sentiments. People had expressed surprise on seeing an Indian witch. She has used this hurtful incident as an eye-opener and combined it with the tremendous impact that the declaration of Civil War in Pakistan made on the narrator's parents and Mr. Pirzada. Mr. Pirzada was a Pakistani who had been awarded a grant by the Pakistan government to study the foliage of New England and had left behind seven daughters and a wife in the strife torn Dacca.

> What I remember during those twelve days of the war was that my father no longer asked me to watch the news with them, and that my mother refused to serve anything other than boiled eggs with rice for dinner. I remember some nights helping my mother spread a sheet and blankets on the couch so that Mr. Pirzada could sleep there. . . . Most of all I remember the three of them operating during that time as if they were a single person, sharing a single meal, a single body, a single silence, and a single fear. (40-41)

The above extract is from the story "When Mr.Pirzada Came to Dine," that is partly autobiographical according to Lahiri. When the narrator speaks of the trauma of her parents and Mr. Pirzada during the Pakistan Civil War, she places herself in the role of a bystander who is watching a fierce emotional upheaval. She feels just as intensely maybe but cannot do more than popping a candy given by Mr. Pirzada into her mouth at night and praying for the well-being of his seven daughters. This incident marks the role she is to assign herself for always, a person who is marginal both here and there. Lahiri is not struggling to discover her identity. Rather, having found hers that can be comfortably called a dual one, she views both the worlds with a pinch of salt.

While Mrs. Sen carries her homesickness on her sleeve, the narrator in "The Last and the Final Continent" makes a compromise and a celebration of his assimilation. He is an Indian bachelor who happens to live for a short while in the house of an old woman called Mrs. Croft. He is agonized by the fact that she lives on her own at her age. He remembers his own mother whose nails he had scrupulously cleaned with a pin before her cremation because she used to play with her faeces in her senility. The depth of the son's sentiments is reflected in the hesitant concern he shows for Mrs. Croft. However, he makes a deliberate effort to outgrow his past, accepts his newly wed Indian bride, goes on to make a properly assimilated man out of their only son. Yet, he and his wife make it a point to speak to their son in Bengali because they are apprehensive of a time when he will cease to speak Bengali.

Lahiri's sketch of the above characters spins them through a period of turbulence when their identity seems lost in the newness of the surroundings but she makes them come to terms with reality and compromise with the situation.

However, with her second-generation protagonists she is not so kind. In "A Temporary Matter," she speaks about the inability of a couple to come to terms with the loss of their first-born baby. An inability to share the intense grief draws them apart. They communicate only in darkness during a temporary power cut. It reaches a sad state when Shukumar deliberately sets his table in the room they had planned for the baby because Shoba avoided the room. Their little game of revealing untold secrets to each other ultimately leads to Shoba revealing her plans of moving out and Shukumar's below the belt retaliation that he had seen their baby boy after he was born. Their failure to cope with the crisis seems to have been brought about by the routine of living one's own life, away from prying questions and the interference of well-meaning adults. Marriages fail everywhere but in a country where one is accountable for one's actions to family and society, one feels obliged to give it another chance. The title "A Temporary Matter" seems a comment on the nature of marriages in the west.

Yet another instance of an immigrant's identity being lost in the clash of cultures is the title story "Interpreter of Maladies." Here we come across an America-born Indian couple who are holidaying in Orissa in India. A guide-cum-driver called Mr. Kapasi drives them around. They, especially the wife, are intrigued by the other part-time job that Kapasi does. He acts as an interpreter for a Gujarati doctor who has the ailments of his patients interpreted by Kapasi. This earns both of them their money and more importantly relieves the poor patients of their agony. Mrs. Das takes the healing capacity of Kapasi a little too seriously and expects him to provide her with a remedy for the suffering within her. She confesses to him that one of her sons is not that of her husband but the result of a torrid encounter with her husband's friend. Lahiri's attempt to divine hidden insecurities of the lady beneath an apparent nonchalance that says "To hell with values" is her characteristic disapproval of behavior unsanctioned by a code of conduct, which has its roots in her home country. Mrs. Das rebuffs Kapasi's question "Is it really pain you feel, Mrs. Das or is it guilt?" (66) because she has known of a different set of rules in India even though she has followed another in America.

When second generation immigrants are termed as ABCDs i.e. America Born Confused Desis, one must look at the confusion with the perspective of a second-generation woman writer. When an Indian or for that matter anyone migrates to a foreign country, he carries with him certain values which he imposes upon his children, especially the daughters. Lata Mani says: "Given that there is no rupture in patriarchal power with migration, merely its reconfiguration, the consequences of diaspora are specifically different for women and men."[11] Lahiri dwells upon this confusion because she has known the presence of "invisible walls" around their home. In "Heaven without Dying," she writes: "Growing up I was admonished not to behave like an American, or, worse, to think of myself as one. Actually, being an American was not an option." Most immigrants are confused about their identity regarding their identity, whether first generation or second. They are all Janus-faced with one face looking ahead and the other behind which causes them to stumble a few times. All immigrant writers write of the nostalgia and the identity crisis. Jhumpa Lahiri has presumably gone through both but has proved to be surprisingly resilient. Her portrayal of the immigrant trauma is without the tinge of hopelessness. She seems to suggest an antidote for the warped personality that results due to the cultural discrepancies. She allows the chiffon sari theory of Feroza Jussawalla to gain weight and then proves with her narrative that chiffon saris, which are a metaphor for the confused exile or immigrant, are in fact much sought after because of their flexibility and adaptability to all occasions. Thus, she finds her identity through her protagonists who do look back but pick and choose the best of both the cultures, that of their homeland and of their host country.

NOTES

1. Feroza Jussawalla, "Chiffon Saris: The Plight of Asian Immigrants in the New World," *Massachusetts Review*, 29.4 (1988-89), pp. 583-95.
2. Jhumpa Lahiri, "To Heaven without Dying," *FEED Books Issue, Essay*, 7.24.2000 (Internet source).
3. *Ibid.*
4. Bharati Mukherjee, "Prophet and Loss: Salman Rushdie's Migration of Souls," *Village Voice Literary Supplement*, 72 (March 1989).
5. Feroza Jussawalla.
6. Uma Parameswaran, *Trishanku* (Toronto: TSAR Books, 1988), p. 66.
7. Sandip Roy Chowdhury, "India Currents," *New California Media Online*, October 8, 1999.
8. Bharati Mukherjee, "American Dreamer," *Mother Jones*, January-February 1997.
9. Bharati Mukherjee, Interview by Alison B. Carb, *Massachussetts Review*, 29, no. 4 (1988), pp. 645-54.
10. Jhumpa Lahiri, *Interpreter of Maladies* (U.S.A.: Houghton Mifflin Company, 1999), pp. 122-23.
11. Lata Mani, ed., "The Women of South Asian Descent Collective," *Our Feet Walk the Sky: Women of the South Asian Diaspora* (San Francisco: Aunt Lute Books, 1993).

Interpreter of Maladies: A Study in the Use of Doubling

MADHOO KAMARA

Doubling is not a new concept in literature. "Doppelganger motif," or twinning or doubling or fragmentation elucidates; the technique which uncovers the complexity and contradictions within one single personality and highlights the idea of multiple personalities. Shakespeare, Dostoevsky, Henry James, Melville and others have presented innumerable characters with such facets. It dramatizes the intrapsychic and extrapsychic conflicts—the protagonist in the web of the situational surroundings to describe, define and delineate the man-nature inter-communicating impulses and its aftermath or end-product.

Robert Rogers in his book *A Psycho Analytic Study of the Double in Literature* describes doubling as an act of splitting oneself into two halves or meeting oneself as two different entities. Classifying doubling, he gives a number of categories like implicit or explicit doubling. Implicit doubling is the fragmentation of a single character with no concrete extension of personality outside its frame whereas explicit doubling concerns the distribution of a single selfhood into various characters. Here the self extends to encompass "selves" further. Roger describes fragmentation as "dual" or multiple. Dual fragmentation occurs when the personalities contain two conflicting images and multiple when it houses more than two images.

Another category of fragmentation is that of doubling by multiplication and by division. Doubling and multiplication is characterized by two or more persons striving to define a particular concept or attitude; on the other hand doubling by multiplication takes place when characters with opposing qualities are contrasted with each other.

Interpreter of Maladies represents one or the other category of fragmentation in each of the nine stories.

In "A Temporary Matter," Shukumar is reconciled to the loss they had suffered in the form of losing their baby but Shoba keeps her wounds green. Shukumar is practical but Shoba is hypersensitive and her elusiveness is its by-product. To her, the death of her baby is a personal injury but to Shukumar a common one for it had poisoned the happiness they shared earlier. Shoba had found her cocoon by getting a new residence but Shukumar hungers togetherness. To him Shoba exists very much as she used to be after the loss took place; but Shoba, nursing her private gloom, stands on the threshold of alienation.

R.D. Laing in his fundamental study entitled *Self and Others* describes the state of mind as:

> Self receives and gives. Other is needed to give and to receive. The more self receives the more self needs to give. The more other cannot receive, the more self needs to destroy. The more self destroys others, the more empty self becomes. The more empty the more envious, the envious the more destructive.
>
> A prototype of the other as giver but not receiver, unresponsive or impervious, tends to generate in self a sense of failure.[1]

Similarly Mr. Pirzada and his friends in the story "When Mr. Pirzada Comes to Dine" make one hemisphere against Mr. Pirzada, his wife and seven daughters left in Decca. The two locale complete the domestic architecture although the geographical split exists until the close of the story. Further, the narrator's fascination towards Mr. Pirzada as a "hero" reveals the myriad forms of love of which the father and the child are constructively blessed in their growth as an individual and the realization of the humane within. When the enamour disappears, the narrator character joins the large group of well-wishers and rejoices in Pirzada's rejoining the family in his own country.

Every relationship gives "satisfactions" to the self, every successful relationship gives gratification of the potency to communicate successfully. Laing remarks: "relationship implies a definition of self by other and other by self. This complementarily can be central or peripheral, have greater or less dynamic significance at different periods of one's life." (69)

"A Real Durwan" puts the two phases of life seeped in apparent hostility at opposite poles. Old age emblematic of immense reciprocity, undemanding volunteer and a patient sacrificer stands in opposition to the adulthood which rejects all threats to ego and is self-interested in its motive. It is robust, highly volatile to offences and status conscious. But these two phases give a complete whole to life which undergoes changes as one passes from one period to another. Further, Boori Ma, recollecting her past and dead regality, is illustrative of the past that man's consciousness cannot shun through which it has passed out for another venture into time. Time in its collective form—present, past and hopes making the future—reveals an alive psyche that breathes in creativity to construct the mental perception of one's own existence. Besides, it is also a reflection upon the quality and flux of the form of living to which we individuals have little contribution. Our success lies in our labour but not in our rewards. The juxtaposition of the haves and have nots is another image of doubling. Besides, the Boori Ma, treasuring the keys to the chest which once upon carried her riches, but no more now, reveals that man derives much from false hope to overcome the vicissitudes of life. She is very particular about the keys as if its loss would prevent her from opening the chest. Although it is ridiculous on the superficial level to label Boori Ma as a neurotic, yet the sense of pity makes you identify her with her keys. At the climax, she loses her keys which adds much to her emotional disorder (the unhealthy situation is initiated by her neglect at the chaal): A vacuum creates in her although its physical co-relation did not ever exist. Her keys are her way to the world of imagination. Once the connector is lost, the real and the unreal separate making the lady wretched.

> "Identity" is that whereby one feels is the same, in this place, this time as at that time and at that place, past or future it is that by which one is identified."[2]

In social context, the Boori Ma again is an image of the unreal whereas her survivors are embodiments of the real. To construct dreams, concrete reality efforts are demanded. Here Boori Ma and the chaal fellows make the whole of the imaginary in process.

"Sexy" presents Dev and Miranda on the double of Laxmi and Dev's wife at one level; Dev and Miranda at another level and Miranda and Laxmi on the other. Laxmi's cousin is the double of Dev's wife. Dev and Miranda are animal passion against social norms but because human beings have learnt the trick of deception. Miranda knows it but is so enamoured by Dev that at the crux of lust, she doesn't realize the futility of being involved with a married man. A sense dawns upon her as she stays for a day with Laxmi's cousin whom she baby-sits for they have gone for a film show. Dev's allurement loses its magic and Miranda is guilty of being a home-wrecker. She avoids Dev intentionally and purposefully takes up fresh engagements to fill the void which being new is poignantly painful. Dev's wife as a contrast to Miranda is ceremonial love sanctified by religion and society and dutiful to husband and children. She stands for well-lessoned domesticity and Dev is her belief in honest participation in conjugality. She is suggested as perfect feminine Indian beauty, an image of purity, sacrifice and sanctity in marriage. Perversity and adultery do not exist anywhere.

Laxmi and Laxmi's cousin represent the marriage structure—fruitful conjugal bliss or broken families and estranged or separated spouses. Miranda represents the attack that reduces conjugality to rubbles. Miranda mending her ways is suggestive of the ways marriage may survive after a short turmoil. She can be imaged as a temporary illness affecting the health of domesticity.

"A Blessed Home" shows the impact of the blessedness of religion to a proper recipient. Conservative attitude is not rigid adherence and practice of religion. An open mind receives the good no matter it travels down through which agency. Twinkle treasures the image of Christ one after the other from the nooks and corners of the newly occupied house and feels that the house is a blessed-one. God is present everywhere and at each approachable place. The nearness of God overwhelms her but Sanjeev is full of annoyance for Jesus is no Hindu deity. A borrowed deity may subject him to ridicule during the house-warming party is his lurking fear. Luise Eichenbaum and Susie Orbach in *What Do Women Want* describes the need of this demand: "Many people are extremely sensitive to the way others see and think about their partners. We may be concerned with the way our partner talks about various topics in a social situation—is he or she saying the right things, does everyone think this person is witty, weird, etc.? We begin to see our partner as an extension of our self. We feel as if we are being judged at the same time we imagine other people to be judging our partner."[3] Sanjeev stops Twinkle but she is adamant and compromises on the ground that she would have it in her study. The split in their attitude to the figures of Christ destroys the symphony of the love rejoinders. The omniscient narrator describes the two attitudes in conflict:

> He studied the items on the mantel. It puzzled him that each was in its own way so silly. Clearly they lacked a sense of sacredness. He was further puzzled that Twinkle, who normally displayed good taste, was so charmed. These objects meant something to Twinkle, but they meant nothing to him. They irritated him. "We should call the Realtor. Tell him there's all this nonsense left behind. Tell him to take it away."
>
> "Oh, Sanj." Twinkle groaned. "Please. I would feel terrible throwing them away. Obviously they were important to the people who used to live here. It would feel, I don't know, sacrilegious or something."
>
> "If they are so precious, then why are they hidden all over the house? Why didn't they take them with them?"[4]

Through these two characters, the story presents doubling by division. In the essay "False and Untenable Positions" Laing writes: "Actions may be attributed, by self to self or self to other, as revealing or concealing, 'strong' or 'weak,' 'fulfilling' or 'emptying'; making 'real' the being of the doer making him more 'unreal,' more creative, or more destructive." (112)

"The Treatment of Bibi Haldar" contains complementary characters which again reveal fragmentation by division. Bibi Haldar stands in contrast to Haldar who is robust in health whereas Bibi suffers from an ailment "that battled family friends, priests, palmists, spinsters, gem therapists, prophets and fools." Her fits of unconsciousness and shameless delirium annoyed Haldar who expressed his animosity at every available occasion. Whereas Haldar enjoyed conjugal bliss, Bibi Haldar's demand directly or indirectly for "a man" was overlooked and Bibi was made to suffer in isolation. Whereas Haldar enjoyed and participated in "events and entertainment of the world," Bibi was deliberately kept away from it. She was regarded as a bane for business, "a liability and a loss." Bibi Haldar represents the fragmentation of a single character and hence is a picture of implicit doubling. At the very outset we are told that Bibi Haldar suffers from strange ailment and it defeated all allopathic homeopaths and ayurvedics. No amount of X-rays, probes and injections could cure her. Her illness is described by the omniscient narrator:

> The nature of her illness, which struck without warning, confined her world to the unpainted four-story building in which her local family, an elder cousin and his wife, rented an apartment on the second floor. Liable to fall unconscious and enter, at any moment, into a shameless delirium, Bibi could be trusted neither to cross a street nor board a tram without supervision.
>
> For her services Bibi received no income but was given meals, provisions, and sufficient meters of cotton at every October holiday to replenish her wardrobe at an inexpensive tailor. At night she slept on a folding camp cot in the cousin's place downstairs. (159)

Bibi Haldar is molested by an unidentified culprit and as the result of the assault, she becomes the mother of a son. The identity of the evil doer could not be traced but then she managed to raise the boy and run a business in the storage room to make money for his nurture. This cured Bibi's prolonged illness. With the blessing of illegitimate motherhood, Bibi Haldar learns the worldly ways of living. She now knows how to cook; how to stitch; how to prepare fire and how to dress gracefully.

No sooner did Bibi Haldar possess what belonged to her own self and was a part of her flesh, life grew meaningful to her. Her illness disappeared all with suddenness and with miraculous results. Her normalcy was restored and she was more or less perfect in her roles of a mother and a business-woman. This gain is explained thus: "In relationships people become psychologically merged. In many ways it is an extremely pleasurable experience. It represents a letting go of a firmly fixed position of 'mine.' If one feels secure enough in oneself, then sharing and merger don't represent loss of self. They show that developmentally one has achieved a secure sense of selfhood and is able to move into the world of 'mature' relationships."[5]

"Interpreter of Maladies" presents implicit fragmentation and also doubling by division. As an adjunct story to the title of the collection, "Interpreter of Maladies" puts into contrast the characters of Mrs. and Mr. Das, and also at the level of Mr. Das set against Mr. Kapasi. Mrs. Das appears as an attractive woman to Mr. Kapasi and Mrs. Das longs for his companionship not for fun but for cleansing of self-accusations with which she nagged herself for a little less than a decade. Mr. Kapasi who interprets the maladies of patients to the doctor offers a patient listening to the tormenting guilt of Mrs. Das. Mrs. Das is relieved of the shame of adultery after she makes a confession to Mr. Kapasi. The omniscient narrator describes the event thus:

> "I've just told you about my secret, and about how terrible it makes me feel. I feel terrible looking at my children, and at Raj, always terrible. I have terrible urges, Mr. Kapasi, to throw things away. One day I had the urge to throw everything I own out the window, the television, the children, everything. Don't you think it's unhealthy?"
>
> He was silent.
>
> "Mr. Kapasi, don't you have anything to say? I thought that was your job."
>
> "My job is to give tours Mrs. Das."
>
> "Not that. Your other job as an interpreter."
>
> "But we don't face a language barrier. What need is there for an interpreter?"

> "That's not what I mean. I would never have told you otherwise. Don't you realize what it means for me to tell to you?"
>
> "What does it mean?"
>
> "It means that I'm tired of feeling so terrible all the time. Eight years, Mr. Kapasi I've been in pain eight years. I was hoping you could help me feel better, say the right thing. Suggest some kind of remedy." (65)

The story does not have the trajectory of a romantic story. At first, it expects a love affair between Mrs. Das and Mr. Kapasi but the story takes an unanticipated turn. It conveys a subtle idea and defines the psychological effect of civil confessions in an unorthodox manner.

Mr. Das and Mr. Kapasi are also complementary figures. The closeness of Mr. Das makes Mrs. Das weary of guilt pangs but the presence of an unknown stranger reveals her of what had made her "a cannibal of her own heart." The proximity of Mr. Das in his husband role was no comfort to Mrs. Das, but the presence of Mr. Kapasi is assuring, encouraging, and reviving to her dull spirit. Mr. Kapasi renders help to Mrs. Das with an efficiency of a medical practitioner. Mr. Kapasi wants to help the lady as he had been helping the patients in expressing their symptoms to the doctor. The omniscient narrator records his willingness to help Mrs. Das with sufficient details:

> Mr. Kapasi believed it was his duty to assist Mrs. Das. Perhaps he ought to tell her to confess the truth to Mr. Das. He would explain that honesty was the best policy. Honesty, surely, would help her feel better, as she'd put it. Perhaps he would offer to preside over the discussion, as a mediator. He decided to begin with the most obvious question, to get to the heart of the matter, and so he asked, "Is it really pain you feel Mrs. Das, or is it guilt?" (66)

When Bobby is attacked by monkeys, Mr. Kapasi shoes them away, gathers Bobby in his arm and carries him back to his parents and siblings. The boy is comforted and his wounds are treated with medicine. This is a gesture of reciprocity—a pardon to the weary soul and a great relief to an anxiety-stricken mind. Mrs. Das finds a message of pardon through Mr. Kapasi as someone representing Mr. Das for she lacked courage of informing Mr. Das of the sin she had committed unknowingly. In her mind Mr. Das is the accuser, the charge levelling mouth and a judge announcing judgement. But Mr. Kapasi is a speaker to God for fellowmen who come for the benediction of God.

"Mrs. Sen's" represents doubling by multiplication, for the image of perfect mother is what puts Mrs. Sen and Mrs. Linden into a contrastive slot. Eliot is a boy of eleven and because his mother is a career woman, he has no one to stay with him at home. Eliot loves Mrs. Sen and the mutual dependency is as real as it exists between a real mother and his son. When Eliot meets with an accident owing to the callousness of Mrs. Sen who is new to the art of driving, Eliot receives minor injuries but Mrs. Sen's motherly image is shattered for she believes that a mother is a protector and not a damage-doer. Mrs. Sen's resignation from the already held position as a tutor to Eliot is soul-stirring.

"The Third and Final Continent" presents the intradiegetic narrator who puts Mala, his wife, as the segment of completion for his personality value. The character speaker has migrated to England where he settles down permanently and rears a family. He remembers his stay with Mrs. Croft as a tenant and had developed warmth and affection for her. Mrs. Croft is an old lady who lives all alone in a big house, religiously at her small round table in a starched white shirt and a long black skirt. Although she was no sight of beauty with:

> long pallid fingers, with swollen knuckles and tough yellow nails. Age had battered her features so that she almost resembled a man, with sharp, shrunken eyes and prominent creases on either side of her nose. Her lips, chapped and faded, nearly disappeared, and her eyebrows were missing altogether. Nevertheless she looked fierce. (178)

Mr. Croft, with his miserly speech habits, did not communicate much with the speaker narrator, yet he loved being connected with her and felt as much responsible to her as grown up children take care of their aged parents. When the speaker narrator shifted to another house, he carried Mrs. Croft as a figure of eternity in his mind. Although Mala was introduced to Mrs. Croft yet she could not perceive the lady with her virtues even though she had the blessedness of femininity. When Mrs. Croft died, the speaker narrator felt an emotional vacuum as if he had lost someone connected to him in blood:

> I came across Mrs. Croft's obituary. I had not thought of her in several months—by then those six weeks of the summer were already a remote interlude in my past—but when I learned of her death I was stricken, so much so that when Mala looked up from her knitting she found me staring.

Mrs. Croft as a universal mother is encompassing in love and transcends cultural polarities. Mrs. Croft's attachment to the speaker narrator who is an outsider insider (Indian by birth) is a foster son to Mrs. Croft, whereas the son of the speaker narrator doesn't exhibit any amount of passionate love although Mala and his son are biologically of the same human structure. The speaker describes this relationship thus:

> We have a son who attends Harvard University. Mala no longer drapes the end of her sari over her head, or weeps at night for her parents, but occasionally she weeps for our son. So we drive to Cambridge to visit him, or bring him home for a weekend, so that he can eat rice with us with his hands, and speak in Bengali, things we sometimes worry he will no longer do after we die. (197)

The speaker narrator and his son are complementary characters with opposing qualities marked out in the story which, according to the canons of Ian Reid, is "Sketch." The speaker is Ulyssesian in spirit who explores the new continent and manages to carve his personal private room for himself whereas his son who studies in Harvard University is discouraged by the feel of a strange world around. He says:

> In a few years he will graduate and pave his way, alone and unprotected. But I remind myself that he has a father who is still living, a mother who is happy and strong. Whenever he is discouraged I tell him that if I can survive on three continents, then there is no obstacle he cannot conquer. While the astronauts, heroes forever, spent more hours on the moon, I have remained in this new world for nearly thirty years. (197-98)

Structurally, the technique of doubling is a uniting thread that connects the opposing characters and forms symbolically a psychological perspective. The significance of this technique is well pointed out in the article entitled "The Bright Chimera" by Rawdon Wilson: "Characters may be seen as products of the author's mind . . . functions of the text . . . constructs to be analyzed in terms of the compositional techniques and the characters as actual persons."[6]

Hence the fictional consciousness produced by Jhumpa Lahiri is fully life-like and open to interpretation. It is from this point of view that doubling is a necessary adjunct to the short stories and gives grasp of the intricacies of human understanding with meaningful communication.

NOTES

1. R.D. Laing, *Self and Others (*London: Tavistock, 1961), p. 68.
2. *Ibid.*, p. 70.
3. Luise Eichenbaum and Susie Orbach, *What Do Women Want* (Toronto: General Publishing, 1983), p. 112.
4. Jhumpa Lahiri, *Interpreter of Maladies* (UK: HarperCollins, 1999), p. 138.
5. Eichenbaum and Orbach, p. 113.
6. Rawdon Wilson, "The Bright Chimera: Character as a Literary Term," *Critical Inquiry*, Vol. 5 (1979), p. 730.

The Native and Acquired Selves of the Tormented Souls in the Fictional World of Jhumpa Lahiri

BHAGABAT NAYAK

The last decade of the twentieth century witnessed a remarkable growth in fiction in the global literature. While in general the Indian writers in English have their substantial achievements in this field, some women writers in particular have been honoured with prizes both at home and abroad. After Arundhati Roy's Booker for *God of Small Things*, Jhumpa Lahiri has bagged the prestigious Pulitzer award for her *Interpreter of Maladies*. This has added another feather to the glory of Indian English literature in the midnight to the Millennium generation. The book is a collection of nine superbly created stories set in Bengal, Boston and beyond. The stories display her American and Calcutta chromosomes with the lives of the Indians in exile. "The nine stories included in the book can be considered as bold attempts at exploring the landscape of the inner world of the protagonists who are mostly Indian immigrants in the United tates."[1] Lahiri has presented how they navigate between the strict traditions they have inherited, and the baffling "New World" they must encounter everyday.

The year 2000 stands as a milestone not only in the Indo-American socio-political relationship with president Clinton's visit to India but also for an Indian immigrant Jhumpa Lahiri's winning of America's greatest award for literature. Lahiri has been credited with a number of awards for her title story, which include O'Henry Award, Transatlantic Review Award for the best fiction, Louisville Review Fiction Prize, and the *New Yorker*'s nomination among twenty best writers under forty for the twenty first century. Like the millions of Indians in America she enjoys a "sense of emotional exile" in her living in America. Though she lacks the cultural ambidexterity to write about the Indian life and characters in an authentic way, still it seems that she has adopted the Indian setting for her stories as a device to woo the western audience with exotica. While living in America she presents her un-American self, and being an Indian she expresses her outsider's views about India and America.

The fictional world of Lahiri is a new one of its type as a setting for her narrative work and art. Although she is an Asian in origin in America, her understanding of India and America is apparently visible in her stories. The stories in the collection present her trans-continental and trans-cultural experiences of India, England and America that justify the full title of the book, *Stories of Bengal, Boston and Beyond.* While living in the multilingual and multicultural heritage of this new world her parents have struggled much in the theory of social Darwinism for existence. She has adopted certain liberal democratic values between the actual and the ideal. She has learnt to live by stretching her imagination to Bengal where her stories are originally rooted, and she is unable to cut off completely that umbilical cord. Her characters are mostly Indians with Bengali identity and she has tried to identify her immigrant self through them. The facts she narrates in the stories are trivial and mundane, but her characters are sometimes autobiographical and unlike herself, they have the multi-cultural experiences in which they are being oxygenised by the thinking of home issues. All the stories in the collection offer a wonderful variety of experiences gathered largely from the cultural clashes rippling outward in diverse directions. The stories chronicle the traumas and sufferings of the Indians settled abroad, who fail to find their identity in a world where they cannot have a sense of belongingness. She portrays faithfully the trauma of cultural dislocation, disorientation and displacement suffered by the millions of "exited Indians," and they try desperately to balance themselves between "home and abroad." Lahiri has done her best to interpret the maladies of their major issues. The stories also bear multiple identities and the strain of double coding for the Indians and the western audiences.

As an immigrant writer, Jhumpa Lahiri has presented her insider's as well as outsider's views, and native and acquired self in her stories. She admits; "neither as a tourist nor as a former resident . . . I think as a writer. I learned to observe things as an outsider and yet I also know that as different as Calcutta is from Rhode Island, I belong there in some fundamental way, in the ways I didn't seem to belong in the United States."[2]

She has also expressed her views in a response to her parents' nostalgia about which she says: "my writing, these days, is less a response to my parents' cultural nostalgia and more an attempt to forge my own amalgamated domain."[3] Lahiri's preoccupation with her parental home in Calcutta has made her to think of the home issues. During her terminal visits to Calcutta with her parents, she finds less of cultural separation between America and India due to greater communication and access although she has enjoyed a "sense of emotional exile" like her parents.

Understanding the history of civilizations in Indian subcontinent during her continental tours, she has realised how history is the story of integration and disintegration of human aggregates but culture as the greatest integrating force in men. In her story "When Mr. Pirzada Came to Dine," she has presented how culture does not continue in social systems or in institutions but rather in the norms of human conduct. It is like a flowing stream in the life of the people. The story is a turning point in her literary career. It is set on the American soil with an Anglo-American protagonist. She portrays Mr. Pirzada, a Bangladeshi scholar in America and shows how he is more close with her father and family. Lahiri conveys how this intimate alien Bengali focuses his support to India during Pakistani Civil War of 1971. Although the story reminds of the caricaturing style of Dickens, it conveys the message that culture is the greatest integrating force that unites men with others. In the story Mr. Pirzada and Lahiri's father are the persons of separate national identities but they have been preoccupied with their respective countries and cultures living in America's neo-cultural matrix. Lahiri enjoys all social systems, individual urges and fundamental values.

Sometimes she becomes bilingual and bicultural in her secret desire for seeking her identity like her characters. She has disclosed this in her authorial freedom in writing fiction. She feels how her distinct Bengali culture is endangered and how in order to preserve this she makes her terminal visits to Calcutta. She reminisces: "Calcutta nourished my mind, my eyes as a writer and my interest in seeing things from a different point of view."[4] She has tried to remember her native self during her wedding with Alberto Vourvoulias, an American with Hindu rituals in Calcutta. This expresses her urge for the revitalizing of the cultural soul by mixing the Indian genres with the American context.

After her return from a visit to India in 1992, she had written "A Real Durwan." It does not express her sharing of feelings and emotions with a Bangladeshi refugee as temporary matter, rather it expresses her poignant feelings over the suffering Boori Ma undergoes in a fretful present by "gloating over a glossy past." She describes Boori Ma's derision against the residents of the flat and registers "her approbation of Boori Ma as the REAL DURWAN, with maternal love and care, though incapacitated by senility."[5] Boori Ma's life is a series of losses and misfortunes and her final suffering and second banishment from the means of "her livelihood drag her into alienation, deprivation and uncertain future. "A Real Durwan" and "The Treatment of Bibi Haldar" are set in India. In both the stories, Lahiri captures the Indian ethos effectively. In these stories, her characters speak Bengali which she thinks is an "unwise decision" but she defends it: "Bengali is essentially a spoken language for me, because it occupies such an aural presence in my mind."[6] She expresses her native self in Bengali language and way of life even in America.

Since 1969 Lahiri's parents have made their home in America but she has felt the invisible walls erected around their home intended to keep American influence at bay. She is undoubtedly more American than her parents and faces the challenges like the millions of Indian immigrants, who live in America. Reacting to the challenges "She has undergone the trauma of failing to find her identity in a world where she could never have a sense of belongingness and so tries to fall back upon the treasured memories of what Rushdie calls "Imaginary Homeland," which, with its vibrant colours and versatility, gave life to her starving existence and stimulated her very being."[7] This makes her attempt to write stories on India, about Indians and her culture. She thinks of her life as in an exile and unlike her parents she feels a strong tie to their country of origin who move like her characters in loneliness and alienation between the two worlds grappling bravely their cultural displacement.

Being "homesick" in her sensation and diasporic in her immigration, she feels culturally displaced in the fascinating metropolis of America. In order to avoid complications over her knowledge of India she writes:

> I am the first person to admit my knowledge of India is limited, the way in which all translations are. I am impeded not only by my own lack of proximity but by the fact that my parents' impressions—one of my main resources when writing about India—are also arrested in time; the country they left in the sixties is in many respects, unrecognizable to them today. Still my translation of India has evoked for some readers and reviewers here and there, the illusion of cultural accuracy and resonance.[8]

Lahiri has presented her experiences through her protagonists of how to live in a multicultural milieu. It is as vital as preserving cultural distinction in the pluralistic society of America.

"Mrs. Sen" is a story on Bengali life, culture and habits. She presents Mrs. Sen's struggle to become an American in her pan-American situation, while she is not ready to leave her inherited Indianness in America. She is torn between the worlds and braves the New World like the author's mother. Lahiri admits in an interview with Vibhuti Patela: "Mrs. Sen is based on my mother. . . . I saw her one way but imagined that an American child may see her differently, reacting with curiosity, fascination or fear to things I took for granted,"[9] Mrs. Sen is nostalgic for Calcutta, has love for the Calcuttans, fish, Bengali fashion and way of life. Her job as a baby-sitter, adjusting with her professor husband and learning to drive a car really express her braving the new world. Mrs. Sen tries to be an American never leaving her Bengali self and appears to be more and more Indian everyday.

The more Indian she becomes, the stranger she seems in her surroundings. Through Mrs. Sen Lahiri brings to light the intense loneliness experienced by Indians, especially unemployed Indian women, who are transplanted into a new culture which cuts them off from the sustenance and peace provided by their traditional, moral, and spiritual sources. Susan Ram writes: "In this beautifully observed story East meets West on the shared experience of loneliness, and the poignancy of Mrs. Sen's situation is handled with utmost delicacy and control unsullied by any hint of mawkishness,"[10]

"Sexy" is a story of "semantic research." It describes the theme of extra-marital relationship between Devajit, a married Bengali, and Miranda, a married American lady. Lahiri has made it clear how Devajit has kept his extra-marital relation with Miranda even though his wife Laxmi resembles the Bollywood actress Madhuri Dixit and represents the women of conventional propriety. He is attracted towards Miranda as she appears sexy, forceful, beautiful and curious. She is not only sexually adventurous but also possesses the qualities which are loved by a man without knowing the implicit meaning of philosophy of love. Equally, Miranda's curiosity about Dev is a way for her to gain access to her married and increasingly unavailable lover. Thus, Lahiri has presented the "vicarious descriptions of extramarital relations"[11] in the trivial matters of love. She hypothises "love as not profound but a nauseating apology" in the story.

"A Temporary Matter" and "The Blessed House" are the stories with Indian and American setting. Shukumar, the protagonist of "A Temporary Matter" is a research scholar who believes that his love with his wife is a temporary matter for the sake of knowledge and research. This makes Shoba to find herself in emotional frigidity like her husband. In the classical theory of "Sringaara" both of them have numerous objective correlatives in the joy of union, the pain of separation and the trauma of conflict, or rejection. On the other hand in Shoba-Shukumar relationship, "We find Tiresian detachment and impotency reigning their brief temporary sessions of sharing, punctuated with unduly long intervals of silence."[12] In "The Blessed House," education makes Twinkle and Sanjeev attracted towards each other and secular in thinking. This makes their life happy and enjoyable. Education is also a factor in keeping the house blessed. In the story, Lahiri conveys a message to her readers that if the inmates of a house are ready for compromise, sacrifice and adjustment, it remains blessed.

"The Third and Final Continent" is the best in the collection about her protagonist's continental tours. While the protagonist finally stays in Boston with his landlady, he is not ready to quit his native self in language and culture that he had left in India. When his wife Mala arrives there he talks with her in Bengali by breaking the shell of the acquired self. She tells his wife about his son: "if I can survive on three continents then there is no obstacle he cannot conquer."[13] The rhythm and tone of Lahiri's life becomes identical with her protagonists in the story. "The Treatment of Bibi Haldar" is a moving story. Bibi Haldar is a 29 years old orphan girl suffering from a mysterious disease. But after a series of blood tests, the doctor in charge of Bibi "concluded that a marriage would cure her." (161) After serious lapses of the Haldars she enjoys her life in prolonged isolation until one day Bibi discovers her "about four months pregnant" (172) and finally delivers a son leaving the question who in the town disgraced her or with a positive note graced her by curing. Lahiri's Boori Ma and Bibi Haldar are the tormented souls in their native selves.

The title story "Interpreter of Maladies" is a narrative that appears to be a pilgrim's progress of a guilt conscious tormented soul. With a woman's "pain" and "guilt," the story is set in Orissa and the woman is in search of "solace through her soul's pilgrimage to Konark (Arka Khetra), the place of Sun God and Khandagiri and Udayagiri. Mr. Kapasi, a part-time tourist guide of Gujarati origin and driver, often remains engaged as a "doctor's assistant." His job is to translate the language of Gujarati patients to a local doctor for maladies. But he "found nothing noble in interpreting people's maladies." (51) He had a longing to be an interpreter for diplomats and dignitaries, resolving conflicts between people and nations, and settling disputes. Incidentally, when he guides this Bengali-American family to Konark, Mrs. Das becomes attracted towards his professional acumenship and seeks a relief from him for her secret pain as she had a son through her husband's friend, a Punjabi, who had come to stay with them for a few days. The guilt she committed in a moment's passion made her obsessed with it. For this she requests Kapasi:

> Don't you see? For eight years I haven't been able to express this to anybody, not to friends, certainly not to Raj. He doesn't even suspect it. He thinks I'm still in love with him. Well don't you have anything to say? . . . About my secret, and about how terrible it makes me feel. I feel terrible looking at my children, and at Raj, always terrible. I have terrible urges, Mr. Kapasi, to throw things away. One day I had the urge to throw everything . . . Don't you think it's unhealthy. (65)

Mrs. Das's seeking of Kapasi's help to interpret a malady is only to get redemption from her sins and to purify her soul. But Mr. Kapasi's sympathy for Mrs. Das ends with a hesitation and detachment, between the lyrical and satirical, between romance and realism, and between love and laughter. Her eight years of suffering from guilt and waiting for a purgation come to a finality with a spiritual catalysis after her visit to Konark and Khandagiri.

In her diasporic identity, Lahiri has expressed her personal background and Indian lineage of her Eastern origin. The nine stories in her collection offer a wonderful variety of experiences gathered from the cultural clashes rippling in many directions. Lahiri has attempted to present the trauma of the Indians in loneliness, and successfully balances their native and acquired selves in their home and foreign issues. It appears that "Most of her characters keep hanging in the limbo—between two identities—non-Indian and Indian—a fact that brings Jhumpa Lahiri fairly close."[14] What makes Lahiri special is not just her mingling of the expected and the unexpected through telling in detail about cruelty and betrayal, the motifs of her tales of married life. Yet Lahiri's subtle airbrush touch of defining the experience of life long transcontinental voyages comes from her stories.

Through her characters she tells about the human conditions that have universal resonance in her immigrant identity that forms the core of her stories.

Lahiri wears the different hats of culture—the Indian, the British and the American. Sometimes her descriptions are with the Indian way of thinking and at others she presents a wonderful multi-cultural world with the forces of universalism. Presenting the native traditions and language, she has internationalized her own culture. Of course in the diverse forces of the world, she has a hard time in selling multiculturalism. Parmanand Jha writes: "The trauma of dislocation, an acute sense of loneliness and the pangs of estrangement suffered by the millions of 'exiled Indians' who try unsuccessfully to balance them selves between 'home' and 'abroad' are the major maladies Lahiri attempts to interpret."[15] By deconstructing the self of her tormented souls she has become a cultural broker and a cultural breaker. She has successfully delineated the selves of her tormented characters who search for a panacea. Unlike herself her characters overcome their acquired selves. Her stories about the exiled Indians are called by the Indian academics a "diaspora fiction" and the American academics call it an "immigrant fiction," lodging both the Indian and American contexts in her stories and her position between the different transcontinental situations one may call her an Indian-American author. In Bengal, Boston and beyond she has chosen the plots of her stories for reflecting her emotional problems.

Lahiri's protagonists are the continental immigrants but they suffer from their cultural introspection. They have their conflict of consciousness between two selves—the native and the acquired, the real self and the community to which they belong. She has unraveled modern man's facts of crises and despair in the labyrinths of life, existence and reality. They have their circular journey toward home and identity, being recognised as an unsettling race through alienation, cultural dismemberment, sex, modernity, urbanism and muted boundaries between time and space, life and death, identity and authenticity. In their strong cultural obsessions at home, they face difficulty in their actual living and comprehend their survival to adopt to the dominant Euro-American societies. Alienation leads them to emancipation, but emancipation from one world enslaves them to another world. The native self is tormented in the acquired self and with an obsession for the native land it appears to them as the land of "some secrets, some mystery."[16] But as the product of a mixed race and a mixed culture Bulbul, Lahiri tries to get the complete approval of her self precisely because India is her home. Thus, her stories are the real social documents on tormented souls not with the usual sound and fury but rather through imaginative re-construction.

NOTES

1. S. Parvathy, "The Fictional World of Jhumpa Lahiri," *The Journal of Literature and Aesthetic,* VIII, 2 (July-December 2000), p. 111.
2. Lavina Melwani, "Interpreting Exile," *The Hindustan Times*, 23 April 2000.
3. Jhumpa Lahiri, "My Intimate Alien," *Outlook (*Collector's Edition, 2000), p. 120.
4. Surabhi Khosla, "Beauty, Brains, Bounce and Bengal," *Swagat* (November 2000), p. 155.
5. Parvathy, p. 114.
6. "My Intimate Alien," p. 118.
7. Parmanand Jha, "Home and Abroad: Jhumpa Lahiri's *Interpreter of Maladies*," *The Indian Journal of English Studies*, Vol. XXXVIII, 2000-2001, pp. 106-17.
8. "My Intimate Alien," p. 118.
9. Vibhuti Patel, "Maladies Belonging: An Interview with Jhumpa Lahiri," *Newsweek International*, 20 September 1999.
10. Susan Ram, "Chronicle of Cultural Interface," *Frontline*, 22 October 1999, p. 71.
11. Ramchandra Ragini, Jhumpa Lahiri's *Interpreter of Maladies*: A Temporary Matter?" *The Journal of Indian Writing in English.* Vol. 29 (January) 2001, pp. 50-54.
12. Parvathy, p.112.
13. *Interpreter of Maladies* (New Delhi: Harper Collins, 1999), pp. 197-98.
14. Jha, p.115.
15. *Ibid.*
16. A.R. Wylie, *The Daughter of Brahma* (London: Mills and Boon, 1912), p. 33.

"Beyond" Ethnicity: A Study of *Interpreter of Maladies*

BRATI BISWAS

Jhumpa Lahiri's *Interpreter of Maladies*,[1] a collection of short stories, offers the reader a variety of experiences that are both familiar and foreign—all concern Indian (often Bengali) protagonists living either in India, or in the United States. The stories are rich in details of Indian life, and of cultural values and customs. The domestic routines, for example, Indian food and cooking provide an important backdrop in several stories. Most of Lahiri's characters occupy a space in between cultures. They date, have vacation, emigrate and work across cultural and national boundaries; they constantly move between India and Unites States. They are not traumatized refugees but are negotiating a path in a country that seems to provide opportunities ("Mrs. Sen's," "When Mr. Pirzada Came to Dine," "The Third and Final Continent"); or they are the westernized children of such Indian families ("A Temporary Matter," "Interpreter of Maladies," "This Blessed House"). There is a powerful sense of cultural transition and loss. Yet in their struggle for dignity and their attempts to love and overcome loneliness they transcend their ethnicity and reflect the universal predicament of modern humanity.

Jhumpa Lahiri draws heavily on her Indian heritage. She was born in London of Bengali parents and grew up in Rhode Island, U.S.A. She has travelled several times to India, where both her parents were born and raised and where a number of her stories are set. These stories are an evidence of the fact that India is not just a physical entity but something that is created in the mind as well, in one's memories or through one's ancestors. The stories speak eloquently of what it means to be an "outsider," whether in

India or in the West and consequently raise questions about the concept of "home." One does not have to travel far from "home" to feel like an outsider. The central protagonist of the story "The Treatment of Bibi Haldar" is an outcast within her own home. The concept of "home" is closely associated with the idea of selfhood, a sense of identity, and a feeling of rootedness. On being asked about her Calcutta roots, Lahiri explained:

> When I began writing fiction seriously, my first attempts, for some reason, were always set in Calcutta, which is a city I know quite well from repeated visits with my family. These trips to a vast, unruly, fascinating city so different from the small New England town where I was raised shaped my perceptions of the world and of people from a very early age. I learned that there was another side, a vastly different version to everything. I leaned to observe things as an outsider, and yet I also knew that as different as Calcutta is from Rhode Island, I belonged there in some fundamental way, in the ways I did not seem to belong in the United States.[2]

But as she grew in confidence, her stories were based increasingly in the United States which to her was the "greater challenge." Her stories in *Interpreter of Maladies* explore what it means to be an "outsider" whether in India, in the West, or in ones home.

On the question of identity, Jhumpa Lahiri says in the internet conversation that it "is always a difficult one, but especially so for those who are culturally displaced, as immigrants are, or those who grow up in two worlds simultaneously, as is the case for their children. The older I get, the more aware am I that I have somehow inherited a sense of exile from my parents, even though in many ways—superficial ones, largely—I am so much more American than they are. In fact, it is still very hard to think of myself as an American. For immigrants the challenges of exile, the loneliness, the constant sense of alienation, the knowledge of and longing for a lost world, are more explicit and distressing than for their children. On the other hand, the problem for the children of immigrants, those with strong ties to their country of origin, is that they feel neither one thing nor the other. The feeling that there was no single place to which I fully belonged bothered me growing up. It bothers me less now." Growing up involves the process of assimilation that is both arduous and continuous. As an adult she is more comfortable with her multicultural heritage and has a more secure sense of identity. This she feels is because there is less of a cultural divide between American and Indian culture now, due to greater communication and access. Some of the young protagonists of her stories; reflect the veracity of this observation. They, like her, enjoy both Indian and Italian food while preferring to listen to Jazz than Kishore Kumar. This says something about the universal theme of changing times and differences between generations.

Lahiri, one of the youngest recipients of the Pulitzer Prize for fiction, explores the so-called "immigrant" experience with fully fleshed out characters whose ethnicity is secondary to their humanity. Through the myriad voices of Indians, Indian immigrants, their children and Americans, she explores the difficult grey areas between the American self and the "other." Lahiri does not use her ethnicity as the story but integrates it into a larger tale. The first story in *Interpreter of Maladies*, "A Temporary Matter," gives us a young married couple troubled by the wife's miscarriage, in a rapidly disintegrating relationship. Shukumar, the young husband, is completing his degree while his wife works as an editor to support them. The details of the couple's ethnicity—how Shukumar "rubbed a lemon half along his fingertips," (5) or the characterization of his mother-in-law as "polite to Shukumar without being friendly" (9)—weave in the details of culture without being didactic or heavy handed. Her portrayal of a troubled marriage is sensitive and subtle and the fact that the couple is Indian seems almost incidental.

In "When Mr. Pirzada Came to Dine" as well as other stories, there is the recurring theme of children caring for their elders. Lilia, only ten, frets over Mr. Pirzada's family in peril; Eliot, an American boy in "Mrs. Sen's," retrieves the mail of his unhappy babysitter, Mrs. Sen. The middle-aged narrator of "The Third and Final Continent" checks on his centenarian landlady, Mrs. Croft, "to make sure she was sitting upright on the bench, or was safe in her bedroom." (189) Their concerns underscore Lahiri's interest in the variables of other cultures.

Although the stories in *Interpreter of Maladies* use the device of multiculturalism to express separation and loneliness, these are universal human experiences. The theme of emotional and cultural, estrangement, exile, loss, separation, grief, displacement and marginality form the common matrix of the stories. Commenting on the title of the book, Jhumpa Lahiri says in the internet conversation: "It best expresses, thematically, the predicament at the heart of the book—the dilemma, the difficulty, and often the impossibility of communicating emotional pain and affliction to others, as well as expressing it to ourselves. In some senses I view my position as a writer, in so far as I attempt to articulate these emotions, as a sort of interpreter as well." She is the prolocutor for the afflicted; giving voice to the "maladies" of our times.

The full title of the book *Interpreter of Maladies: Stories of Bengal, Boston and Beyond* is subtly suggestive. "Bengal" and "Boston" suggest that the stories are located in a specific place and may be time. In a sense this is true the stories have fixed locales and they deal with a period ranging from the Sixties to the present times. But the word "Beyond" in the title destabilises this motion of fixity, stability and rootedness. It suggests that there is a truth *beyond* these fixed notions of place and time. This is very true of characters in exile who belong to no one place. It opens up a world *beyond* the specificities of "Bengal" and "Boston." The word alternately suggests a reality that lies "*beyond*" the narrow limited boundaries of geographical locations, nationality, ethnicity, politics and culture. It further suggests another kind of reality that exists *beyond* the realistic details of ordinary/ everyday living that imbue her stories. This is the equally real realm of imagination, fantasy, dream and memory. In a more philosophical sense, it is also suggestive of that which lies *beyond* the narrow limitations of the self and relationships. For the immigrant, "Home" is always that which lies *beyond* his present physical location; but which is ever present in his consciousness, occupying a realm that is *beyond* the physical. *Beyond* social, cultural, political confines lie the hope of assimilation, integration, companionship, love and security; dimly described; appearing *beyond* reach, but within the horizon of hope. Jhumpa Lahiri refuses to be circumscribed/limited by boundaries. She goes *beyond* the surface to present the other side of the picture. Transcending the ethnic, she presents the larger humanist spectrum.

In the story "When Mr. Pirzada Came to Dine," the little girl Lilia is at a loss to understand why her father insists on calling Mr. Pirzada a Pakistani and not an Indian:

> It made no sense to me. Mr. Pirzada and my parents spoke the same language, laughed at the same jokes, looked more or less the same. They ate pickled mangoes with their meals, ate rice every night for supper with their hands. Like my parents, Mr. Pirzada took off his shoes before entering a room, chewed fennel seeds after meals as a digestive, drank no alcohol. . . . Nevertheless my father insisted that I understand the difference. . . . "Mr. Pirzada is Bengali, but he is a Muslim," my father informed me. "Therefore he lives in East Pakistan, not India." (25-26)

Though she does not understand the politics of partition or the reason for Bangladesh's war of independence, Lilia's empathy with Mr. Pirzada is at a humane level. She goes beyond the artificial boundaries of nation, religion and ethnicity (these preoccupy her father) and highlights Mr. Pirzada's essential humanity. Not only does he not look different from them, Mr. Pirzada is no different from any other concerned father who is away from a besieged home. Mr. Pirzada and Lilia's parents belong to different religions and nations, yet are culturally similar. A shared sense of displacement and rootlessness brings them together in a foreign land, which is not theirs by birth but by adoption. Their sense of identity is derived from their native country, which is "home." This "home," physically inaccessible, is always accessible in one's memories. The sense of time is displaced. In Boston, Mr. Pirzada's watch is always set to Dacca time, the place he really belonged. Like Mr. Pirzada, Lilia's parents too precariously balance themselves between two different nations and cultures. Lilia who is an American-born Indian, does not share her parents, sense of alienation, but her interaction with Mr. Pirzada does unsettle her and makes her aware of a different world that lies *beyond*.

Alienation and estrangement are "maladies" that universally afflict people irrespective of class and nationality. The protagonists of "A Real Durwan" and "The Treatment of Bibi Haldar" find themselves in exile in their native milieu. Both these stories are set in Calcutta. Boori Ma is poor, while Bibi Haldar belongs to the lower middle class. In "A Real Durwan," Boori Ma, an old woman, who came from East Bengal as a refugee, has been living in the stairwell of a block of flats for many years. She does the job of a charwoman and virtually guards the whole building. Her services resemble those of a real durwan and the residents of the flats are thankful to her for this. Sometimes the residents welcome her to their flats and offer her tea. The following lines highlight Boori Ma's outsider status: "Knowing not to sit on the furniture she crouched, instead, in doorways and hallways, and observed gestures and manners in the same way a person tends to watch traffic in a foreign city." (76) The condition of Boori Ma becomes miserable when Mr. Dalal, a benevolent resident of the building, goes to Simla for an outing. One day she goes out for a walk and finds a basin fitted on the stairwell missing when she returns to the building. The blame falls on Boori Ma and she is thrown out of the house for neglecting her duty. In the beginning of the short story, Boori Ma is introduced as a refugee and at the end of the story we see her again as a homeless exile.

In "The Treatment of Bibi Haldar," an ailing woman finds herself forlorn even among her relatives. Bibi Haldar stays with her cousin in an apartment and spends her days recording inventory for the cosmetic shop of her cousin in a small room in exchange for her shelter, food and clothes. Her permanent illness confines her world to the four-story building and she lives in isolation even among her own people. "She wanted to be spoken for protected, placed on her path in life." (160) She is lonely and desperate to find a husband. Her marriage is impossible as she suffers from epilepsy. Meanwhile, her cousin winds up his business and moves away leaving Bibi alone at the mercy of fate.

This finally allows her a sense of freedom: "Now I am free to discover life as I please." (170)

Lahiri's "Mrs. Sen's" presents a young Indian woman who immigrates to America after marriage. Hers is a poignant story of physical estrangement from her homeland. Having nothing to do, she grows lonely and decides to baby sit. As she does not know how to drive, she baby-sits Eliot, the son of a young American working single mother. Eliot becomes her companion and listens to her nostalgic brooding about Calcutta. He quickly becomes aware of Mrs. Sen's loneliness, her bewilderment in a strange new culture. She alarms him by asking: "Eliot, if I began screaming right now at the top of my lungs, would someone come?" At home in India, she explains: "just raise your voice a bit, or express grief or joy of any kind, and one whole neighborhood and half of another has come to share the news, to help with arrangements." (116) She spends a good part of the afternoon chopping vegetables for the elaborate meals she prepares for herself and Mr. Sen. She tells Eliot that she brought the huge blade she uses from India. Whenever there is a large celebration, "my mother sends out word in the evening for all the neighborhood women to bring blades just like this one, and then they sit in an enormous circle on the roof of our building laughing and gossiping and slicing fifty kilos of vegetables through the night." (115) Her attempts to connect to Eliot's mother are unsuccessful. Mrs. Sen lives for two things that make her happy: letters from home, and whole fresh fish from the sea. She wears a sari, coral gloss, golden bangles, vermilion paste in her parting of hair. Food and dress become reassuring bits of the homeland. Mrs. Sen and Eliot are more than just accidental companions. Eliot is the product of social dysfunction, which Mrs. Sen is encountering for the first time. They are both very lonely people.

In "This Blessed House," we encounter the Americanized couple of Sanjeev and Twinkle, who rush into marriage because they both liked P.G. Wodehouse, disliked Sitar music and were lonely. Their marriage is under strain. Twinkle is not an organised housekeeper and this irritates the methodical Sanjeev. Trouble starts when their new house proves to be a treasure trove of objects related to Christianity like St. Francis Postcards, a plaster virgin Mary and a white porcelain Christ. Fearing for the dignity of his "Hindu" home, Sanjeev threatens to throw the icons out. He ultimately bows to Twinkle's obstinate will and relents. Twinkle has breathed her own life into the Christian icons humanely and demands that her husband respond to this achievement with mercy and respect. Like Twinkle, Lahiri makes us go *beyond* mere surface reality and see things in a new light.

In the title story, "Interpreter of Maladies," Lahiri again explores the theme of a failed marriage. The opening sentences of the story describe the bickering that symptomizes the failing marriage of the American Indian couple Mrs. and Mr. Das. The story is narrated from the point of view of Mr. Kapasi, their tour guide, whose own marriage too is faltering. Mr. Kapasi works as a tour guide only on weekends, and has another job during the weekdays as an interpreter in a doctor's office—translating the Gujarati spoken by some of his patients. Mina Das, the wife proclaims his job as an interpreter of maladies as "romantic." (53) Her interest in him makes him fantasize a romantic relationship with her. At the crisis point of the story, when the two of them are in the car, Mina discloses to Mr. Kapasi that one of the couple's two boys was clandestinely fathered by her husband's Punjabi-Indian friend, during a brief visit. This is the malady which she hopes Mr. Kapasi will provide a remedy for. However, all the interpreter of maladies can say is: "Is it really pain you feel Mrs. Das, or is it guilt?" (66) Mrs. Das seeks out Mr. Kapasi to expiate her guilty soul.

Shoba and Shukumar, the young couple in "A Temporary Matter," are children of Indian immigrants. Their marriage reaches an impasse after Shoba has a miscarriage. Their responses to grief are opposite as Shoba stays away, working late, burying herself in work even at home; Shukumar becomes a hermit, and cannot focus on his work at all. They use a temporary electricity blackout as an excuse to exorcise some of their secret demons, but no cathartic solution is easily available, and the couple remain alienated from each other. A more optimistic view of bonding is offered in "The Third and Final Continent" wherein a young Indian bride flies to Boston to join her reluctant husband. However, the two grow accustomed to each other, and love eventually starts to flourish. The husband's meditations at the end read like a soft-spoken humanist credo: "I am not the only man to seek his fortune far from home, and certainly I am not the first. Still there are times I am bewildered by each mile I have travelled, each meal I have eaten, each person I have known, each room in which I have slept. As ordinary as it all appears, there are times when it is beyond my imagination." (198)

The author of the prefatory note to "A Conversation with Jhumpa Lahiri" succinctly puts Jhumpa Lahiri's vision in perspective: "Maladies both accurately diagnosed and misinterpreted, matters both temporary and life-changing, relationships in flux and unshakable, unexpected blessings and sudden calamities, and the powers of survival—these are among the themes of Jhumpa Lahiri's extraordinary, Pulitzer Prize-winning debut collection of stories. Travelling from India to New England and back again, Lahiri charts the emotional voyages of characters seeking love beyond the barriers of nations, cultures, religions and generations. Imbued with the sensual details of both Indian and American cultures, they also speak with universal eloquence and compassion to everyone who has ever felt like an outsider."

Jhumpa Lahiri has the rare gift of being able to convey human emotions of tenderness and loneliness without extravagance. Her subject matter is often rooted in the ordinary, everyday existence of people in different walks of life. Like the best humanist artists, she has the gift of erasing boundaries. She is able to translate the thoughts and words of characters immersed in specific cultures and situations into themes that universally resonate.

NOTES

1. Jhumpa Lahiri, *Interpreter of Maladies* (New Delhi: HarperCollins India, 1999).
2. Internet conversation with Jhumpa Lahiri Jhumpa/interpreter_maladies.shtml

Exi tential Irony through Optic Motifs in *The Interpreter of Maladies*

V. SAM SAHAYAM

Jhumpa Lahiri, the new Pulitzer winner is no mean talent, so far as her awareness of the potential of strategies in her prodigious literary arsenal is concerned. Her short story collection, *Interpreter of Maladies*, that sky-rocketed her to fame and instant recognition worldwide, reveals, under close scrutiny, several imaginative literary features of crafts(wo)manship which all go into the making of the fine fabric of her fiction. This paper focuses its attention only on the author's skill in marshalling and deployment of optic imagery, which, in the context of the story "Interpreter of Maladies," turn symbolic, thereby enhancing the ironic perception of its existentialist theme.

Perhaps the most striking trait in Lahiri's central piece—"central" in the sense that the entire anthology owes its title to this item, that is accorded also a "central" space in the over-all format of the book—is the plethora of optic images employed in it. Each character in the story has his/her own individualistic perspective, and each of them presumes that the reality he perceives, is the "real" or the "right" one, so long as the "vision" lasts. Paradoxically, there are so many, almost countless perceptions possible, the author seems to suggest, which, in her view, can even negate or nullify someone else's—or several others'—perceived reality. In other words, in existentialist terms, comprehension of the composite reality is possible, only in ironic terms.

The story, almost in the Faulknerian sense, makes an attempt to present such a comprehensive view of reality, through its multiple perspectives. Mr. and Mrs. Das, a couple of Indian origin in their thirties with three children, currently settled in the U.S., trip to the well-known Sun Temple of Konark, famed for its erotic sculptures. They hire a taxi from their tourist hotel. Subsequently, Mr. Kapasi, their middle-aged taxi-driver, is bowled over by the voluptuous charms of Mrs. Das at first sight. A highly knowledgeable man, given to also some linguistic pretensions, Mr. Kapasi goes dramatically up in the visiting lady's esteem, when the latter happens to learn that he is working as an "interpreter" for a local doctor to whom he interprets the complaints of patients. She obviously takes him to be a very understanding and kind counsellor endowed with empathy, who can plumb the psyche of every patient who comes to him for help. For, she too has her own peculiar need for such a person in life.

They reach Konark and study the luxuriant erotica the sandstone sculptures present there. Mr. Kapasi, in particular, goes drooling secretly over the sexual fantasies the ambience of the place generates in him, and gets almost irresistibly infatuated with Mrs. Das. The tourists decide to prolong their trip, at Mr. Kapasi's suggestion, proceeding to the hills at Udayagiri and Khandagiri, noted for some ancient monastic ruins there. On their arrival in that secluded spot, the naive Mr. Das takes away the children for sight-seeing, leaving his wife behind, as she feigns some pain in her legs. As soon as they are out of sight, Mrs. Das slips in beside Mr. Kapasi's seat, and starts confiding to him about an episode of her infidelity in the past to her rather colourless husband, falling for a Punjabi youth who happened to be a guest in their home at that time, as a result of which, she bore her second male child. However, Mr. Kapasi's response to the lady's confession turns out to be extremely dumb and utterly devoid of empathy, much to the chagrin of the tourist. The story closes underlining the gulf that divides the worlds of the driver and the lady. The "interpreter" who is supposed to understand and articulate the "maladies" of others himself, is, ironically, left utterly bewildered and baffled.

This open-ended short story communicates the existential angst and isolation of human individuals, by defining their respective limits of perceptions. Mr. Das totally self-complacent with job and home, is happily lost in a world of love of his children, as his wife remains only in the background. Mr. Kapasi, fighting for survival and struggling to make both ends meet, is also racked with obsessive fantasies, bordering on the prurient, even as he is psychologically conditioned by the ethos of the Indian middle class, desperately making a vain attempt to reconcile his dreams with reality. Mrs. Das, easily the most sophisticated, most daring and the most curious amongst the characters of the story's cast, is largely self-absorbed, suffering from in-built taboos, conflicts and inhibitions, thanks primarily to her innate disposition to indulge, and exposure to contrary claims of different cultures, and remains strangely vulnerable. The children, on the other hand, experience life totally in their own limited worlds, which await fulfillment and fruition only in the years to come, though it should be conceded at this point, none of them is provided with any in-depth treatment by the artist, perhaps due to want of space on the canvass, or because of the basic preoccupation of the story which deliberately focuses its attention on the problems and issues of adults.

It is interesting to note that the artist makes deliberate attempts to define perspectives of characters throughout, employing optic imagery, which gradually turn symbolic. The Das children, for instance, wear "translucent visors." (44) Mr. Das, on the other hand "had a sapphire blue visor." (44) Even more important is the fact that, to the artist at least, what distinguishes Mr. Das from his children is the camera that he carries around, standing for the adult's capacity to "freeze" reality, often, from a preferred angle, under desired conditions of light and shade. Even the manner in which the camera is referred to in the work under discussion is ironic:

> A clean-shaven man, he looked exactly like a *magnified* version of Ronny. He had a sapphire blue visor, and was dressed in shorts, sneakers, and a T-shirt. The camera slung around his neck, with an impressive telephoto lens and numerous buttons and markings, *was the only complicated thing he wore.* (44, Italics mine)

It is significant that characterization is done in the above passage using the optic imagery of "magnification" of an image, as for instance, in a photographic studio. There is also an implicit suggestion here that he is blissfully unaware of the fact of the illegitimacy of the birth of one of his sons, a secret pertaining to the adult world. Besides, the blue visor Mr. Das wears gives him a distorted or illusory view of the world, in which he finds himself more at home; and he is not capable of seeing things in the reality of daylight. Hence, his ignorance of and indifference to his wife's growing boredom and her consequent falling for the young visitor; and, above all, his total unawareness of the fact one of the three children he devotes himself to, Bobby, is not his own. His "telephoto lens" suggests his personal preference for seeing and recording the world of reality, from a certain (safe?) preferred distance. In fact, the "distance" maintained by Mr. Das from the world of daylight reality can be seen from the objects he captures with his camera. He is interested in taking a picture of monkeys· "He asked Mr. Kapasi to stop the car so that he could take a picture." (48)

> They were seated in groups along the branches with a face, silver bodies, horizontal eyebrows, and crested heads. Their long gray tails dangled like a series of ropes among the leaves. A few scratched themselves with black leathery hands, or swung their feet, staring as the car passed. (47)

If this instance highlights only the fact of his identifying himself with the children, there are other telling episodes in the work to show that Mr. Das has gone so far away from the real country around the country he originally hails from—and he has become almost an alien voyeuristic visitor, obsessed with sights of exotic misery and squalor, merely touring India, from a distant perspective:

> "Hey, do you mind stopping the car. I just want to get a shot of this guy."
>
> Mr. Kapasi pulled over to the side of the road as Mr. Das took a picture of a barefoot man, his head wrapped in a dirty turban, seated on top of a cart at grain sacks pulled by a pair of bullocks. Both the man and the bullocks were emaciated. (49)

Meanwhile, in sharp contrast, Mrs. Das is lost in a totally different spectacle, suggestive of freedom and nature, not at all concerned with what her husband is doing: "In the back seat Mrs. Das gazed out of another window, at the sky, where nearly transparent clouds passed quickly in front of one another." (50)

It is also interesting to note that Mr. Das never takes a photograph of his attractive wife in the whole story. It is indeed true that other devices are also pressed into use in the work, like the sartorial imagery, to drive home the relative immaturity and lack of full development, on the part of Mr. Das. For instance, while children are shown as dressed "in stiff, brightly colored clothing and caps," (44) Mr. Das "was dressed in shorts, sneakers, and a T-shirt." (44) However, it is the optic imagery which figures as the dominant—and recurrent—thematic motif in this work.

Mr. Kapasi's viewing of Mrs. Das has all the accuracy, vividness and colour of a good close-shot photograph:

> He observed her. She wore a red-and-white-checkered skirt that stopped above her knees, slip-on shoes with a square wooden heel, and a close-fitting blouse styled like a man's undershirt. The blouse was decorated at chest-level with a calico applique in the shape of a strawberry. She was a short woman, with small hands like paws, her frosty pink finger-nails painted to match her lips, and was slightly plump in her figure. Her hair, shorn only a little longer than her husband's, was parted from one side. *She was wearing large dark brown sunglasses with a pinkish tint to them,* and carried a big straw bag, almost as big as her torso, shaped like a bowl, with a water battle poking out of it. (46, Italics mine)

It is significant that Mrs. Das too wears sunglasses which screen her eyes off from the perspectives of all those around her. In fact, she remains a mystery till the very end. There is another optic image associated with Mrs. Das, suggestive of a world of glamour and illusion, referring to her interest in the news concerning celluloid world: "She fanned herself with a folded Bombay film magazine written in English." (47) Mr. Kapasi finds both the parents and the children, collectively immature, with Mr. Das being obsessed with his photography and wanderlust, and Mrs. Das, lost in her world of vanity and self-absorption, wrapped in a kind of mystery of her own, a fact emphasized through optic imagery again:

> They were all like siblings, Mr. Kapasi thought, as they passed a row of date trees was hard to believe they were regularly responsible for anything other than themselves. Mr. Das tapped on his lens cap, and his tour book, dragging his thumbnail occasionally across the pages. . . . Mrs. Das continued to polish her nails. She had still not removed her sunglasses. (49)

It is only when the taxi-driver informs that he is also doing a part-time job of interpreting what the patients say to a local doctor, relatively a stranger to Gujarati, that Mrs. Das starts taking an interest in Mr. Kapasi, and steps out of her inner world of self-obsession and mysterious self-absorption, an important development in the narrative, conveyed through another optical image, namely, her sunglasses, and directly looking at him:

> "But so romantic," Mrs. Das said dreamily, breaking her extended silence. She lifted her pinkish brown sunglasses and arranged them on top of her head like a tiara. For the first time, her eyes met Mr. Kapasi's in the rearview mirror: pale, a bit small, their gaze fixed but drowsy. (50)

What impresses Mrs. Das about Mr. Kapasi is his expertise in articulation of the complaints of his patients and the latter's total dependence on him. In other words, he is one who could be a confidant. Mr. Kapasi finds the lady's attention "mildly intoxicating" (53) and it is significant that the artist describes the forty-six year-old driver's growing interest in this woman, using the optic image of the rear-view mirror, suggestive of his bygone youth and romantic preoccupations:

> From time to time he glanced through the mirror at Mrs. Das. In addition to glancing at her face he glanced at the strawberry between her breasts, and the golden brown hollow in her throat. . . . Mrs. Das listened attentively, stroking her hair with a small plastic brush . . . and Mr. Das was absorbed by his tour book . . . so it seemed like a private conversation between Mr. Kapasi and Mrs. Das. (53-54)

The shadowy, unreal quality of the budding contact between Mr. Kapasi and Mr. Das is deftly with the significant imagery of the rear view mirror in this context.

Optic imagery of the camera is employed again when Mr. Das takes a picture of his wife along with the taxi-driver, when they stop *for* lunch in a wayside restaurant. Ironically enough, the lens of the camera is responsible for promoting the physical proximity of Mr. Kapasi and Mrs. Das, however fleeting the occasion may be; that too, at the instance of Mr. Das:

> By now the children had gotten up from the table to look at more monkeys perched in a nearby tree, so there was a considerable space between Mrs. Das and Mr. Kapasi. Mr. Das placed the camera to his face and squeezed one eye shut, his tongue exposed at the corner of his mouth. "This looks funny, Mina, you need to lean in closer to Mr. Kapasi."
>
> She did. He could smell a scent on her skin, like a mixture of whiskey and rosewater. (54-55)

The irony in this context lies in the fact that what the lens of the camera can see, remains invisible to the voyeur in Mr. Das. Mrs. Das asks for Mr. Das's address voluntarily, on a scrap of paper she rips "from a page of her film magazine," showing a "tiny picture of a hero and heroine embracing under a eucalyptus tree." (55) Again, the celluloid world that churns out illusions is appropriately brought in here, by the artist in Lahiri.

As they arrive at Konark, the adults get carried away at the wealth of erotica at the Sun Temple. While Mr. Das is lost in tour book giving details and his photography, Mr. Kapasi and Mrs. Das have a leisurely look at the sculptures on the walls: "countless friezes of entwined naked bodies, making love in various positions, women clinging to the necks of men, their knees wrapped eternally around their lovers' thighs." (57) As for Mr. Kapasi, he grows more and more enamoured of Mrs. Das: "He had never admired the backs of his wife's legs the way he now admired those of Mrs. Das, walking as if for his benefit alone." (58) Further, she seems to him preferring his company above that of the rest. Still she remains wrapped in the mystery of her sunglasses:

> Mr. Kapasi was anxious to be alone with her, to continue their private conveisation, yet he felt nervous to walk at her side. She was

> lost behind her sunglasses, ignoring her husband's requests that she pose for another picture, walking past her children as if they were strangers. (58)
>
> He had an overwhelming urge to wrap his arms around her, to freeze with her, even for an instant. (59)

But all what he does is: "He stole glances at her in the rear-view mirror." (60) As they reach at dusk in the secluded hills, Mrs. Das refuses to get out of the car, when all the others go out: "My legs are tired," she said, sinking low in her seat. "I'll stay here. . . . Anyway, those monkeys give me the creeps." (61) When Mr. Kapasi is about to follow them, Mrs. Das stops him:

> "No. Stay a minute," Mrs. Das said. She got out of the back seat and slipped beside Mr. Kapasi. "Raj has his dumb book anyway." Together, through the windshield, Mrs. Das and Mr. Kapasi watched as Bobby and the monkey passed the stick back and forth between them. (62)

Mrs. Das even offers Mr. Kapasi, some puffed rice, which she has the habit of "not offering . . . to anyone." (47) She confides that Bobby was not born to Mr. Das. The father of Bobby was a Punjabi youth who happened to stay with their family for a week and how "He made love to her swiftly, in silence, with an expertise she had never known." She even suggests to Mr. Kapasi to "stop calling me Mrs. Das" (64) She tells him further, how she gets sudden urges:

> I have terrible urges, Mr. Kapasi, to throw things away. One day I had the urge to throw everything I own out the window, the television, the children, everything. Don't you think it's unhealthy? (65)

The irony in the story stems from the dumbness and nervousness Mr. Kapasi exhibits at the most crucial moment of the trip, and the consequent frustration and bitter disappointment Mrs. Das meets with at the end. Mr. Kapasi is a depressed man now, having utterly failed to help her feel better; by saying the right thing or making the right gestures.

That Mr. Kapasi fails at the most truthful moment in the story is vividly brought out once again through optic imagery. He fails to look at her directly:

> He knew that Mrs. Das was watching him, but did not turn to face her. Instead he watched as the figures of Mr. Das and the children grew smaller, climbing up the steep path. (62)

At the close of the story, the reunion of the family is again highlighted with the efforts of Mr. Das, "kneeling on the ground, focussing the lens of his camera." (67) Mrs. Das, who is currently out of the range of the camera, rushes forward: "Wait for me," Mrs. Das called out. "I'm coming." (67) "God, let's get out of here," she says, relieved when Bobby is rescued from the monkeys by Mr. Kapasi. As regards Mr. Kapasi, all his illusions end when the slip of paper on which he has written his address gets blown off in the wind. The story closes with the optic image of "the picture of the Das family he would preserve forever in his mind." (69)

Thus, Jhumpa Lahiri's *Interpreter of Maladies* makes a masterly attempt to delineate and define various moods, subtle vicissitudes in human relationships and the world view of the work itself, through a skilful and imaginative employment of optic images which, in their turn, gradually assume a symbolic tone, thus rendering the vision of the work existential and universal.

NOTE

1. Jhumpa Lahiri, *Interpreter of Maladies* (Boston, New York, Houghton Mifflin Company, 1999).

Human Relationships in *Interpreter of Maladies*

KISHAN H. PAWAR and SAVITA A. PATIL

Jhumpa Lahiri's *Interpreter of Maladies*,[1] the Pulitzer Prize winner of 2000, is no more a new name for the lovers of literature. The book is a collection of nine stories that deal with the characters from Bengal, Boston, Calcutta and other locales of the U.S. This collection of short stories deals with the modern problems of the so-called modern and material world. People like Shoba and Shukumar are the ones who are struggling to come to their dilapidated home, knowing that it is hardly possible to keep it on. But this book has Mr. Pirzada too, who is longing for his home in Daka. Being abroad, he is homesick. There are human beings like Mr. and Mrs. Das too, who are thinking that they are really happy living with each other, which is merely an illusion. Mrs. Das has deceived her husband. Her son Bobby is not her husband's but was conceived from Mr. Das's Punjabi friend. It was just a matter of a moment. Another character in this story, Mr. Kapasi, who is the interpreter of maladies in a hospital, gets attracted towards Mrs. Das only because she praised Mr. Kapasi's profession. Even his wife never praised his job. But he hates Mrs. Das after knowing about her adultery. These and such characters of these stories are the living people of this very century. No character is self-sufficient, happy and fulfilled one. The relationships they have are equally weak and morally shattered. Some of them like Boori Ma are struggling for bread and butter and six by six shelter to hide themselves; and most of them are suffering from self-created maladies, all psychological ones. In this sense, this attempt of writing the book is an impressive effort at interpreting the psychological maladies of this century.

The characters of this book have maladies like alienation, guilt-complex, self-insufficiency, over-ambitiousness etc. But there are some people who try to carry on life as it really is. Such people set an example before the readers—an example of ideal husband, ideal wife, and good citizen. That shows that if life is lived quietly without creating problems, it really becomes a pleasure to live. In "The Third and Final Continent," Jhumpa Lahiri has created such a couple that really sets an example of a perfection match. The narrator and his wife Mala live such self-sufficient life. Living abroad also they don't adopt those mis-leading modern ways of life of the so-called ultra-modern people for whom a normal way of living is to have extra-marital affairs.

The human relationships in the first story "A Temporary Matter" also look temporary. Man-woman relationship becomes a burden to carry on unwillingly and reluctantly. Shoba and Shu-kumar are such husband and wife who don't really enjoy the company of each other. But they carry on the life as if it is a task to live the life. They often have to struggle to find out the topics to discuss in the moments of leisure so that the communication-gap can be lessened. They often feel that the past was a beautiful moment whose beauty enhances when it goes deeper into the history. They reel the present to be unbearable even in the company of each other.

Shukumar prepares food every now and then, and Shoba eats it silently. This small thread of their relationship became thinner after the loss of their child. Shukumar enjoys cooking because "It was the one thing that made him feel productive. If it weren't for him, he knew, Shoba would eat a bowl of cereal for her dinner."[1]

The opportunity to sit hours together to eat together and to speak leisurely comes to them, due to the failure of electricity. In the candle-lights, they dig-up their darkened past and try to find the gems of sweet memories. Drinking wine together for hours, they search interesting topics to get involved in each other. What Jhumpa Lahiri wants to suggest here is that life is not a one-way tour to an unknown destination but a deliberate journey into the selves of each other for fixed and unfixed destinations. It seems that Shoba and Shukumar's journey has not even set for that destination yet. Writes Jhumpa Lahiri:

> They weren't like this before. Now he had to struggle to say something that interested her, something, that made her look up from her plate, or from her proof-reading files. Eventually, he gave up trying to amuse her. He learned not to mind silences. (12)

And then, continues Shoba, that during power failures at her grandmother's house they had to say something. It is a monotonous lifestyle. No one can enjoy such yoke of life placed on one's back against one's wishes. To meet the dangerous gap, they both tell their past experiences. Now each day, Shukumar noticed her beauty which had once overwhelmed him seemed to fade. The cosmetics that had sound superfluous were necessary now, not to improve her, but to define her somehow. It all shows that the relationship of the husband and wife, after losing the child, has not crossed the boundary of body, beauty and sex. With time, the husband and wife should grow up and should come out of the mire of sex and should raise themselves to the level of further growth. When he tells her that their dead child was a boy of five pounds, they sit together and weep.

"When Mr. Pirzada Came to Dine" is the experience of a Dacca citizen living abroad. The division of East and West Pakistan is the reason why human beings suffered that much. The capital of Bangladesh Dacca was the eastern frontier's locale which was fighting for autonomy from the ruling regime in the Western Pakistan. Mr. Pirzada's seven daughters were living in Dacca. Ayesha, Amira, Amina and Aziya are remembered by him very anxiously. The love that is offered by Lilia's parents to Mr. Pirzada is really unusual. They share every anxiety he feels, when there was action in Dacca and young women were raped and killed. Mr. Pirzada could do nothing but to listen to the news and pray to the Allah. The writer says that during those twelve days of war, Mr. Pirzada watched the news and contorted himself. He forgot to bring candy to Lilia:

> Most of all I remember the three of them operating during that time as if they were a single person, sharing a single meal, a single body, a single silence, and a single fear. (41)

These three persons were Lilia's mother, father and Mr. Pirzada himself. The support offered to Pirzada by these people is worth admiration. Beyond all the boundaries of race and religion, they behaved like one single family. This is important. Such human relationships are realty encouraging and enhancing the prospects of human race.

"Interpreter of Maladies" has three characters and some children. It's all about grown ups who know the life and its problems. In "A Temporary Matter" the couple carries on their dilapidated home by deliberate attempts, but in "Interpreter of Maladies" all the people are frail minded. They have hardly any morals to be proud of—even the taxi driver Mr. Kapasi gets prepared instantly to break his wife's confidence and to love Mrs. Das, just because Mrs. Das has praised his job. Mrs. Das's dress, her open legs, sexy eyes and inviting smiles corrupt the driver's soul. They exchange their addresses and the phone numbers and he dreams of having extra-marital relationship with her. For no reason Mrs. Das tells to Mr. Kapasi that her Bobby was not the child of her husband but of his Punjabi friend who had once stayed at their home:

> Bobby was conceived in the afternoon, on a sofa littered with rubber teething toys, after the friend learned that a London pharmaceutical company had hired him, while Ronny cried to be freed from his playpen. She made no protest when the friend touched the small of her back as she was about to make a pot of coffee, then pulled her against his crisp navy suit. He made love to her swiftly, in silence, with an expertise she had never known, without the meaningful expressions and smiles Raj always insisted an afterward. (64)

Kapasi, the tour guide and interpreter of maladies, cannot guide as well as interpret this immoral and psychological malady of Mrs. Das. He does not understand why she has told this immoral deed. Mr. Kapasi is a common human being who observes this failed man-woman relationship. Mrs. Das hates the thrifty nature of her husband and she is a very showy and fashionable young woman. Kapasi watches that people live as if they are obliging the life by living it. No mutual understanding, no compassion is shown towards each other. She does not understand her husband. She asks him with a hating accent: "Why do you do this, Raj, just to save a few stupid rupees. What are you saving us, fifty cents?" (49) She wanted to hire a car with A.C, but Raj avoided it; hence this anger. She praises Kapasi's job of interpreting the maladies as romantic and responsible. He instantly gets attracted towards her. But that was all his infatuation . But still Mr. Kapasi is unable to interpret this lady's dilemma:

> Don't you see? For eight yarn years I haven't been able to express this to anybody, not to friends, certainly not to Raj. He doesn't even suspect it. He thinks I am still in love with him. Well, don't you have anything to say? (65)

She further tells Kapasi that she feels terrible looking at her children and at Raj: "I have terrible urges, Mr. Kapasi, to throw things away. One day I had the urge to throw everything I own out the window, the television, the children, everything. Don't you think it is unhealthy?" (65) But Mr. Kapasi was accustomed to the physical unhealthiness of the patients. Mrs. Das's unhealthiness was somewhat psychological. He is unable to interpret her malady. Actually she wanted Mr. Kapasi to endorse her guilt complex as a very normal thing to be overlooked by her. She wanted him to encourage her to bury the sinful act of adultery in her conscience. But he keeps silent. And she gets shattered by his uninterpretable silence.

> "Mr. Kapasi, don't you have anything to say? I thought that was your job."
>
> "My job is to give tours, Mrs. Das."
>
> "Not that. Your other job. As an interpreter." (65)

But Mr. Kapasi's job is to interpret the language of patients into the language of the doctor. His job was not to interpret the extra-marital relationship into the language of the sinner's conscience.

That is what she says: "I was hoping you could help me feel better, say the right thing. Suggest some kind of remedy." (65)

No doubt, she was aware of the sin she had committed long back. Now, she seeks a divine guidance from the interpreter of physical remedies. Perhaps, she took him as the priest of some church who not only listens to the confessions of the sinner but suggests the right spiritual remedy. But alas this was neither a priest, nor a spiritual authority, to console her sinned soul. He was just looking at her, the sexy, attractive woman, who neither loved her husband nor her children, who had already fallen out of love with life. She might have confessed to lighten her heart from sinful guilt, but it depressed him. He thought of telling her to confess it before her husband but he could not. He just observed this unsuccessful human relationship. How people deceive each other even in their beds! Jhumpa Lahiri focuses on psychological suffocation even a sinner can feel. Living together is not sufficient, the feeling of togetherness is as necessary.

The fourth story in this collection is "A Real Durwan" which is about an old woman called Boori Ma. She lives in the shelter given by people in an apartment. She had had a glorious past, a rich life, in her youth. This is the turn of her fate, from heights of glory to the bottoms of misfortune. She works there as a durwan or sentry, living understairs waiting for donations. This old woman has descended from the heights of kingly glory to the dust. She recalls: "Our bath-water was scented with petals and attars. Believe me, don't believe me, it was a luxury you cannot dream." (78-79)

Residents of the apartment finally decided what they needed was a real durwan. So they tossed her bucket and rags, her basket and reed broom down the stairwell. Then they tossed out Boori Ma. She kept telling them all: "believe me, believe me." (82) This is another end of the failure of human relationships. The relationship called humane is a failure since it was made. We expect something more from each other than we can offer to them, or can do for others. Basically, human beings are selfish and they can hardly love beyond the spheres of practicality.

The fifth story in this collection is "Sexy," another story on the extra-marital relations. Laxmi's cousin's husband falls in love with another woman after nine years of marriage. This story narrates adulterous relationship. Miranda is the name of this sexy woman who is young and beautiful American. She has adulterous relation with Mr. Dev, a married Bengali youngman, who is a banker in America. His wife has left for India, for a few weeks. Dev uses his wife's absence as an opportunity. In their love, the words like moral and selfless love, sacrifice and devotion do not exist. Dev and Miranda live as if they are husband and wife. They make love every night, go for shopping, watch movies in theatres, drink to their full and eat various foods. Dev praises Miranda by calling her sexy. In the world of these adulterous people, there is no value of real responsibility. As an adventure, they have sex with others.

As Dev's wife arrives, Miranda loses her grip over Dev. She understands that it is difficult for her to manage to live without Dev. When she looks after Rohin, the nephew of Laxmi, she feels a bit relaxed. Rohin asks Miranda to put on the cocktail dress. He calls her sexy in this dress. When asked by Miranda what the meaning of the word sexy is, Robin answers, "It means loving someone you don't know." (108) Miranda felt Rohin's words under her skin. When Dev had called her sexy, she had felt hot within. But now she felt numb. Miranda suddenly realizes her futile infatuation towards Dev because he had been made for his wife that resembled Madhuri Dixit, the Indian heroine. It was the child Rohin whose innocent narration of his father and mother's quarrel over his extra-marital affair with a woman he had never seen, changed Miranda's mind. The end of this story is symbolic. Miranda goes to the place where Dev had kissed her for the first time. She sat outside the church, "gazing at its giant pillars, and its massive dome, and at the clear blue sky spread over the city." (110) It shows that like the clear sky her mind became clear now, without any dot of sin over it. The church was standing on the solid pillars. Her mind also got a solid base to live with, and that was perhaps, spiritual attitude.

She understood her mistakes, and like the church her mind too, stood on the unmovable.

The sixth story is "Mrs. Sen's." Mrs. Sen is the wife of a professor of mathematics. To overcome her loneliness in American milieu, she gets a job to look after a child Eliot whose mother has hardly any time for him. Mrs. Sen is shown struggling against her own inability to learn driving. If she has to keep her job, she must learn driving. People in America live the professional life in which every relation wants certain return. Indian women face certain problems in America. Susan Ram comments on this situation "In this beautifully observed story, East meets West, in the shared experience of loneliness and poignance. Mrs. Sen's situation is handled with utmost delicacy and control unsullied by any hint of mockishness."[2]

The seventh story of this collection is "This Blessed House" which dwells on the same difficult situation of husband-wife tense relationships. Lahiri has presented a couple which tries to cope up with a new world they have just entered. They are Sanjeev and Twinkle. Their arranged marriage had not given them sufficient time before marriage to understand each other. Therefore, they are now trying to peep into each other's selves. Sanjeev does not like her behaviour and her excessive respect for the statues of Christ and Mother Mary. She wishes to adopt the new culture where she is living and Sanjeev thinks it to be a superfluous act. None of them surrenders. Both stretch the matter as much as they can. The matters are very trivial but the tension they build is very tiresome. It often seems that this tender thread may be cut. One recalls the couple in "A Temporary Matter" who tried to cope up with such difficult situations by weeping in each-other's arms. Jhumpa Lahiri writes:

> Though she did not say it herself, he assumed then that she loved him too, but now he was no longer sure. In truth Sanjeev did not know what love was, only what he thought it was not. (147)

This couple has a hot debate and quarrel over the Virgin's statue. She wanted to put it in her study or in the garden but Sanjeev wished to move it to the garage, just because people should not think them to be Christian. Instead of making life beautiful, they make it rotten.

The eighth story is "The Treatment of Bibi Haldar" that sounds like "A Real Durwan." This story shows that male member of society is still unable to face a woman with her problems—the problems created by him only. The men in this story have been shown escapist and the woman is the one "who can face the pains created by man. Bibi Haldar is a young lady with mediocre looks. Naturally, no man gets attracted towards her. Her guardians leave her back and go away, leaving a few hundreds for her. Bibi's dream of marrying someone who will love her is broken, She is an immature woman, who had been treated as a patient of some undetectable disease. Finally, it is leant that she is expecting. She never tells the name of the man whose child she is expecting. With the help of women of neighbourhood, Bibi runs a shop after begetting the baby boy. It sounds to be the feminine voice in this story to prove the abilities of woman in the society where male appears as an escapist, and female a daring entity. Bibi Haldar is an individual who maintains her individuality against all odds.

The last story in this collection is "The Third and Final Continent." This is one of the most beautiful stories. The two Indians, husband and his wife Mala, move in America, and settle there. The changes in culture and people don't affect their livelihood, like the couple in "This Blessed House." The narrator is the husband whose nature and behaviour in America is very much like an Indian. The old lady at whose house the narrator stays as tenant is impressed by his gentlemanly behaviour. Even his wife Mala impresses this old lady.

This couple is the only one in this book who have been living a successful arranged married life. But unlike Sanjeev and Twinkle, this couple shows great respect for each other's desires and needs. At the house of Mrs. Croft when they go to see her, they smile and laugh, looking at each—other for the first time after their marriage. When Mrs. Croft declared, "She is a perfect lady," (195) they laughed very sweetly. This was a step taken by this couple towards their inner personalities. He says: "Now it was I who laughed. I did so quietly, and Mrs. Croft did not hear me. But Mala had heard, and for the first time, we looked at each other, and smiled." (196)

It was when the distance between this married couple began to lessen. It is the ideal couple Jhumpa Lahiri has created in this book. She has set an example before the readers of this machine-age—the example of a peaceful couple whose life is smooth, like a gust of cool breeze. They live life listening to the inner music of their souls, very gradually moving towards perfection.

These nine stories portray various human relationships. The characters live, cut off from their solid base called culture and faith. Jhumpa Lahiri has proved her uncommon merit picturing these much human relationships.

NOTES

1. Jhumpa Lahiri, *Interpreter of Maladies* (New Delhi: Harper Collins, 1999), p. 8.
2. Susan Ram, "Chronicle of the Cultural Interface," *Frontline*, Oct. 22, 1999, p. 71. Qtd. Parmanand Jha, "Home and Abroad: Jhumpa Lahiri's *Interpreter of Maladies*," *The Indian Journal of English Studies*, Vol. XXXVIII, 2000-2001.

Lahiri Does Not Interpret Maladies in *Interpreter of Maladies*

SHYAM S. AGARWALLA

In a 1987 interview, Gayatri Chakravorty Spivak[1] describes herself as "bicultural," but she then explains that this means that she is "not at home in either of the places" she inhabits. Like Edward Said, she views this as an advantage, since she feels that "it's important for people not to feel rooted in one place." (37) She expresses scepticism about identity labels, since "There are many subject positions which one must inhabit; one is not just one thing." (60) She describes herself as "born a Brahmin, upper-class, senior academic in the United States, highly commodified distinguished professor, adding, ironically, "What do you want?" (86) More seriously, she asserts that "being an Indian without nationalism and being a Bengali without regionalism" is the biggest problem for her. (115) Like Said, Spivak rejects notions of identity based on national or regional identity.

Jhumpa Lahiri was born in 1967 in London, raised in Rhode Island and is now settled in New York. Both her parents—a librarian father and teacher mother—were born and raised in Calcutta. When she arrived in Calcutta, she talked about her predicament to Ashish Kumar Sen[2]:

> The older I get, the more aware am I that I have somehow inherited a sense of exile from my parents, even though in many ways—superficial ones, largely—I am so much more American than they are. . . . In fact, it is still very hard to think of myself as an American (partly so because I was born in London). . . . On the other hand, the problem for the children of immigrants, those with strong ties to their country of origin, is that they feel neither one thing nor the other. This has been my experience, in any case. . . . If I say I'm from Rhode Island, people are seldom satisfied. . . . Alternatively, if I say I'm from India, a place where I was not born and

> have never lived, this is also inaccurate. It bothers me less now. But it bothered me growing up, the feeling that there was no single place to which I fully belonged.

The exile of Spivak and Lahiri from India is not like the exile of Sita from the kingdom of Lord Rama. Their doorplates are still fondly cleansed by their fellow Bengalis, in Kolkata, by applying cleansing cream of their love, affection, and swank on them. I do not observe any maladaptive maelstrom either in their writings or interviews for their "exile" in America. Nor is it necessary to write a book of martyrology, for they are not martyrs. What they need, instead, are mudflaps in the vehicles of their lives, which are racing with the intellectuals of the Third World in the First World. Their whining in public for their "unhousement" in foreign lands as well as in India is, to use a half-credible metaphor, timocratic in nature.

My observations on them do not lead me to the unconscious cerebration of their literary achievements. The contribution of Spivak in the post-colonial discourse is immense, next to Edward Said, though her language often snarls up the traffic of even the minds of galumphing university professors, not to talk of a toddler like me. Jhumpa Lahiri, mercifully, is within our reach. A wonderkid, with the spiritual mind, and comprehensive vision, she writes *Interpreter of Maladies*, a collection of stories, which is a sort of spritzer. Some stories are based in America and some in Calcutta. Her literary admirers call her a metropolitan writer but what I feel, after reading some of her stories, is that she, like Amitav Ghosh, is more inclined towards the depiction of the subaltern characters than Rushdie, Seth, and Mistry.

Mr. Kapasi, in "Interpreter of Maladies," suffers from a cacoethes that Mrs. Das is attracted towards him. His impercipient and inchoate mind fails to see the limitary nature of her job of a driver-cum-tourist guide. He was "forty-six old, with receding hair . . . but his butterscotch complexion and his unlined brow . . . made it easy to imagine what he must have looked like at an earlier age."[3] As a guide, he is trying to interpret some tourist spots in Orissa to Mr. and Mrs. Das, Bobby, Tina and Ronny—their children. Mr. Das and Mrs. Das, like Jhumpa, "were both born in America. . . . Our parents live here now, in Asansol." (45) Kapasi reveals to them that he works with one doctor, as "an interpreter." (50) The family has never heard of anything like that of an interpreter to a doctor and, therefore, Mrs. Das exclaims: "But so romantic." (50) It is one thing to interpret a patient's maladies to the doctor but it is difficult to interpret a woman's exclamation. Let me digress for sometime.

Jhumpa Lahiri tells her interviewer, Ashish Kumar Sen, about the origin of the phrase "interpreter of maladies." She situates an incident that happened to her at Boston University in 1991. She meets a man in Brookline, who worked at a doctor's office, interpreting for him, since he had a number of Russian patients who had difficulty explaining their ailments in English. "As I walked away from that brief conversation, I thought continuously about what a unique position it was and by the time I'd reached my house, the phrase 'interpreter of maladies' was planted in my head. I liked it enough to write it down and I told myself, one day I'll write a story with that title. . . . About five years passed. . . . When I was putting the collection together, I knew from the beginning that this had to be the title story—the dilemma, the difficulty, and often the impossibility of communicating emotional pain and affliction to others, as well as expressing it to ourselves."

The malady of Mrs. Das was that a Punjabi friend of Das "made love to her swiftly, in silence, with an expertise she had never known, without the meaningful expressions and smiles Raj (Das) always insisted on afterward." (64) Bobby was conceived that afternoon. She tells Kapasi: "For eight years I haven't been able to express this to anybody, not to friends, certainly not to Raj. He doesn't even suspect it." (65) She wants Kapasi to suggest a remedy to her emotional pain or over-burdened guilt. Like Raju in Narayan's *The Guide*, Kapasi is also not a temporizer. But, he is in a dilemma, again like Raju. Kapasi, like Raju, gauges that Mrs. Das is indifferent to Das. So, he is out to impress her. He misreads the reason behind this indifference. He thinks he can entrap her in his love-net. But, when she collogues with him about her infidelity to Das and seeks remedy, he is dumb-founded. It is one thing to conjure up a fictive future but it is another thing to interpret and solve one's ailment. Raju guided Rosie to the path of self-recognition. So does Kapasi. Kapasi asked her, "Is it really pain you feel, Mrs. Das, or is it guilt?" (66) Mrs. Das grabs the one. Her sullen face radiates light. For seven years, Bobby was not her son. Now, she is relieved of her emotional pain. Like Rosie, she gains self-recognition. She embraces Bobby. A sourpuss Mrs. Das oozes confidence whereas a confident Kapasi turns sourpuss.

Bibi Haldar, in "The Treatment of Bibi Haldar," suffers "from an ailment that baffled family, friends, priests, palmists, spinsters, gem therapists, prophets and fools." (158) No "pathy" is able to diagnose or cure her ailment. Her elder cousin and his wife dislike her She, as the story tells us, suffers from hysteria, goes through bouts of collapse. Jhumpa situates this story in Bengal, in India. She writes to tell us that Bengalis are still superstitious, ignorant, aleatory, and gradualist. Bibi's impudicity and salacious nature, combined with her illiteracy, ignorance, unworldly gestures, make her unfit for marriage. She was not allowed to watch the television. Nobody in the village could find or interpret the reason of her malady. Only a few persons suggest to Haldar that she be married at once. But he scouts their suggestion. Scarified by his neighbours and well-wishers, he leaves the village. This is the beginning of the independent life of Bibi Haldar. She becomes pregnant. And after the birth of a child she becomes a normal human being. Jhumpa tries to tell us about Bengal in the 1990s. Her portrayal of the subalterns of Bengal is unconvincing, for they cannot allow a tainted woman to live with them. I think Jhumpa Lahiri is trying, unsuccessfully, to mix the wine of the West with the sodawater of the East and to present a reasonably reformed, improvised and modern Bengal to the Western readers. This story should be stored in a Bollywood cinemasque.

The story, "Mrs. Sen's," is about a middle class Indian woman living in America. Mrs. Sen's predicament in America is half-hypogean and half-limitary. She can offload her hypogean feelings to Eliot. For instance, she tells Eliot about a large celebration of any kind in Bengal, which was always rip-roaring and sociable. Her mother "sends out word in the evening for all the neighborhood women to bring blades just like this one, and then they sit in an enormous circle on the roof of our building, laughing and gossiping and slicing fifty kilos of vegetable through the night. . . . It is impossible to fall asleep those nights, listening to their chatter. . . . Here, in this place where Mr. Sen has brought me, I cannot sometimes sleep in so much silence." (115) Her *Sehnsucht* for the life-giving Bengal is contrasted with lifeless America, by Lahiri. Her relatives in Bengal, living in their self-created rosy world of swanky delusion, believe that "I press buttons and the house is clean. They think I live in a palace." (125) But, Mrs. Sen's story is that of the subaltern woman. She has lived a tweedy life in Bengal but, in America, life is formal and funereal, at least for Mrs. Sen. She cannot fill this yawning gap nor can Lahiri or Spivak. Neither Mrs. Sen (an Indian) nor Mrs. Eliot (an American) is a *rara avis* in any cultural encounter between the West and the East on the foreign soil.

Jhumpa Lahiri, as I mentioned earlier, is neither fully Indian nor fully American. She does not belong to a single place. Yet, she tries to interpret maladies of Indians to her Western readers and of maladies of Western people to Indians. Her stories are a veritable feast for those who know neither the Eastern culture nor the Western. Lahiri is vendeuse, wears a telegenic appearance and sells her *Interpreter of Maladies* to us as if it were an example of her developed serendipity of India and the U.S.

NOTES

1. Gayatri Chakravorty Spivak, *The Post-Colonial Critic; Interviews, Strategies, Dialogues*, ed. Sarah Harasym (London & New York: Routledge, 1990), p. 83.
2. *The Asian Age*, 16 April 2000.
3. Jhumpa Lahiri, *Interpreter of Maladies* (New Delhi: Harper-Collins, 2000), p. 45

Ambivalent Expatriate Sensibility in *Interpreter of Maladies*

PUSHP LATA

In the last two decades, an increasing number of Third World writers have emigrated to the West. Corollary the style and the content of their writings have been greatly influenced by the extent to which they have been able to identity and adapt to their new surroundings. This is how we can have two broad categories. In the first category we can place those writers who still feel alienated in their new country and who tend to write about people and events which are typical of their motherland. They also seem to be anxious to infuse their native color in their writings. The feeling of loss, prevalence of longing, and loneliness have been reflected in the works of quite a few emigrant writers. In fact the manifestation of such a disjuncted, defunct and uprooted mood has been so frequent and dominant that in modern criticism, it has acquired a currency in the name of expatriate sensibility. In the past few decades, this aspect has been focussed by many noted Indian critics, as an exiled self has been quite overwhelmingly portrayed by most of the anglo-Indian writers living in the western countries. For instance, Viney Kirpal in her book *The Third World of Expatriation (*1989) and Uma Parameswaran in her essay, "What Price Expatriation" (1976) think in the same vein. Alastair Niven in his Foreword to the book, *The Commonwealth Writer Overseas*, has emphatically brought the point home that the time has come in Commonwealth literature to consider the expatriate sensibility as a literary term. At this juncture it is important however, to define and fix the phrase expatriate sensibility in the context it is required to be understood. Though many people have tried to define this term in their own peculiar ways, what comes very close to summing up the expatriate sensibility is the statement made by Manju Sampath in her paper, "Bharati Mukherjee: The Fiction of Alienation and Identification" has tried to trace the dictionary meaning of the words identity: "Identification can be on many levels, psychological, sociological, linguistic, cultural and emotional and the extent to which identification has been achieved . . . how complete one's assimilation has been to the new surroundings . . . 'alienate' means to make hostile where previously friendship has existed." (141) Further she says: "So in an expatriate writer's case, this would imply a sort of hostile distancing from the homeland as well as a latent hostility implied or experienced for the adopted country."

However, the second category writers have been able to identity themselves with their new host country to a certain extent. They are more part of their host society rather than their native society. These writers are blessed with bi-cultural perception. This is what we find in writers like Bharati Mukherjee. In Bharati Mukherjee's fiction, we find her writing about West Indian, Hispanics and Vietnamese as immigrants in America with great ease and conviction.

On the contrary, Jhumpa Lahiri, the Pulitzer Prize Winner for the year 2000 for her work *The Interpreter of Maladies* can not be put in either of the categories. On reading this collection of Jhumpa Lahiri's superbly crafted short stories, one is reminded of Meenakshi Mukherjee's celebrated remark as her felicitous comments seem to concur with what we observe in Jhumpa Lahiri's works. This is what the noted critic had to say on the intriguing aspect of the inside outside sensibility of the writers in her paper "Inside the Outsider" (1977): "Today it is not at all rare to find a writer for whom the multi-cultural situation is not only a subject matter, but a mode of perception as well."

The strength of Jhumpa Lahiri's *Interpreter of Maladies* lies in the fact that the work refuses to manifest a pellucid or bigoted vision of character. In fact, all her characters appear tentative and irresolute in their approach to resolve matters like society, culture, ambience and one's consequent adaptability or lack of it.

Such issues, the otherwise usual afflictors to one's psyche, do not much perplex Jhumpa Lahiri's characters as they look beyond this thin veil of social edifice and prefer to concentrate on the other wider, cosmic and universal aspect of existence.

That is why an expatriate sensibility or an exiled self is not easily the keynote in Jhumpa Lahiri's work as in the case of other modern writers living in other countries. The writer of Indian milieu in fact assumes an ambivalent posture to issues like self and society and prefers to focus on more profound, intense and subtle intricacies of our existence. Thus we find in her a deliberate detachment and aloofness that alienates the writer from her work and also quite interestingly refuses to propitiate the reader who expects her, an emigrated soul herself, to sing the mournful nostalgic tunes to the countrymen of her lost paradise i.e. her own country.

In "A Temporary Matter" and "Interpreter of Maladies," we see a complex weaving of two cultures and find that Lahiri still has strong ties with India, her homeland. Born in London, she grew up in Rhode Island and has travelled several times to India. Her stories draw richly from her visits to Calcutta. In an interview to rediff.com. she says. "It is the place where my parents are from, a place I visited frequently for an extended time and formed relationships with people and with my relatives and feel a tie over time even though it was a sort of parenthesis in my life to be there." After spending nearly 30 years in the United States, she says, "It is home to me but I feel a bit of an outsider too."

Marriage, an essential Indian social ritual, is at the very core of Jhumpa Lahiri's modes. Some of them are arranged, some have been rushed into, some are betrayed and some are exhausted. Besides, she depicts cultural clashes between the residents of different countries in a very subtle, penetrating and compelling manner. She seems to believe that culture conflicts ripple outward in many directions, providing that there is much more subtlety and craftiness than most of us assume about living on an ethnic divide. Her sense of separation is never as simple as this sounds. Seen through the eyes of a child, no matter what their ethnicity, all adults seem foreign and inexplicable. And even within the same household, between husband and wife, there is no agreement about the costs and benefits of adapting to a new environment. Her characters do not get perfectly assimilated into the host society even after living for several years. They are trying to break the umbilical cord with their homeland linguistically and physically, but at the psychological level they display their Indianness.

"Interpreter of Maladies" is a well-knit and insightful tale in which a young affluent American couple traces their Indian heritage under the guidance of Mr. Kapasi, their English speaking Indian guide-cum-driver. With three kids, Ronny, Bobby and Tina, they visit the Konark Temple and other typical tourist spots, seeing them through the eyes of ordinary Americans. During their conversation on route, Mr. and Mrs. Das come to know that Mr. Kapasi, besides his part time job of a tour—guide, works as an interpreter in a doctor's clinic where he translates the Gujarati spoken by some of the patients. Mr. Kapasi who found nothing noble in interpreting people's maladies (51) is flattered to hear Mrs. Das describe it as "romantic." The real turning point, however comes in the story when Mrs. Das discloses to him in the car, that Bobby, her second son, was conceived from her husband's Punjabi-Indian friend. This fact justifies the title of the story, as Mrs. Das is able to divulge her malady to Mr. Kapasi, the interpreter.

"A Temporary Matter" unravels complex emotion through a simple situation that is familiar to a Calcuttan: a power cut. Repairs on a faulty cable line in Boston lead to five days of hourly power cuts. Diasporic Bengalis Shoba and Shukumar, coping with a disintegrating marriage, use this time to exchange secrets that have driven them apart since the loss of their first baby. They try to bridge the yawning distance that threatens to overwhelm them. Thus a small-scale heartbreak is dealt within the framework of this story. When the current goes off, Shukumar, the protagonist of the story tells Shoba:

> I cheated on my Oriental Civilization exam in college. . . . I could see the blue book of the guy next to me. He was an American guy, a maniac. He knew Urdu and Sanskrit. I couldn't remember if the

> verse we had to identify was an example of a ghazal or not. I looked at his answer and copied it down. (17)

Though it had happened over fifteen years ago but he feels alleviated now after having told her the long hidden secret. Somehow, without saying anything distinctly the power cut hour turns into an exchange of confessions—the little ways they had hurt and disappointed or thwarted each other and themselves. While narrating, Jhumpa Lahiri tells how Shukumar starts looking forward to this hour and spends time to think about what to say to her. On the third night during the power cut hour, he admits to her how he once ripped out a photo of a woman from one of the fashion magazines she used to subscribe to when she was pregnant and carried it in his books for a week. He also discloses the fact that he felt an intense desire for the woman but it turned to disgust finally. He also expresses that it was the closest he'd come to infidelity. On the fourth night he tells about the sweater-vest which was presented by her on their first marriage anniversary. He has not lost it but exchanged it for cash at filen's, as he did not like it and got drunk at a hotel.

Shukumar, on the morning of the fifth night, finds a notice from the electric company, which communicated that the line has been repaired ahead of schedule. It rather disappoints him. In fact he expresses this to Shoba when after her returning home at seven thirty he finds her reading the notice. He says: "I suppose this is the end of our game," and she replies back that he could still light candles if he wanted.

As the story progresses we find on the fifth night they eat in darkness and finish off one bottle of wine. But as the candle has nearly burned away, Shoba blows out the candle and stands up, turns on the light and sits down again. She does it purposefully as she wants him to see her face while she tells him something. She says that she has looked for an apartment for herself and got one. She adds that no one is to be blamed and they have been through enough. Undoubtedly she knows her own mind and heart. Shukumar realizes that this was the point of her game and this was what she had been trying to tell him for the past four evenings. It relieves yet sickens him. And as it was Shukumar's turn to speak, after a few moments of silence, he tells her that their baby was a boy and his fingers were curled shut, just like hers in the night. This statement proves that the blame of his coming late from Baltimore was absolutely wrong. He had arrived in time to see the baby. In fact, he had held their son close to his chest before burying the little one. Thus the loss of their first-born child, which kept haunting both of them individually, suddenly becomes bearable and shareable. Further we are told that they wept together, for the things they now knew. Their individual pain and anguish becomes a unified pain, which helps them strengthen their bond.

In the above story, Jhumpa Lahiri portrays marital boredom that is typical of Indian society. Shoba has been represented as an American woman. This is one reason that after she has realized that it will be difficult for her to get along with Shukumar, she decides to live separately. This reflects the non-conformist attitude of the protagonist. But at the end of the story when she comes to know the fact about the child and realizes how much Shukumar still loves her, she weeps along with him. With this confession, the grief of the parents becomes a reality, a grief which they can share and become close once more. It does not remain a secret burden which is shouldered by individuals and creates a void in their lives. It also reflects a clash of two cultures. In spite of her Western outlook and education she feels alienation, yet at the crossroads we get the impression that she cherishes the traditional Indian values. She still feels some warmth; she certainly cannot get back to India, a country where sex is not a taboo, Shukumar feels a sense of guilt even when he rips one picture of a woman from a book and keeps it for weeks hidden inside his book. This particular fact indicates the changed perspective regarding sex and marriage. He may not think of coming back to India but he does not establish extra-marital affair in spite of liberal sex prevailing in American society.

The second story, "When Mr. Pirzada Came to Dine" is narrated from a child's point of view. This story is set in Boston but has 1971 Indo-Pak war and the birth of Bangladesh as the backdrop. The exiled Indian is usually anxious to hobnob with compatriots but in this case although Mr. Pirzada spoke the same language as the child's parents, he belonged to East Pakistan. In Dacca he had a three storey home, a lecturership in Botany at the university, a wife of twenty years and seven daughters between the age of six and sixteen whose names all began with the letter 'A'. (23) Lilia, the child narrator, is an expert in American history but is completely ignorant about the division of Bengal between Hindus and Muslims. Lilia and Mr. Pirzada become fast friends and the child quite understandably prays for the safety of her friends, seven daughters in the newly developed war situation. All of a sudden Mr. Pirzada disappears from the child's life to find out the whereabouts of his family. Jhumpa Lahiri attempts to delineate the child's perception of the things happening around her. The little one knows a little about human relationships and does not have a clear idea of what would have meant for Pirzada to have been away from his family for so long.

"A Real Durwan" is a story in which the protagonist, Boori Ma is a self-appointed sweeper of the stairwell of a multi-storeyed building. Her services came to resemble those of a real durwan, as she kept the crooked stairwell spotlessly clean. We also come to know that the residents liked that Boori Ma who slept each night behind the collapsible gate, stood guard between them and the outside world. However, the same residents accuse her of the theft of the basin and throw her out as they think Boori Ma has endangered the security of the building. The lady lives in the past in order to forget her intolerable present. This story is pathetic but certainly a powerful pen-portrait of an old lady who possesses her own maladies, which she wants to be heard.

The reasons affecting the conjugal bliss adversely of a newly married couple have been excellently explored in the story, "This Blessed House." Sanjeev who is an ambitious corporate Vice-president has recently married Twinkle, a 27 year-old girl. They have come to live in a new house where they keep finding strange Christian relics: a white porcelain Christ, St. Francis postcards and Noah's arclight switch plates left behind by the previous tenants. Twinkle calls it treasure hunt whereas it is deeply disturbing and unsettling for Sanjeev as Twinkle gets infected with the religious mania of the erstwhile occupants of the house. She has a strange fascination for these Christian paraphernalia while Sanjeev is scornful and dismissive. Though it is only the second month of their marriage, certain things began to nettle. Jhumpa Lahiri successfully portrays these baffling and intriguing moments of their lives.

In "Interpreter of Maladies" when Kapasi, the driver-cum-guide introduces himself, he presses his palms together in greeting, but Dr. Das squeezes hands like an American. Moreover, when Kapasi asks Mr. Das: "You left India as a child?" he replies: "Oh, Mina and I both were born in America. Born and raised. Our parents live here now, in Asansol. They retired. We visit them every couple years." With this statement it appears that they prefer living in America. Again, they are Americans in their physical appearance. Dr. Das wears a sapphire blue visor, shorts, sneakers and a T-shirt, with camera slinging around his neck whereas Mrs. Das puts on a red and white-checkered skirt that stops above her knees and a close-fitting blouse styled like a man's undershirt. Mrs. Das uses Kapasi to unburden her guilt by telling the secret of Bobby not being Mr. Das's son. She says:

> And no one knows, of course. No one at all I've kept it a secret for eight whole years. . . . But now I've told you. (64)

Mr. Kapasi is disturbed to know this and also wonders why she has told this to him. During conservation Mrs. Das tells that Mr. Das does not even suspect it. Even the Punjabi boy who made love to her and was responsible for this does not know that he is Bobby's father. The question arises when they are born and brought up in America, where having extra-marital affair is not considered a sin, what makes her keep it a secret. It is perhaps the inheritance of values at the psychological level. Perhaps she thinks he could suggest her some remedy, as she feels terrible looking at her own children. She finally asserts:

> It means that I'm tired of feeling so terrible all the time. Eight years, Mr. Kapasi, I've been in pain. I was hoping you could help

> me feel better, say the right thing. Suggest some kind of remedy. (65)

Her confession rather depresses Mr. Kapasi. He thinks of telling her that honesty is the best policy. It would surely help her. But he starts with the most obvious question to get to the heart of the matter: "Is it really pain you feel, Mrs. Das, or is it guilt?" She opens her mouth to say something, but as she glares at Mr. Kapasi, certain knowledge seems to pass before her eyes. She does not wait for further discussion and rather starts climbing the hill to reach Mr. Das and kids. This scornful silence and move of Mrs. Das shatters the fantasy of Mr. Kapasi and thus puts an abrupt and early end to their strange intimate relationship. Though this reaction suggests her self-centeredness, yet it makes the fact translucent that she does not feel free to communicate her pain, agony and guilt even to her husband. Thus it can be realized that Mrs. Das has not perfectly assimilated into her host country. Prema Srinivasan, in her article "Beyond Bengal and Boston" appositely comments on the theme of the story in the following words: "The story moves and finishes in an almost pedestrian manner. Whether Boston or Bengal, the maladies are similar and the interpreter is charged with the onerous burden of conveying the right problem in the right words. Though the end is quite predictable, yet she tells the story with ease and eloquence. In a very subtle manner she is trying to interpret the meaning of distance and dislocation. She attempts to identify the discrepancies that exist between 'home' country and 'New home' i.e. abroad in both the stories."

To sum up, it can be said that usually the expatriate writers do not write too much about their adopted country, as it is very difficult to get behind the actualities of the mind of a new country. Even when an Indian writer born in America faces colour and racial discrimination as a child, he does not grow with the children of the host country. So is the case with Jhumpa Lahiri. When Vibhuti Patel asked her in an interview: "as a second-generation immigrant, are you still an outsider?" she replied that India is home for her parents even after living for 30 years in

America. So she never felt fully at home in America. But to another question, "So you felt at home in India?" she said that she did not grow up in India; she was not a part of things. She says, "We often visited India but we did not have a home. We were clutching at a world that was never fully with us." At other point she admits: "As I grew older, going to India was frustrating, because growing up in America is different."

Thus Jhumpa is a writer who bubbles over with the trauma of dislocation and loneliness, as she herself does not feel a part of this society or that society and the same sensibility is reflected in the characters of her stories. She clearly vocalizes the pangs of estrangement suffered by millions of Indians living in the other countries. In this collection of short stories, she displays great mastery over voice and vocabulary and the true versatility of her range is visible as she writes in many different styles. She does not strive to impress. She nowhere deliberately uses witty remarks or phrases to catch the readers' attention. Her style of writing is just simple, direct, lucid, elegant and sparkling. As mentioned earlier, identification and alienation exist on a linguistic and psychological level, this is something, which Jhumpa seems to have perfected in her timeless treatise, *Interpreter of Maladies.*

Bibliography

http/www.rediff.com.site

Viney Kirpal, *The Third World Novel of Expatriation (*Delhi: Sterling, 1989).

Jhumpa Lahiri, *Interpreter of Maladies* {Delhi: HarperCollins, 1999). Vibhuti Patel, "Interview with Jhumpa Lahiri," *Newsweek International*, 20.9.99. http:/www.umiacs.umd.Edu/saw net.

Meenakshi Mukherjee, *Inside the Outsider,* Paper read at the Fourth Triennial Conference in New Delhi, 2-8 January 1977.

Manju Sampath, "Bharati Mukherjee: The Fiction of Alienation and Identification," *Indian-English Fiction 1980-90: An Assessment*, ed. Nilufer E. Bharucha and Vilas Sarang (Delhi: B.R., 1994).

Prema Srinivasan, "Beyond Bengal and Boston," *The Hindu*, February 2, 2001.

The Enigma of Cultural Multiplicity: A Study of *Interpreter of Maladies*

JAYDEEP SARANGI

Philip Carey, the doctor protagonist in William Somerset Maugham's "Of Human Bondage," whose encounter with human misery prompts the thought: "There was neither good nor bad there. There was just facts. It was life." Jhumpa Lahiri's Pulitzer winning collection of short stories *Interpreter of Maladies* has close proximity with Maugham, who described himself as 'a craftsman, not a genius.' Jhumpa Lahiri's work seems to be more of a product of craftsmanship than genius. As Vimala Rao says: "Jhumpa writes well. But it is too much to claim the birth of a new star. One must wait and see if she develops a distinctive style and voice and creates characters who are individual and memorable. Till then there is no need to speak of a new star rising or shining."[1] Like Maupassant, a nineteenth century French writer, she adopts verisimilitude and a detached and straightforward narrative mode.

After Arundhati Roy's Booker for *God of Small Things*, Jhumpa Lahiri becomes the first South Asian to win an individual Pulitzer for the year 2000. She was born in 1967 in London to Bengali parents who emigrated from Calcutta, the capital city of West Bengal, and was raised in Rhode Island, U.S.A. Thus, Lahiri had the experience of three continents. In "The Third and Final Continent," Jhumpa Lahiri indirectly speaks of her multicultural (rootless?) identity through the mouth of an unidentifiable I who seems to be the narrator as well as an active participant in the dialogue format of the last chapter of the book: "Whenever he is discouraged I tell him that if I can survive on three continents, then there is no obstacle he cannot conquer while the astronauts, heroes forever, spent more hours on the moon, I have remained in the new world for nearly thirty years."[2] The author-narrator does not stop at this point and says: "I am not the only man to seek his fortune far from home, and certainly I am not the first. Still, there are times I am bewildered by each mile I have traveled, each meal I have eaten, each person I have known, each room in which I have slept." (198) Jhumpa Lahiri claims that her stories in *Interpreter of Maladies* are "stories of Bengal, Boston and beyond." The stories reflect the multiple identity of the author-narrator. Her yearning for the Indian sensibility (as that is her root) bears the stamp of a vagrant searching for her lost home. She is as if in self-exile. Jhumpa Lahiri's Indian characters and the Indian sensibility are not all misfit in the American permissive society. She sincerely accepts the problems of settling somewhere else far from the native land:

> I have spent many months with relatives here and learnt about my parents' home and where they lived. I have always felt integrated with the place. . . . My parents never felt at home. Being the child of immigrants I did not feel at home too. It's taken a longtime for me to feel at home anywhere.[3]

Feeling at home can be an indication of a process which is known as adaptation. Man cannot be uprooted thoroughly from his socio-cultural fixity. Yet none can transcend his cultural identity, said Marx. *Interpreter of Maladies*, with sub-title "Stories of Bengal, Boston and Beyond," projects the problems of the immigrants in a foreign soil: "the yearning of exile, the emotional confusion, et al."[4]

Jhumpa Lahiri can be grouped with Salman Rushdie or Bharati Mukherjee for her status as a 'migrant' writer. The migrant writers project their identity as plural and partial. 'Migrancy' and the 'vagrancy' give birth to the question of crisis of 'identity.' Jhumpa Lahiri can never have the sense of belongingness. She feels as if she is cut off from her roots. Her mind yearns for the 'Imaginary homeland.' She admits her condition, "neither as a tourist nor as a former resident—a valuable position, I think as a writer. I learned to observe things as an outsider and yet I also know that different as Calcutta is from Rhode Island, I belong there in some fundamental way, in the ways I didn't seem to belong in the United States."[5] This is undoubtedly a common scene in Indian green-card holding diaspora. The writers of this genre are in a fix. In *Interpreter of Maladies*, six of the nine stories are set in America, but deal with the lives of Indian immigrants—the Indians in the U.S.A. These immigrants live in America but they still belong to their 'home' community. These people are caught "between the strict traditions they've inherited and the baffling New World they must encounter everyday." The rest three stories are set in India.

The opening story "A Temporary Matter" portrays an ontological condition dealing with the conjugal crisis of a young couple—Shoba and Shukumar. The decline of their mutual attachment in Boston prepares the readers for the problems of self-exile. Memories of India come in their intimate conversation:

> "It's like India," Shoba said, watching him tend his makeshift candelabra. "Sometimes the current disappears for hours at a stretch. I once had to attend an entire rice ceremony in the dark. The baby just cried and cried. It must have been so hot. (11)

This story is an in-depth study of human psychology. The Americanized Bengali couple exhibits the trends of typical post-colonial diaspora where the characters carry different socio-geographical identities with them. India is discussed in a foreign soil. These trans-cultural references give an advantage to Jhumpa Lahiri to have a wide range of readers.

The second story is set again in Boston. The readers are introduced to Mr. Pirzada. He is from Dacca, "the capital of Bangladesh, but then a part of Pakistan." (23) The story has the civil war in Pakistan as well as the birth of Bangladesh as a free state (in 1971) as the backdrop. Mr. Pirzada befriends a Bengali family in Boston. He seemed to be disturbed as his family stayed in Dacca. Later in the story, he was reunited with his family:

> He was reunited, he wrote, with his wife and children. All were well, having survived the events of the past year at an estate belonging to his wife's grandparents in the mountains of Shillong.

"Interpreter of Maladies," the title story, is set in Puri, India. The readers are introduced to Mr. Das and Mrs. Das. There is an elaborate description of the Sun Temple at Konark, Orissa. They visit the great Sun Temple in an "ideal weather for sightseeing." Jhumpa Lahiri, like a veteran craftsman describes the dress of the family: "The family looked Indian but dressed as foreigners did, the children in stiff, brightly colored clothing and caps with translucent visors." (44) Jhumpa presents the family as if they are of mixed/hybrid cultures. In language, Jhumpa Lahiri follows the American tradition of spellings favouring color to colour and so on. Interestingly, she makes use of Indian words/phrases '*Astachala-Surya*' (setting sun), '*hanumun*' (monkey) '*Nagamithunas*' (act of sex), '*villa*' (place).

Jhumpa Lahiri is careful in her details. There is reference to a paperback tour book *India*. More interestingly, the book has been published abroad. "*India* which is about real India must have been published from India."

In this complex story of an Indian American couple, Mr. Kapasi, a tour-guide-cum-chauffeur plays an important role. Mrs. Das discloses the real identity of Bobby to Kapasi. We come to know that a Punjabi-Indian friend of her husband is his father.

The 'most obvious question' gets to the 'heart of the matter' and Mr. Kapasi asks, "Is it really pain you feel, Mrs. Das, or is it guilt?" Mr. Kapasi, the interpreter of people's maladies, fails to offer any remedy to Mrs. Das's malady. A multiple identity may be a reason for Mrs. Das's queer sexual behaviour. In this context her cultural uprootedness cannot be rejected in disdain.

"A Real Durwan" begins with Boori Ma, 'sweeper of the stairwell' of a multistoried building. Her services "come to resemble those of a real durwan." (73) The streets and place names of Calcutta are mentioned at random in this story of Boori Ma. College Street,' 'Circular Road,' 'Jodhpur Park 'Howrah Bridge' add realistic appeal to the story. Parmanand Jha claims "the vagaries of material possession plaguing human relationship forms the matrix of this story. The story is based on the search for a real durwan." (82)

"Sexy," the fifth story of this collection depicts Miranda, a young energetic American who falls in love with Dev, a married Bengali banker. Dev's wife is away for some days. This story again highlights weak conjugal ties. And we are stuck in the basic-'out of sight out of mind.' Miranda and Dev refer to breaking of commitment in the husband-wife relationship again and again in the story.

Mrs. Sen, in the story named after her, has a distinctive as well as individualistic speech: "Every one, this people, too much in their world" is her impression of America. Her evocation of homeland is convincing and extremely enjoyable:

> She had brought the blade from India, where apparently there was at least one in every household. "Whenever there is a wedding in the family," she told Eliot one day, "or a large celebration of any kind, my mother sends out word in the evening for all the neighborhood. Women to bring blade just like this one, and then they sit in an enormous circle on the roof of our building, laughing and gossiping and slicing fifty kilos of vegetables through the night.

Simple household activities in India are mentioned in this story with accuracy. Mrs. Sen wants the job for an engagement to fill up her loneliness in afternoons. There is reference to the people of Kolkata for their fascination for fish: "in Calcutta people ate fish first thing in the morning, last thing before bed, as a snack after school if they were lucky." (1 23)

This story projects the difficulties faced by Indian wives in a foreign culture. A sense of alienation preoccupies the hearts of people culturally as well as geographically cut off from their homeland. A sense of loss runs all through the stay:

> "Do you miss your mother, Eliot, these afternoons with me?"
> "You must miss her. . . ."
> "I see her at night."
> "When I was your age I was without knowing that one day I would be so far." (122-23)

Jhumpa Lahiri, a perfect interpreter of cultural multiplicity, is faithful enough to project Indian culture and tradition in realistic terms. She portrays Mrs. Sen as she is. Jhumpa Lahiri knows that fish can be palatable and enjoyable for Mrs. Sen as she has her roots in Bengal: "The other thing that made Mrs. Sen happy was fish from the seaside." (123)

Bibi Haldar, too, in the story, "The Treatment of Bibi Haldar," is presented against an Indian socio-cultural backdrop. She is about 29 years old. She suffers from "an ailment that baffled family, friends, priests, palmists, spinsters, gem therapists, prophets, and fools." (158)

Bibi finally has a miraculous cure. She becomes pregnant. She says, "I'm contagious, like the pox. She says I'll spoil the baby." Later on she delivers a 'forceps' baby. The child proves to be a panacea for Bibi. The final authorial remark confirms Bibi's comparatively better health condition: "she was, to the best of our knowledge, cured."

Interpreter of Maladies is a monuments of cultural multiplex which is multinomial as well. Jhumpa Lahiri, through her experience of different cultural identities, comes to know the basic properties of different cultures. The nations are not merely geopolitical identities. One who is born and brought up in a cultural situation makes his own root there. When he is planted elsewhere he becomes a member of that culture. But the total adaptation in a new set-up is next to impossible. One who is in exile ('self' or 'forced') may find himself in the crux. Is it cultural multiplicity? Why can't we brand it as cultural uprootedness? One is migrated means he is uprooted societally and psychologically. When it is psychological, there must be an inclination for the homeland. And the self is divided. One must fall back to nostalgic past. He may experience an alienation from a stream of life, a tradition and bondage for what he was known for. His identity becomes plural and partial. If plural, he symbolizes cultural multiplicity, and if partial, he stands for cultural uprootedness. The stories are perceptive critique of human relationships, bonds and commitments that one has to make with homeland as well as the migrated land. Man in exile has dual responsibilities to carry out.

Oksaor (1983) defines bi-culturalism on the basis of a broad view put forward by Soffleti (1955) which uses culture as "the ways of a people." Multi-culturalism (Oksaor uses the term bi-culturalism and multi-culturalism as synonymous) of a person is realized in his ability to act according to the requirements and rules of different cultures. The immigrants like Jhumpa Lahiri project two or more cultures to accomplish different, sometimes divergent roles and functions, their distribution in different contexts and geopolitical identities. Bi-culturalism, or multi-culturalism in whatever way we interpret Jhumpa Lahiri's stories, a socio-cultural criss-cross is there. Her experiences seem to be total than partial.

Bapsi Sidhwa, an immigrant writer is often asked, "As a recent migrant how comfortable are you writing about America?"[6] Bapsi Sidhwa has the answer:

> The compulsion to transpose experience into narrative, to convey a personal vision, is what makes one write in the first place. Creating fiction is essentially subjective and my assessment of what is striking in America, and of how my family and I have coped in our new circumstances, are bound to insinuate their way into my writing.

Bapsi Sidhwa confesses the hardships the immigrant writers are bound to be troubled with:

> Of course, it is not easy to portray the nuances of a culture one is not born to, and it entails a risk to get inside the skin of a character that is shaped by another culture.

The immigrant writers are like journeymen who are caught between two cultures. *An American Brat* is a cultural compromise between the East and the West. The characters of cross-cultural writings are to compare life as they perceive in the New World (in which they are in) with the ways and values in the native world in which they are more accustomed to.

The chronic uprooting of the immigrant writers as well as the characters demand adjustments which cause tensions. Jhumpa Lahiri's sense of being an outsider remains. It is shared by her characters: "Jhumpa Lahiri's elegant stories tell the lives of Indians in exile, of people navigating between the strict traditions they've inherited and the baffling New World they must encounter every day."[7]

Jhumpa Lahiri has close proximity with V.S. Naipaul. Naipaul's relationship to India or the Caribbean closely resembles Jhumpa Lahiri's relationship to India and Rhode Island. Jhumpa Lahiri's 'Pulitzer prize for fiction 2000' pays gracious tribute to the U.S.A. and India, the two civilisations which matter to her. The thirst for roots drive Jhumpa Lahiri and her characters to India. In the process, Jhumpa Lahiri looks for Indian traditions, cultural heritage, sculpture and the life-style of the Indians. And she finds an oblique relation to them.

East, West by Salman Rushdie, published in 1994, forms a link across the oceans. David Malouf's *Antipodes* connect Australia with Italy, Belgium and Austria. *Interpreter of Maladies* explores what Naipaul has so appropriately defined "the enigma of arrival." Stories of cultural multiplicity or cultural distance succeed one another. There are "undisclosed connections" among the characters of different stories. Jhumpa Lahiri's stories are the gateways into the large submerged territory of "cross-culturalism." "Cross-culturalism" goes beyond biculturalism or multi-culturalism. It is a metaphor to share cultures. Both Malouf and Rushdie "work on edges, Botiders, thresholds, and boundaries, looking for "links," "bridges" something that will allow them/us to share, instead of dividing, what is on either side."[8] In this connection, we may refer to the last words of Moraes of *The Moor's Last Sigh:* "Our need for flowing together, for putting an end to frontiers, for the dropping of the boundaries of the self."

Jhumpa Lahiri does not work for the "dropping of boundaries." Her characters move within a limited space. They bear their respective cultural flags. They never 'grow' or make an attempt to cross the limits of cultural boundaries. Her writing becomes restlessly nomadic: she visits different locales and gets into these localisms. At the same time, one must not read *Interpreter of Maladies* as a travel book like *An Area of Darkness,* which is a record of V.S. Naipaul's travels in India. There is hardly any special perception or vision that distinguishes Jhumpa

Lahiri's stories from the common run of writers. She seems to be a faithful portrayer of life.

NOTES

1. Vimala Rao, "Prognosis: Hospital; Interpreter of Maladies," *JIWE*, Vol. 29. No. 2, July 2001.
2. Jhumpa Lahiri, *Interpreter of Maladies* (New Delhi: Harper-Collins, 1999).
3. *The Times of India*, Kolkata edition, 21 Jan. 2001.
4. Parmanand Jha, "Home and Abroad: Jhumpa Lahiri's *Interpreter of Maladies*," *IJES*, Vol. XXXVIII, 2000-2001.
5. Lavina Melwani, "Interpreting Exile," *JIWE*.
6. *The Atlantic Literary Review*, Vol. 1, No. 2, Oct.-Dec. 2000.
7. Introductory note of *Interpreter of Maladies*.
8. Elsa Linguanti, "Origin, Origins, Originality: Salman Rushdie's *East, West*, David Malouf's *Antipodes* and Wilson Harris' *The Womb of Space*," *ALR*, Vol. 1, No. 2, Oct.-Dec. 2000.

The Problems of Immigrants in an Alien Land: *Interpreter of Maladies*

SATISH BARBUDDHE

Jhumpa Lahiri's first book *Interpreter of Maladies*, an anthology of nine delightful stories forced Amy Tan, the distinguished novelist, to utter the following words about her: "Jhumpa Lahiri is the kind of writer who makes you want to grab the next person you see and say 'Read this!' She's a dazzling storyteller with a distinctive voice, an eye for nuance, an ear for irony. She is one of the finest short story writers I have read."

All the nine stories in the collection have coherence and some of the characters in these stories are manic-depressive. Having grown up in America and spent many months in Calcutta as a child, she sees things in a way that not everyone around her can. Therefore, her experiences may be painful for some readers but for most of them it is a refreshing experience.

When Jhumpa Lahiri, born in London but living in the United States for 30 years, began writing seriously about a decade ago, she set her stories in Calcutta, which she has visited many times. Her stories deal with the problems of the immigrants in an alien land.

Lahiri did not straightway became storyteller. Initially she was disappointed as several schools rejected her graduate School application. These rejections at last turned into blessing in disguise. Very soon she joined a non-profit institution in Cambridge, Massachusetts. There, she worked as a research assistant. She had a computer of her own there, which helped her a lot in her first creation. Most of her characters take surefooted steps without any fear.

The first story in the collection, "A Temporary Matter," begins with these words. "The notice informed them that it was a temporary matter: for five days their electricity would be cut off for one hour, beginning at eight p.m. A line had gone down in the last snowstorm, and the repairmen were going to take advantage of the milder evenings to set it right. The work would affect only the houses on the quiet tree lined street, within walking distance of a row of brick-faced stores and a trolley stop, where Shoba and Shukumar had lived for three years."[1]

This story narrates the subtle relationship of a young couple—Shoba and Shukumar. Shukumar remembers their first meeting. They met at a lecture hall, where a group of Bengali poets were giving a recital. He got bored but could not leave the place. Instead he started reading a newspaper, especially the temperatures of cities around the world. "When he turned his head to the left, he saw a woman next to him making a grocery list on the back of a folder, and was startled to find that she was beautiful."[2]

The announcement of hour long power-cuts in the evening—though a temporary matter—tremendously helps both. Shukumar went to Baltimore for an academic conference. He did not want to go, but it was Shoba who insisted him as 'it was important to make contacts.' But when he returned to Boston it was all over. "The baby had been born dead." (4) The doctor's smile was professional. The sad incident did not indicate that she would not be able to have children in future. But 'the born dead baby' made Shoba and Shukumar "experts at avoiding each other in their three-bedroom house." (4) They started spending much time separately.

The temporary hour-long power-cut made them happy. Shoba was a typical lady who kept the bonuses from her job in a separate bank account in her name. Shukumar was least bothered about it. He liked that Shoba was different. (5) She had a powerful capacity to think ahead. Shukumar's mother-in-law "was polite to Shukumar without being friendly." (9) She hardly mentioned about Shoba in her talk. She was a typical example of a very quiet mother-in-law who prayed twice a day for healthy grand-children in future.

Shukumar's wife hadn't prepared for such an ordinary emergency, i.e. power-cut, therefore, he found it difficult to locate the candles. There is a reference to 'their first meals.'

> He remembered their first meals there, when they were so thrilled to be married, to be living together in the same house at last, that they would just reach for each other foolishly, more eager to make love than to eat. He put down two embroidered place mats, a wedding gift from any uncle in Lucknow, and set out the plates and wineglasses they usually saved for guests. (10)

Shukumar was disappointed when he found the notice from the electric company, that the line had been repaired. He had a plan for Shoba like buying 'malai' for her. The end of power-cut was unbearable for him. He had no energy to buy anything for cooking. He found the coconut milk tin dusty and overpriced. Still he bought them. "Something happened when the house was dark. They were able to talk to each other again." (19) Shukumar declared that their baby was a boy. He narrated all the minute details of the baby. At this moment Shoba looked sad. The story ends with the words: "They wept together, for the things they now knew."

The second story "When Mr. Pirzada Came to Dine" has the Indo-Pak war as the backdrop. Mr. Pirzada came to Boston on a grant from the Government of Pakistan to study the foliage in New England. He came from Dacca where he was a lecturer in Botany at the university. He had a wife of twenty years and seven daughters between the ages of six and sixteen.

Mr. Pirzada was always worried about the incidents in Dacca. "In March, Dacca had been invaded, torched and shelled by the Pakistani army. Teachers were dragged onto streets and shot, women dragged into barracks and raped." (23)

Lila is the narrator in the story who says, "A glass for the Indian man." (25) She is immediately corrected by her father. 'Mr. Pirzada is no longer considered Indian.'

The partition is described thus: "like a pie we were sliced up. Hindus here and Muslims there." Little Lilia did not understand anything as Mr. Pirzada and her parents spoke the same language. Lilia's father told her that Mr. Pirzada was a Bengali, but he was a Muslim. That was the reason why he lived in East Pakistan. A map was shown to Lilia. She was told by her father the current situation in East Pakistan. Lilia nodded without understanding a word.

Lila's curious eyes noticed the act of Mr. Pirzada, which he used to do before dining.

> Before eating Mr. Pirzada always did a curious thing. He took out a plain silver watch without a band, which he kept in his breast pocket, held it briefly to one of his tufted ears, and wound it with three swift flicks of his thumb and forefinger. Unlike the watch on his wrist, the pocket watch, he had explained to me, was set to the local time in Dacca, eleven hours ahead. For the duration of the meal the watch rested on his folded paper napkin on the coffee table. He never seemed to consult it. (30)

Lila watched Mr. Pirzada very carefully, when she learnt that he was not an Indian. She carefully looked at the pocket watch that night: "Life, I realized, was being lived in Dacca first." Lilia had a clear picture before her now. It was morning in Dacca, Mr. Pirzada's daughters getting up from their sleep one by one. Lilia thought that their meals, their actions were "only a shadow of what had already happened there." She at one time wondered "what would happen if suddenly his seven daughters were to appear on television, smiling and waving and blowing kisses to Mr. Pirzada from a balcony. I imagined how relieved he would be. But this never happened." (31)

Mr. Pirzada finally reunited with his family in Dacca. Lilia had no memory of his first visit or his last visit. Her father drove Mr. Pirzada to the airport one afternoon when she was at school. They did not hear anything from him for a long time. The only missing things at the dinner time were Mr. Pirzada and his extra watch. Several months later he informed the family in Boston that he was happy with his wife and children, living in an estate belonging to Mr. Pirzada's wife's grandparents in the mountains of Shillong. Lilia felt Mr. Pirzada's absence on that day. 'It was only then . . . that I knew what it meant to miss someone who was so many miles and hours away." (42)

Mr. Pirzada's friendly relations with an Indian Bengali family in Boston are narrated in the story. The characters in the story literally live in two different worlds. Though Mr. Pirzada lived in Boston with an Indian Bengali family, he always remembered his own family in Dacca. He kept a watch ready in his pocket, which was set to the local time in Dacca. The social background of Mr. Pirzada is totally different from the Bengali family. Still the Bengali family open-heartedly supports Mir. Pirzada till 'he flew back to his three-storey home in Dacca.' The story's main focus is the relationship of the two different families. Mr. Pirzada narrated in his letter that 'his seven daughters were a bit taller, but otherwise they were the same, and he still could not keep their names in order.' The good news of Mr. Pirzada's family's reunion made Lilia's mother happy, who prepared a special dinner that evening.

The third story "Interpreter of Maladies" is set in Puri, India. The phrase 'interpreter of maladies' has its origin way back in 1991. Lahiri got the phrase in a conversation with a person in Boston. She says, "I asked him what he was doing and he said he was working as a translator for a doctor who had a number of Russian patients who had difficulty explaining their ailments in English. I had never heard of a job like this, but realized that it was necessary in places where doctors and patients didn't have a common language."[3]

An Indian-American couple visits India, Mr. Das, his wife Mina and their three children Tina, Ronny and Bobby are guided by a tour guide Mr. Kapasi. He also works as an interpreter in a doctor's clinic, where he translates the Gujarati spoken by some of the patients. He is a Gujarati tour guide, working as an interpreter for Gujarati patients.

The Das family is on their way to see the Sun Temple at Konark. He is surprised to find Mr. Das referring to his wife by her first name when speaking to the little girl. Mr. Kapasi closely observes Mrs. Das: "She wore a red-and-white-checkered skirt that stopped above her knees, slip-on-shoes with a square wooden heel, and a close-fitting blouse styled like a man's undershirt." (46) She teaches Science at Middle School in America.

When Mr. Kapasi declares that he is not a doctor, but he works as an interpreter, Mrs. Das reacts: "Interesting. I've never heard of anything like that." (50) She finds the job very much romantic. She wants to know more about Mr. Kapasi's job. She wants 'to picture what happens.' Kapasi's wife has little regard for his career. She thinks that he is just a doctor's assistant. She hardly shows any interest in his work. She never asks him about his patients. She never thinks that his job is full of responsibility, while Mrs. Das is so inquisitive about his job. Her sudden interest in his job makes Mr. Kapasi happy. Mr. Kapasi thinks that his job is a thankless occupation. But Mrs. Das thinks that his job is full of challenges. The word 'romantic,' which is used by Mrs. Das, makes Mr. Kapasi think:

> She did not behave in a romantic way toward her husband, and yet she had used the word to describe him. He wondered if Mr. and Mrs. Das were a bad match, just as he and his wife were. (53)

Mr. Kapasi's life is full of indifferences, the protracted silences. The interest shown by Mrs. Das is 'mildly intoxicating' for him. This intoxicating attraction leads him to the conclusion that his choice in selecting the gray suit that morning is a wise decision. Very often he checks his own reflection in the rearview mirror. He is a gregarious guide but this time the centre of attraction is Mrs. Das. He sometimes glances 'at the strawberry between her breasts, and the golden brown hollow in her throat.' (53-54)

On their way Mr. Kapasi narrates the experiences of the patients like the young woman who had complained of a sensation of raindrops in her spine, the gentleman whose birthmark had begun to sprout hairs. Mrs. Das is a patient listener, while Mr. Das is absorbed in a tour book. Normally Mr. Kapasi keeps a distance from the family whenever they stop for a lunch at a roadside restaurant, but this time there is a call from Mrs. Das: "Mr. Kapasi, wait. There's room here."

In a photo-session, Mr. Das wants Mina 'to lean in close to Mr. Kapasi.' When she is close to him, Mr. Kapasi smells a scent on her, like a mixture of whiskey and rosewater. He is restless as his smell of perspiration may widen the distance between the two. Mrs. Das hands over a paper to Mr. Kapasi to write down his address. This scrap of paper is hastily ripped from a page of her film magazine. There was a picture of a hero and heroine embracing under a eucalyptus tree. This picture is enough for Mr. Kapasi to 'fantasy' about their romantic relationship. He thinks that she will send him copies of photographs and very soon they will exchange their ideas, their disappointments and desires. He is hopeful of his growing friendship with her. He hands over the slip of paper containing his address to Mrs. Das, but suddenly notices that he has either misspelled his name or accidentally reversed the numbers of his postal code. He thinks of asking the slip of paper back, but notices that the paper has gone at the bottom of her bag.

When they reach at the Sun Temple at Konark, Mr. Das reads the words from the book.

> The wheels are supposed to symbolize the wheel of life. They depict the cycle of creation, preservation, and achievement of realization. (57)

The exterior of temple is admired by Mr. Das, who takes pictures, "while the children ran ahead, pointing to figures of naked people." (57) Mrs. Das stops at three to four places, stares silently at the carved lovers and the processions of elephants. Mr. Kapasi has been to this place a number of times, but this time in the company of Mrs. Das it is a very different experience. He accepts it in these words.

> He had never admired the backs of his wife's legs the way he now admired those of Mrs. Das, walking as if for his benefit alone. He had, of course, seen plenty of bare limbs before, belonging to the American and European ladies who took his tours. But Mrs. Das was different. Unlike the other women, who had an interest only in the temple—Mrs. Das had taken an interest in him. (58)

There is a strange sense of nervousness in Mr. Kapasi when he walks with Mrs. Das. He has a desire to be alone with her for starting a conversation. His fantasy goes further to becoming an interpreter between nations—he explaining things about India and she narrating things about America. In a frenzy he wants to embrace her, but suddenly recovers and asks her: "When do you return to America?"

At about four thirty they drive back to Hotel Sandy Villa. Mr. Kapasi calculates that in approximate six weeks, he may hear from Mrs. Das, along with developed photographs. On his way back to hotel, he steals glances at her in rearview mirror. For the first time, he wants the tour to last a little longer. The idea of dropping them at the hotel makes him discontented. Therefore he suggests them the idea of visiting the hills at Udayagiri and Khandagiri. His thoughts wander like free birds in the sky.

> He did not know what he would do or say to Mrs. Das once they arrived at the hills. Perhaps he would tell her what a pleasing smile she had. Perhaps he would compliment her strawberry shirt, which he found irresistibly becoming. Perhaps, when Mr. Das was busy taking a picture, he would take her hand. (60)

When they reach the hills, Mrs. Das refuses to get out of car, as her legs are tired. Mr. Kapasi wants to join the group, which has gone ahead, leaving Mrs. Das in the car, but he is suddenly stopped by her. Mr. Kapasi wants to explain the history to Mr. Das, but he is discouraged by Mrs. Das. Together they watch the children through the windshield of the car.

Mr. Kapasi praises Bobby as 'a brave little boy,' but quickly Mrs. Das comments, "It's not so surprising." Mr. Kapasi shows disbelief, and the truth comes out. "He's not his." She opens the floodgates and discloses that he is not Raj's son. She narrates the whole story, how one of her two sons, Bobby, was conceived from her husband's Punjabi Indian friend in her own house. Mrs. Das made no protest 'when the friend touched the small of her back.'

Mr. Kapasi asks her why she has disclosed this secret to him, and prompt comes the reply: "because of your talents." (65) For the last eight years she hasn't been able to express this to anybody. This incident plagues her to the extent that she wants to throw everything she owns out of the window, the television, the children, everything. She thinks that it is unhealthy attitude. She wants Mr. Kapasi to comment as an interpreter. She wants some kind of remedy as she says "I've been in pain eight years." (65)

Her confession depresses him. He thinks that honesty is the best policy. He at last simply asks her: "Is it really pain you feel, Mrs. Das, or is it guilt?" (66) Mrs. Das's silence shatters the fantasy of Mr. Kapasi. He thinks that he is not even important enough to be properly insulted. Mr. Das suggests Mr. Kapasi to take a photograph of the five of them and the search begins for Bobby. Bobby is being beaten by a monkey. Mr. Kapasi rescues Bobby. Mrs. Das tries to find out a bandage from her bag. When she tries to take out the hairbrush to fix Bobby's hair, the slip of paper with Mr. Kapasi's address moves in the air. The piece goes above in the sky. He knows the truth now: "Mr. Kapasi observed it too, knowing that this was the picture of the Das family he would preserve forever in his mind." (69)

Lahiri explains the importance of the title story: "I knew from the beginning that this had to be the title story because I think it best expresses thematically, the predicament at the heart of the book—the dilemma, the difficulty and often the impossibility of communicating emotional pain and affliction to others, as well as expressing it to ourselves. In some senses I view myself as a writer, insofar as I attempt to articulate these emotions as a sort of interpreter as well."[4]

The permissiveness of Mrs. Das shocks Mr. Kapasi. She is unable to answer Mr. Kapasi's question: "Is it really pain you feel, Mrs. Das, or is it guilt ?" Mr. Kapasi is unable to provide any remedy to her. The story expresses mournful lady's anguish through a secret announcement to an interpreter of maladies who is madly in love with her. He shows admiration for her. Mrs. Das's character in the story is of flunky type. She does not hesitate to tell the secret. The inadvertent incident in her life makes her restless. Mr. Kapasi, who at first is attracted towards her, feels unsafe and bewildered in her company.

"A Real Durwan" and "The Treatment of Bibi Haldar" are two stories describing the lives of servants. Boori Ma is the central character in the story "A Real Durwan," who is a self-appointed sweeper of the stairwell of a multi-storied building:

"In short, over the years, Boori Ma's services came to resemble those of a real durwan." (73) The same residents later on throw her out one day. They accuse her that "she informed the robbers." (81) At last the residents toss her bucket and rags; her baskets and reed broom. The residents do not understand her simplicity, they only need 'real durwan.' The service which is rendered by her, is easily forgotten by them.

"The Treatment of Bibi Haldar" is a story of a 29 year orphan, unmarried girl suffering from a mysterious disease. Nobody knows the nature of her illness, as "the treatments offered by doctors only made matters worse." (158) She stays in a married cousin's house. The Haldars do not want to spend money on her marriage and move to a new place leaving her alone. The women in the neighbourhood find her 'four month pregnant' (172) in the month of April. In September she delivers a son but would never "tell us who had done it." (172) Nobody knows the name of the father of the newborn baby. 'She was, to the best of our knowledge, cured.' (172) The story ends without revealing the name of the person who is responsible for her pregnancy. The story exposes the hypocrisy of human nature. Lahiri leaves us guessing 'who had done it.'

The fifth story "Sexy" is about intimate adulterous relationship. A married Bengali investment banker, Dev, falls in love with Miranda, a young American girl. Dev's wife has left for India for a few weeks. When Dev's wife returns, Dev loses interest in Miranda. Miranda is alone now. She offers to look after for a day Rohin, the unhappy nephew of her friend Laxmi. Rohin tells her "you're sexy" (107), when she puts on the silver cocktail dress. Miranda decides to put an end to this relationship and returns the places where Dev had kissed her. "The third Sunday, she got up early and went out for a walk." (110)

"Mrs. Sen's" is a heart-tugging story of the eponymous immigrant, baby-sitting an American Schoolboy and tortured by the culture shock. Lahiri deftly uses the boy Eliot's perspective to portray Mrs. Sen's adjustment problem. Eliot enjoys watching her chop vegetable, seated on newspapers on the living room floor."[5] The story narrates the difficulties of immigrant Indian wives in a foreign culture. The atmosphere is new. They can't cope with it.

"This Blessed House" is the story of Sanjeev and his wife Twinkle. The wife is fascinated by old items left by the previous tenants, while the husband wants to dispose of these items. The distance between the two widens. The story finely portrays the newly married girl and her strange liking.

The last story in the collection "The Third and Final Continent" is about an Indian immigrant and his reminiscences. He remembers the first few weeks in America thirty years ago. The story ends decades later, long after his finding a job with the MIT in Boston, going through an arranged marriage in Calcutta, becoming a father and living a happy superannuated life off social welfare."[6] The story's end is full of wisdom, which comes through life-long voyage.

> Still, there are times I am bewildered by each mile I have traveled, each meal I have eaten, each person I have known, each room in which I have slept. (198)

All the nine stories in the collection are sparkling examples of elegant style. Lahiri's stories are the voices of millions of 'exiled Indians' who are torn within but outwardly cannot express their feelings successfully.

Lahiri is accused of writing not about all Indians, but about the Bengalis, 'and her India hardly stretches beyond Calcutta, except in the story after which the collection is named.' The accusation may be true to some extent but her range of narration is superb. Her skill to narrate the woes of the immigrants is experienced in all the stories of this collection. She herself has observed a sense of exile in her parents, which she says can never go. America is her home, still she feels an outsider there.

Most of her characters do not know their own true identities. They cannot balance between 'home' and 'abroad.' There is a cultural difference. The meanings of values varies. In the title story the guide has more heart than the couple whose life is just adjustment. Though the guide in the story likes Mrs. Das, he keeps a distance. The question of identity is definitely a difficult one. Most of her stories have setting in Calcutta. She says, "There was the necessary combination of distance and intimacy with a place."[7] Khushwant Singh is full of praise for her. He says, "Without striving to impress, without a witty twin of phrase, Jhumpa manages to hold the readers' interest. She reminded me of Somerset Mougham."[8]

NOTES

1. Jhumpa Lahiri, *Interpreter of Maladies* (Delhi: HarperCollins, 1999), p. 1.
2. *Ibid.*
3. Naresh Fernandes, An Interview with Jhumpa Lahiri, *Literature*, 13 June, 1999, p. 18.
4. Lavina Melwani, "Interpreting Exile," *The Hindustan Times*, April 23, 2000.
5. Sumit Mitra with Arthur J. Pais, "Boston Brahmin," *India Today*, April 24, 2000, p. 24.
6. *Ibid.*
7. Arthur J. Pais, "Uncle Sam's Sisters—Jhumpa Lahiri: Calcutta Pilgrim," *India Today*, June 21, 1999, p. 73.
8. Khushwant Singh, "Between Two Continents," *The Telegraph*, May 1, 2000.

Looking beyond the Diaspora: A Reading of *Interpreter of Maladies*

KEYA MAJUMDAR

> Languages are jealous sovereigns, and passports are rarely allowed for travellers to cross their strictly guarded boundaries.
>
> Rabindranath Tagore, 1935

A relatively new development in the postcolonial literatures, Diaspora, has been a favourite topic for disgruntling dialecticism, as well as a source of investigative literary outputs. People who have flown over the distant territories of the globe, their settled assurances of Home and Roots being blown over into smithereens of uncertain insecurities, have been represented in diverse ways in diverse writings all over the world. While Rushdie's search for the ground under one's feet is still going on, the central focus of *Half a Life* of Naipaul, the Nobel Laureate, is about a man "who appeared to have no proper place in the world." Yet, after looking at this established scene of diasporic writing, one can still vote for the Pulitzer prize winner collection of short stories *Interpreter of Maladies* by Jhumpa Lahiri, as rather unconventional. The subtitle of the book "Stories of Bengal, Boston and Beyond" specifically talks about the subject matter. Almost all the stories are about the second generation immigrants of Bengal and their communication with other Americans, who live in and around Boston. Together, they create the stories of disillusionment, loss of faith, search for moorings, creating thus an overview of the essentialism of diasporic characters within given, imagined or hateful physical circumstances. On the whole, the book contextualises the question of emotional-intellectual-spiritual survival of the expatriate Indians, in the foreign land. But in a uniquely created new paradigm, the author also opens up a novel vista of understanding this diasporic problem by getting into the shoes of the Americans sometimes and by looking through the viewpoint of the unbiased, unspoilt children, both Indian and American, at the other times. Thus she exhorts the readers to look for the third dimension, that which is 'beyond' in her words. The purpose of this paper is to examine this 'beyond' in its diverse ramifications.

All the stories of the book mainly give primacy to the yet untapped possibilities of the cross-cultural communion of the Indians and the Americans. Ostensibly focusing on the encounters between these two seemingly diverse cultures, what Lahiri actually attempts to do is to look earnestly for some kind of cultural synthesis, that would go 'beyond' the linear periphery of so-called history, geography, and socio-economic politics of the mapped world. In the story named, "Sexy," Dev takes his girl friend to the Mapparium, where the room was "shaped like the inside of a globe, but looked like the outside of one," (90) and he goes on to explain to her the fascinating changes in the geography "like Siam and Italian Somaliland no longer existed in the same way, the names had changed by now." (90) Likewise are not all the ideologies and issues related, liable to change, or, end for that matter? She cryptically leaves behind such unanswered questions.

While codifying the language of this intercontinental malaise of floating existences, she yearns to go 'beyond' the fixity of language, which is but peripheral, pervertable and permutable. This is not all. The search for mooring for these people with double consciousness, double identity and double vision, takes her beyond the specific barbed wire divisions, to locate a place of love and bliss, for Mrs. Das, for example, "who had already fallen out of love with life." (66) Now this lovelessness of the rootless people appears as a serious malady that she tries to interpret 'to give words to their pains.' (66) The doubly dislocated people like Mrs. Das ("Interpreter of Maladies") or Dev ("Sexy") or the Indian couple ("A Temporary Matter") living dual lives, cheating their partners and themselves, are as much the source of study for her, as the geographically or historically dislocated people like Mrs. Sen ("Mrs. Sen's") or Boori Ma ("A Real Durwan").

If diaspora is about journey back home, journey taken to retrieve the Promised Land, Lahiri tells us that it is at the same time the countless ways of journey of the immigrant moving perennially through circles within circles. We see Mr. Pirzada, in the story "When Mr. Pirzada Came to Dine," the citizen of an already broken country called Bangladesh, takes on another exile, for his career advancement to America. Once there he clings on desperately to the Indian family for his emotional sustenance, as their house provided for him 'a lagging ghost of where Mr. Pirzada really belonged.' (31) And the Indian couple also reciprocates in the same manner, more so, at the troubled times of war in homeland. The little girl observes the whole scene, "I remember the three of them operating during that time as if they were a single person, sharing a single meal, a single body, a single silence, and a single fear." (41)

Taking the journey, thus, from the outer space of immigrational problems and inconveniences, and emotional turmoil to the inner space of understanding and assimilation, her stories and characters outline the emotional map of the peripatetic human soul. For postcolonial literature is much more disposed to acknowledge multiplicity, plurality and even contradiction and dichotomy, both in personal and social relationships, constantly seeking to renew itself.

Incidentally, this is what seems to be the answer to the diasporic trauma. This is supposed to be the recognition of a necessary heterogeneity and diversity by a conception of identity which refuses to be peripheral because it has learnt to live with the differences, as they come, embracing hybridity in that course. This spiritual journey of discovery would lead to an indigenous cultural discovery, if only the dislocated ones try to locate the route of heart and the dispossessed ones disclaim their baggages of possessive ethnicity. As in the story named "Mrs. Sen's," we see Mrs. Sen obsessed with her Bengali food habits, persistently refusing to learn driving (to take on the journey of Americanism) in effect thus bogging down the whole situation into the quagmire of loosing her babysitting job, losing her husband's sympathy, losing the only friendship she ever experienced in that foreign land, that of little Eliot, to whom she confides, "'send pictures' they write. 'Send pictures of your new life.' What pictures can I send? . . . They think I live the life of a queen." (125) Even if she had lived the life of a queen, her heart would have wept poorly all the time. So what is the use? The culture that the immigrant has left behind and the culture of the new, foreign land that he must accommodate, get clashed inevitably and the result is inevitably the jack-o-lantern of the story called "When Mr. Pirzada Came to Dine," that turns into a sheer embarrassing existence, which "wore an expression of placid astonishment, the eyebrows no longer fierce, floating in frozen surprise above a vacant, geometric gaze." (36)

The dynamics of the sense of 'beyond' takes place, when the hum and buzz of the local culture, and cultural fringes are overcome and surpassed by a deeper resonance of expanding connotations, that shuttle back and forth between text and context, margin and centre, inner and outer. Thus exemplified, her vision of the 'beyond' coincides happily with the vision of Tagore expressed so cogently in these lines:

> In an era of mounting anguish and vanishing worth . . . it may sound merely poetic to speak of any emerging principle of world-wide relationships. But Time's violence, however immediately threatening is circumscribed, and we who live beyond it and dwell also in the larger reality of Time, must renew our faith in the perennial growth of civilization towards an ultimate purpose.[1]

In its overburdening propensity towards insistence on the cultural difference, and heterogeneity, diasporic texts remain rooted to the anguish of vacillating consciousness of the migrants and the resultant sense of loss. What Lahiri's text proposes however, is the way out of this parochialism, following the comprehensive milieu of a flowing culture that can assimilate Bengal and Boston by mere humanistic balance—as the protagonist of the story "The Third and Final Continent" finds a reflection of his compliant, weak dead mother in Mrs. Croft, the whimsical, despotic

American land lady. The postmodern ethnicity can work out best when it can represent both the worlds and more. These multiply-linked individuals, whom we see in her book, are connected with the multiple worlds, are richer in the sense of multiculturalism that they proffer, instead of one purist condition of fixed culture. If purity as such is seen to be a fiction and hybridity and cultural pluralism all-pervasive, then areas conceived as 'Marginal' paradoxically attains the position of 'Central.' Inspired by the Upanishadic Mantra of 'Vasudhaiva Kutumbakam'—the whole world as kin, in story after story Lahiri throws the hint that the fixity that discourses of race and ethnicity produces, becomes more malleable, more translatable, more comfortably inhabitable in the dynamics of the world—brotherhood. As the margins of the nation gets displaced by so many historic, cultural happenings and theories even, i.e. the information technology, the Berlin Wall etc., the picture of an organic, artistic/intellectual emerges, which incidentally is the protagonist of the last story, who has reached ultimately the "Final Continent" after traversing through two straggling Continents.

So, while negotiating the distances of the culturally bound souls, she makes us see the indicator of the 'beyond,' prompted by the need to rewrite on the tabula rasa of newborn consciousness. In other words, 'beyond' is also the signifier, that signifies the boundaries of humanism which can and should be stretched to Infinity to accommodate the First World, Second World and Third World global people. All her ordinary characters point to a very extraordinary revelation. They are all "Amritasya Putra" as Upanishad calls human beings, the children of heavenly bliss. Gifted with such immense possibilities and immense resilience, they can never be restricted within the truncated existence of specificities of particular cultural situations.

To the common assumption that diasporic studies generally nurture voices of differences and dissensions, Lahiri's book gives a lie. With patronizing amicability she probes into the confused vision of the diasporic characters. And so, going through the conflicts between cultural hegemony and untutored spontaneity and the dispossessed man's obsessive attachment with memory, history, roots, identity, her text construes itself only in terms of the search for 'beyond.' With Chaucerian compassionate irony and perspicacious observation of a child placed so ideally in some of her stories, she sees and deals with the diasporic and other traumas of the dispossessed ones. Dispossession, as she sees it, could be from the home, state, security, trust, faith, love. So, dispossessed of her scanty bearings, Boori Ma's figure recedes into darkness, as helpless, penniless, she takes to yet another exile, "she shook the free end of her sari, but nothing rattled." (82) Paradoxically enough dispossessed of her virginity, Bibi Haldar gets cured of her strange psychosomatic disease.

As the diasporic literature brings to focus the mixed racial, national and cultural identities formed from dislocations, it also brings to focus the celebration of the hybrid self, thus redefining the metaphor of home. Home is where the heart is, no doubt, but heart that is free from the strings of rigid, monolithic, cultural manifestations, religious dogmas, or, behavioural fixations. "In the Mapparium that day, all the countries had seemed close enough to touch" (108-9) remarks one of her characters who just had lost her love. Yet, the need to rebuild is not lost, as the story ends with the hint of the region, 'beyond,' "she bought a cup of coffee nearby and sat on one of the benches in the plaza outside the Church, gazing at its giant pillars, and its massive dome, and at the clear blue sky spread over the city." (110) The dispossession from the values of life is as terrible as the diasporic identity crises, she seems to say as she goes on presenting the maladies of the homeless ("The Blessed House," "A Real Durwan"), valueless ("Sexy," "Interpreter of Maladies," "The Treatment of Bibi Haldar"), meaningless ("A Temporary Matter"), rootless ("A Real Durwan," "When Mr. Pirzada Came to Dine") people.

Lahiri's writing is ultimately transcultural that traces the need for cultural citizenry, that acknowledges the impossibility of confining migrant writing within the straitjacket of national or regional labels. Hence the need to reach 'beyond,' to the moon perhaps, crossing all sorts of boundaries. Once endowed with that vision, the conclusion comes easy, etched out in the concluding paragraph of the last story of the book, as the character muses: "While the Astronauts, heroes forever, spent mere hours on the moon, I have remained in this new world for nearly 30 years . . . still there are times I am bewildered by each mile I have traveled, each meal I have eaten, each person I have known, each room in which I have slept. As ordinary as it all appears, there are times when it is beyond my imagination." (198) This is her salute to the astonishing resilience of human sprit, his urge for survival against all odds. As the postcolonial literatures are breaking up in diverse fragments, discussing the diversities of place, race, ethnicity, religion, politics et al, her book, placed in an international ambience and shared multicultural experiences, attempts to bridge the gaps through friendship, generosity and tolerance aiming for a new cultural synthesis that promotes cultural plurality through global understanding.

NOTES

1. Krishna Dutta and Andrew Robinson, *Rabindranath Tagore, The Myriad Minded Man* (Rupa, 1997), p. 353.
2. Jhumpa Lahiri, *Interpreter of Maladies* (New Delhi: HarperCollins 1999).

Meaningful Whispers: The Short Stories of Jhumpa Lahiri

O.P. MATHUR

E.M. Forster's "Only connect" has been superseded by all-round globalization and consequent cross-fertilization of different cultures. Its cultural, intellectual and emotional dimensions are being explored in the literature of the diaspora which, on account of its increasing richness, variety and comprehensive coverage, seems to be growing into an independent branch of literature, truly 'inter-national' in its parameters. Its writers, portraying the social, marital, professional and other types of inter-mixture, become the vehicles, sometimes themselves the arenas, of their interaction which has far-reaching impact upon the personalities of the individuals involved. One of the latest born of this diasporic hierarchy, catapulted to the elite of Pulitzer awardees with only one frail collection of nine short stories, is Jhumpa Lahiri, almost a literary phenomenon by herself. She has treated in her own simple, sincere and yet ironic mode the problem of centre, double vision, ambiguity of the ground beneath the writer's feet. She goes on to define her position by viewing herself as an "interpreter of the emotions of pain and affliction."[1] As an interpreter she is also, like her characters, occupying "a middle position,"[2] poised between the two cultures of the East and the West, though there seems to be a marked tilt towards her native land. She goes to the extent of confessing, "I went to Calcutta neither as a tourist nor as a former resident—a valuable position. I think as a writer. I learned to observe things as an outsider and yet I also knew that as different as Calcutta is from Rhode Island, *I belonged there in some fundamental ways I didn't seem to belong in the United States.*"[3]

Out of the nine stories included in her prize-winning book *Interpreter of Maladies*[4] with the sub-title "Stories of Bengal, Boston and Beyond," seven deal with Indian-American interaction, while two exclusively treat the Indian characters in the backdrops of traditional beliefs, superstitions and ways of life. Even in these stories the two narrative attitudes of the author are clearly noticeable—the deeply sympathetic for the fate of a low-caste woman Boori Ma (i.e old mother) in "A Real Durwan," and the ironical one in a female victim of superstition carving out a place for herself in "The Treatment of Bibi Haldar." These two stories focus on some of the important maladies of Indian society. But it is the title story that deserves special consideration, for Jhumpa Lahiri herself has revealed, "When I was putting the collection together, I knew from the beginning that this had to be the title story, for I think it best expresses, thematically, the predicament at the heart of the book—the dilemma, the difficulty, and often the impossibility of communicating emotional pain and affliction to others, as well as expressing it to ourselves."[5] The word 'maladies' is well chosen, for it is a neutral word, comprehensive in its connotation, which can cover anything 'abnormal,' from the mild to the more serious, deviating from the norms of one's native culture, arousing in the observer or interpreter reactions from irony to sympathy. Whatever persona the author adopts—a character involved in the action, an amused, but careful observer, a mediator, or a physician—her stories are vehicles of self-exploration and fulfillment. In the title story the East and the West brush past each other for a while, with the difference that where a local Indian Mr. Kapasi, a tourist-guide and taxi-driver, takes an Americanized Indian family of Mr. Das to see the sun-temple at Konark. This brief business-like encounter reveals how far the Indian characters settled in the West have traveled from their cultural roots. Mr. Das does what is unthinkable In India—he refers to his wife by her first name 'Mina' while talking about her to their small children, and Mrs. Das, only after some bickering, agrees to such a small thing as taking their little daughter Tina to the toilet and that too only after Mr. Das points out that he had given the child her bath the day before. Matters even more serious lie beneath this surface relationship. Their son Bobby is not Mr. Das's son. The lady takes her adulterous relationship with another man so lightly that she casually reveals this fact for the first time to a total stranger like Mr. Kapasi in a far-off land. Her behaviour with Mr. Kapasi borders on flirtation, not unusual in Western society, so that the poor man, slightly self-opinionated, fancies that she is somewhat serious, for she even says that they "have a lot in common." (46) Such behaviour, coupled with the sight of Mrs. Das's body-contours prominent in her tight-fitting dress, goes to the head of Mr. Kapasi, who is probably unused to being treated by a beautiful foreign lady with so much interest, which for him is "mildly intoxicating." (53) When Mr. Kapasi thinks once again how she had said "romantic," the feeling of intoxication grows. (53) This seems to have reached its climax when Mrs. Das asks him for his address, which also makes him dream of becoming even "an interpreter between nations." (59) But his dream is based on a miscalculation of the nature of Mrs. Das. Would the lady who could disregard the marital tie by adultery continue to be friendly to him, a complete stranger in a distant land? Her words so readily lapped by him were for her no more than a casual and light manner of passing time. On her opening her bag, the slip of paper containing Mr. Kapasi's address flies off unnoticed except by him. This is the end of Mr. Kapasi's 'romance' and also of his dream of becoming an interpreter between nations, but it seems to highlight the author's identical objective in the book.

These three stories are located in Bengal. The backdrop of the others is "Boston and Beyond," "Beyond" probably standing for their emotional and spiritual reaching out. A striking story that stands by itself is "Mrs. Sen's" in which Mrs. Sen does baby-sitting for Eliot who is apparently between infancy and boyhood. For Mrs. Sen 'home' means India (116) and her only identity is that of being the wife of Mr. Sen, a teacher of mathematics. Her style of life is almost completely Indian—her outfit consisting of a Sari, vermilion in the parting of her hair, a dot on the forehead, her taste for fish, her cooking in the traditional Indian way down to the knife for pealing and slicing vegetables having a curved blade "like the prow of a Viking ship." (114) As in most Indian families, she has strong ties of affection, and is much upset at the news of her grandfather's death while, contrastingly, even the small American boy Eliot can entertain the thought of putting his mother, when old, in a nursing home. (131) She toys with the silly idea of driving right upto Calcutta and unsuccessfully tries to learn driving, getting involved in a minor accident after which Eliot, though uninjured, is withdrawn by his father from Mrs. Sen's baby-sitting, ironically referred to in the title as "Mrs. Sen's" as if it were a regular institute. Thus end Mrs. Sen's few and half-hearted efforts at getting properly adjusted in the West. Like Mrs. Sen, Mr. Pirzada of the story "Mr. Pirzada Came to Dine" is a Bengali, an East Pakistani who in the course of the story itself becomes a Bangladeshi. He too, like most Indians, is deeply attached to his native place Dacca (the time of which he keeps in his pocket-watch) and his large family of seven daughters back home. While in the U.S.A., he dines every day with an Indian family, of which the small daughter Lilia is the narrator of the story. She is the special object of Mr. Pirzada's affection and so is the best observer of his nature and behaviour. The child-narrator cannot understand the difference between an Indian, a Pakistani and a Bangladeshi, for Mr. Pirzada successively embodies all the three identities which are essentially one for which political divisions are merely notional. Even the long foreign stay of Mr. Pirzada can make no difference to it. The Indian family, while participating in Christian festivals like Halloween, wishes for the safety of Mr. Pirzada's family. The resilient essential Indianness of both parties remains unaffected.

Two stories deal with the problem of inter-relationship of Indo-American couples in a land with different cultural and social norms. In "The Blessed House," the wife Twinkle goes on finding Christian icons in a house into which they have recently moved. Broadminded and tolerant, she likes them and uses them as decoration pieces, but her husband Sanjeev is utterly irritated and begins to hate the icons. The visitors admire them, and ultimately the husband also falls in line with his wife. The all-embracing nature of essential Indianness even in an alien ambience underlies the story. The theme of another story "A Temporary Matter" is also basically similar. The working wife of an Indian couple, Shoba, apparently influenced by the Western stance on the independence of women and the prevalence of separation and divorce, decides to live separately from her husband and even hires an apartment for herself. The catalytic factor was the apparent absence of her husband from the clinic where she delivered her stillborn child and, being unconscious, could not even know its sex. After this they already started avoiding each other. Shoba has not the heart to convey her feelings directly to her husband. Luckily for her, the electricity department announces a power-cut for five days, giving her an opportunity to exchange pieces of information, till now kept secret, in semi-darkness. Shoba's revelation of her plan for separate living makes her husband Shukumar shock her by the fact that their child was male and that he had held him in his arms. These searing revelations made by them to wound each other really unite them in a flood of tears—their reunion being symbolized by the Bradford couple, walking arm in arm on the road outside. Shukumar and Shoba return to the Indian mores after the resolution of 'a temporary matter,' the roots of which lay in the conventionally Indian desire for a male child.

Another story in which the Indian outlook on life sets things right is "Sexy," the title of which refers to one of the chief pursuits of the Western man. Western social life has almost become sex-centered, in which genuine love and friendship have been largely usurped by sex. The chief character Miranda, a professional 'mistress' selling her body, has recently got a catch in Dev whose wife is away for some time. Near the beginning of the story, Miranda gets a glimpse into the Indian psyche when unknowingly his Indian acquaintance Laxmi comments on the adulterous behaviour of her cousin's husbands, "If I were her I'd fly straight to London and shoot them both." (97) Ultimately Laxmi gets a divorce and sends her intelligent seven-year old son Rohin to Laxmi. When at Miranda's place, Rohin calls her "sexy," defining it as "loving someone you don't know." (107)

Rohin also sleeps by her side as if she were his mother. All this makes her realize the depths to which she has fallen when even Dev, an Indian of recent acquaintance, can come and enter her like an animal without speaking a word. (93) She therefore starts avoiding Dev's weekly visits under some pretext or the other and returns to her traditional values symbolized by the church and its giant pillars and a dear blue sky spread over the city (110) against which all evil is dwarfed.

The last story "The Third and Final Continent" also deals with an Indian couple. It is narrated in the first person by the male protagonist, for in it the author wants to portray from within his gradual adjustment with the West. At first he is an 'outsider' but his admiration for his 103-year-old landlady Mrs. Crofts, her exaggerated pride in the American achievement of sending a man on the moon and her clinging to customs, at least a century old, endears her to him so much that after his marriage he brings his wife Mala, herself brought up in Indian traditions, to meet the old lady, who on noticing that she has been following her own cultural norms, calls her 'a perfect lady.' Mala also gradually gets adjusted to American life. The happy spiritual journey of both the protagonist and Mala is portrayed intimately from within—their mutual adjustment making him amazed "that there was ever a time that we were strangers." (197) With a growing son, they attain contentment and happiness in this "third continent," which is also the final one for them. But still the protagonist's Indian moorings occasionally haunt him, as perhaps they still haunt the writer who says, "I am so much more American than they [i.e. her parents] are. In fact, it is still very hard to think of myself as an American." It appears that the Indian 'past' of the protagonist too is embedded deeply in the "Beyond" of his imagination, as it is in that of the author herself who, according to press reports, is going to marry an American, but in Calcutta and according to traditional customs.[6] When the protagonist of the story pores out his nostalgia in the following words, he might well be his creator's mouthpiece:

> I know that my achievement is quite ordinary. I am not the only man to seek his fortune far from home, and certainly I am not the first. Still there are times I am bewildered by each mile I have traveled, each meal I have eaten, each person I have known, each room in which I have slept, as ordinary as it all appears, there are times when it is beyond my imagination. (198)

Jhumpa Lahiri also says, "America is home to me but I feel I am an outsider too."[7] This feeling seems to be common at least among all first-generation expatriates. Ashis Gupta, another such writer, also voices the same feeling in his Interview, "So you will always have people who will come back with the sense of longing for something that is irretrievably lost."[8]

Jhumpa Lahiri's stories are rightly celebrated, for they have a variety of fragrances, subtle nuances of their own. They are deceptively simple on the surface like the calm waters of a deep river. She describes in detail the ripples, only giving to careful reader hints of the deep currents which reveal their forceful significance only when west made to dive, usually at the end. "A Temporary Matter," for instance, is a masterpiece of suggestivity in which the reality underneath Shoba's behaviour is revealed at the very end. This device is reinforced by narrative strategy. Many of the stories have a narrator, sharply observant and with his heart and soul in the right place, who can unveil the layers of reality with an effective seasoning of irony and pathos, simple description and narration, flashbacks and fantasies, streams of thought with dialogues reduced to the minimum. A few of the stories have one of the characters as narrators. This type of narration, whenever used, is a necessary requirement for discerning the point of the story. The basic simplicities of human affection and the irrationality of the Partition can best be rendered through the mind of a child-narrator as in "Mr. Pirzada Came to Dine." In two of the stories, the narrators rightly remain unnamed for they have a representative character. A neighbour is the unnamed narrator in "The Treatment of Bibi Haldar" in which a hysteric girl, supposed to be under the influence of witchcraft is badly treated, often tormented by a superstitious and orthodox society and ultimately treated or cured of her disease when fate makes her independent and she begins to stand on her own feet. Similarly, an unnamed young protagonist, coming to America and then finally getting adjusted, though not without nostalgic moods, and settled there with his Indian wife and son, is representative of a large majority of first-generation Indian Americans.

The sophistication of Jhumpa Lahiri's narrative art is perhaps best revealed in her subtle exposure of the deep structure of her meaning through uncomplicated plots, characters and style, "the extraordinariness of experience . . . evoked by the ordinariness of expression."[9] Some of her stories deal either with the revelation of the essential features of the personalities of their characters or their evolution. But the most significant of them present a sudden transformation springing from their roots, the silent control of their genetic cultural construct. The primary message that seems to permeate the stories is like out of cultivating the best of modernity by a mutually advantageous intermingling of the best in the East and the West, both purified of the accretions of evils and distortions which have disfigured their essence. Her stories thus have global relevance, though they convey their meeting so unobtrusively. Hers is the art of silences suggestive of a 'stream of conscience,' both Indian and universal at the same time, "that peculiarly novelistic continuum, inner-and-outer dialectics of the novel, event by event, under the aspect of an ethical faint"[10]

NOTES

1. Lavina Melwani, "Interpreting Exile," *The Hindustan Times,* Magazine, April 23, 2000, p. 1.
2. INAS, *The Hindustan Times,* April 15, 2000, p. 24.
3. Lavina Melwani, my italics.
4. *Ibid.*
5. *Ibid.*
6. *The Hindustan Times,* September 25, 2000, p. 1.
7. Sumit Mitra with Arthur J. Pais, "Boston Brahmin," *India Today,* April 24, 2000, p. 73.

8. Veena Singh, "The Fragile Self-Image of an Immigrant Writer: Interview with Ashis Gupta," Jasbir Jain, *Writers of Indian Diaspora: Theory and Practice*, p. 212.
9. Gowri Ramnarayan, "Elegant Outsider," *The Hindu*, Literary Review, April 16, 2000, p. IX.
10. Alan Friedman, "The Stream of Conscience," James L. Caldarwood and Harold J. Toliver, *Perspectives on Fiction* (OUP, 1968), p. 383.
11. Jhumpa Lahiri, *Interpreter* of *Maladies* (HarperCollins India, 1999).

In Other Worlds: Reading "When Mr. Pirzada Came to Dine"

SUSHILA SINGH

Edward Said calls for revision in the two aspects of the intellectual frameworks of literature. First, the idea that literature exists within a national framework, and second, the assumption that a literary object exists in a stable or consistently identifiable form, need to be revised. It is commonly accepted that an autonomous aesthetic realm exists, yet how it exists in relation to history, politics, social structures is difficult to specify. Questions and doubts about these have eroded the formerly perdurable national and aesthetic frameworks, limits, and boundaries. The notion of author, of work, of nation is no more dependable. Along with that, the role of imagination, once the central one, and of identity has undergone a total change. Migration and electronic mediation acquire the shaping role in the production of contemporary culture. Changes such as diasporic communities replace settled ones and new mythologies and fantasies energize and also deaden the mind adding to the complexities of location.

The role of writing (literature) in relation to nation has changed tremendously in the twentieth century. Writers have dealt with the interaction between language and literature and a "nation's culture." The recent years have witnessed a major shift towards postnational focus. Challenges to national definitions from within and the forces of globalization have weakened the idea of the nation in many ways. There have been continuities and differences and in the new millennium context becomes important in locating meaning in writing. Writers like Jhumpa Lahiri endeavour to apply the knowledge gained from the past to the questions of the present and the future. Jhumpa Lahiri grapples with the question of grasping reality in today's world and thus intrudes on the hegemonic structures. While addressing these questions she also tries to come out of a disputed aspect of the past—the current rise of the idea of postcoloniality. As Amitav Ghosh believes, under the rubric of postcoloniality, there is an attempt towards a particular "memorialization of Empire."[1]

Imperialism has fractured and dehumanized the world and its people. One such story is told by Jhumpa Lahiri in "When Mr. Pirzada Came to Dine."[2] The narrator, ten year old Lilia, remembers that in 1971 Mr. Pirzada from Dacca used to visit and spend his evenings very often with her parents in the university campus located in the north of Boston. At that time Pakistan was engaged in civil war, the East Pakistan was fighting the West Pakistan for autonomy. Mr. Pirzada's town Dacca had been invaded by the Pakistani army and civilians were subjected to mass scale atrocities. Even teachers were dragged to streets and killed. It is believed that more than three hundred thousand people had died then. Mr. Pirzada held a lectureship in Botany at the Dacca University and lived there with his wife and seven daughters. Mr. Pirzada was in America on a fellowship from the government of Pakistan during the time of the civil war, carrying out research on the foliage of New England. Though the fellowship was a great honour to Mr. Pirzada but when converted into dollars it was very meagre. As a result, Mr. Pirzada lived somehow in a virtually bare graduate dormitory. And, he came to Lilia's house to eat dinner and watch the evening news.

Lilia's parents missed their homeland. Immigrant Indians and other South Asians are closely and poignantly bound to their countries of origin, knowing well the homelands they leave behind can never be regained. The twentieth century has witnessed millions of such lonesome disconnections. Yearning to be connected to their part of the world, it was Lilia's parents' destiny to search for compatriots through the university directory every new semester. They lived in a different world and were disturbed that "supermarket did not carry mustard oil, doctors did not make house call, neighbours never dropped by without invitation." (24) One such search discovered Mr. Pirzada for them, promptly they phoned him and invited him to dinner.

Lilia called him "the Indian man" and was corrected by her father that Mr. Pirzada was not considered any longer an "Indian, not since Partition." Lilia was told that India was divided in 1947. But that date for her was the date of India's independence from the British rule. Her father said, "That too one moment we were free and then we were sliced up like a pie. Hindus here Muslim there. Dacca no longer belongs to us." (25) Ten-year-old Lilia thought it to be so unreasonable. Mr. Pirzada and her parents "spoke the same language, laughed at the same jokes, looked more or less the same. They ate pickled mangoes with their meals, ate rice every night for supper with their hands." Like her parents, "Mr. Pirzada took off his shoes before entering a room, chewed fennel seeds after meals as a digestive, drank no alcohol." (25) Where is Huntington's clash of civilizations.[3] Rather the same people are divided due to the struggle over geography. As Edward Said says, "that struggle is complex and interesting because it is not only about soldiers and cannons but also about ideas, about forms, about images and imaginings."[4]

How geography and historical experience change identities is addressed by Jhumpa Lahiri in her narrator's inability in understanding how Mr. Pirzada could take offence if addressed as an Indian. "Mr. Pirzada is Bengali, but he is a Muslim, therefore he lives in East Pakistan, not India," Lilia's father informed her. And then he became angry, "What exactly do they teach you at school? Do you study History? Geography?" he snarled. She is shown India's map—trailing across Atlantic, through Europe, the Mediterranean, the Middle East, and then to the sprawling diamond that her mother told her once resembled a woman wearing a sari with her left arm extending out. Lilia is trying with great difficulty to recognize her parents' country—Bharat Mata—a different country shown on the map in a different colour. She notices that Pakistan is separated by an expanse of Indian territory. For her, it was as if California and Connecticut constituted a nation apart from the U.S. (26) Lilia's father's frustration at her ignorance and the state of education is obvious:

"What is she learning?" Lilia is learning what she needs to learn in America, now distanced and cut off from India. Her mother pronounced proudly: "We live here [America] now, she was born here." She was happy that Lilia was assured a safe life, an easy life, a fine education, every opportunity. She would not be forced to eat rationed food or obey curfew, or watch riots from rooftops, or hide neighbors in water tanks to prevent them from being shot as her parents had. Lilia is saved from all hazards of growing up in India: "Imagine having to place her in a decent school. Imagine her having to read during power failures in the light of kerosene lamps. Imagine the pressures, the tutors, the constant exams." She is so critical of the Indian education situation. She questions her husband, "How can you possibly expect her to know about Pakistan?" For her mother Lilia is a smart kid. She knows all American history and American geography. Students there constantly study the Revolutionary War, go on field trips to Plymouth Rock, walk the Freedom Trail, climb the Bunker Hill Monument—idolize George Washington and make puppets of King George. It was a matter of pride for her mother that when it came to telling the names of the thirty colonies with dates and capitals, Lilia could do it with her eyes closed.

So Mr. Pirzada of East Pakistan usually arrived at six o'clock and was greeted formally by Lilia's father. Though he was no longer a stranger to them, Mr. Pirzada was always impeccably suited and scarved with silk tie knotted at his collar. He was a compact man in his various ensembles of plums, olives and chocolate browns. He wore on his head a black fez and preferred to walk from his dormitory, a brisk twenty minute walk. Mr. Pirzada appeared so very exquisitely different to Lilia. While hanging his coat on the rack, Lilia noticed that there were no recognizable tags inside his finely checkered gray-and-blue wool coat with striped lining and horn buttons. There was a hand stitched label "Z Syeed, suitors" embroidered on it with glossy black thread. Customized tailored suits are not to be seen in the U.S.—only with brand names and readymade suits there. Entering Lilia's 'Indian' home with the trauma of war in his homeland, Mr. Pirzada quipped, "Another refugee, I am afraid, on Indian territory." Lilia's father informed him that the number of refugees was estimated at about nine million, who came to India as refugees in the 1971 war. Relishing mincemeat kebabs with coriander chutney in the Indian home, Mr. Pirzada wished that Dacca's refugees were as heartily fed in India.

Lilia was charmed by the presence of Mr. Pirzada's elegance and flattered by the seeming theatricality of his attentions as he handed out to her chocolates, honey-filled lozenges or raspberry truffles saying, "For the lady of the house," with an almost imperceptible bow. She could not even thank him, once when she did, he immediately demanded, "What is this thank-you? The lady at the bank thanks me, the cashier at the shop thanks me, the librarian thanks me when I return an overdue book, the overseas operator thanks me as she tries to connect me to Dacca and fails. If I am buried in this country I will be thanked, no doubt, at my funeral." (29) Mr. Pirzada somehow could not get used to this custom of American politeness.

Lilia coveted the candies Mr. Pirzada gave her as she would covet a jewel or a coin from a buried kingdom. Particularly because in some strange manner it connected her to her grandmother she had never known. She would treasure the candy in a small keepsake box made of carved sandalwood, which belonged to her grandmother where she used to store the ground areca nuts she would eat after her morning bath.

Mr. Pirzada had two watches—one plain silver watch he kept in his breast pocket set to the local time in Dacca, eleven hours ahead of the time in New England. The other was with a band on his wrist. He always took out his pocket watch and kept on his folded paper napkin during the meal. Lilia felt very uneasy when she comprehended that life was being lived in Dacca first. In America, their meals, their actions, were only a shadow of what had already happened in Dacca, "a lagging ghost of where Mr. Pirzada really belonged." (31)

Evening after evening, Mr. Pirzada and Lilia's father anxiously watched news on television—it was a catastrophe that ten year old Lilia could not comprehend but she prayed that Mr. Pirzada's family was safe and sound back in Dacca. While she heard her parents and Mr. Pirzada talking and anticipating the birth of another nation on the other side of the world, India and Pakistan drew closer to war with Dacca insisting on independence. The U.S. was siding with the West Pakistan while the Soviet Union with India and what was to become Bangladesh. On December 4, war was declared; after twelve days Pakistani army surrendered in Dacca. The anxiety for relatives and family members in that part of the world brought Lilia's parents and Mr. Pirzada very close, "operating during that time as if they were a single person sharing a single meal, a single body, a single silence and a single fear." (41)

In January, Mr. Pirzada returned to his three storey home in Dacca and Lilia and her parents did not hear from him for long. Lilia would sometimes study the map and try to visualize Mr. Pirzada on the small patch of yellow on the world map, perspiring heavily in one of his suits and searching for his family. But the map had become outdated—a new country had been carved out—the world had been further partitioned.

As I was reading Jhumpa Lahiri's "When Mr. Pirzada Came to Dine" unsettling headlines like "Musharraf's handshake leaves India Cold" (*The Times of India*, 6 January 2002) appeared. How identities change, (General Musharraf) born Indian, changed to Pakistani with partition, ironically today fighting the country of his origin. One suddenly becomes aware of the questions of nationalism, identity, narrative, and ethnicity.

NOTES

1. Amitav Ghosh, Letter to Sandra Vince, Prizes Manager, Commonwealth Foundation, dated 18 March 2001.
2. Jhumpa Lahiri, "When Mr. Pirzada Came to Dine," *Interpreter of Maladies: Stories of Bengal, Boston and Beyond* (New Delhi: HarperCollins India, 1999).
3. Samuel P. Huntington, *The Clash of Civilizations* (New York: Simon and Schuster, 1996).
4. Edward W. Said, *Culture and Imperialism* (New York: Vintage Books, 1994), p. 7.

Imagining Homelands: Bharati Mukherjee and Jhumpa Lahiri

RUDRA PRASAD MAHTO

Canada and India are the members of the Commonwealth countries and by and large they enjoy cordial relations at present. The two countries have worked shoulder to shoulder in a number of fields, for example, in the United Nations' peacekeeping, fighting apartheid and the peaceful use of nuclear power. If India has the second largest population of the globe, Canada has the second largest land mass. Both are multicultural countries.

Despite the importance of geography in the national folklore it is the multicultural nature of Canada—and the efforts that have been made to protect and promote equality rights in the same context. With the exception of the aboriginal People Canada is a nation of immigrants.

Moreover, immigration patterns have changed significantly over the past few decades. While the vast majority of immigrants to Canada once came from Europe, these days immigrants come from Southeast Asia, Africa and the Caribbean. As a result more than nine percent of Canada's population are members of racial minorities, or as they are often referred to in Canada 'Visible' minorities. In some Canadian cities like Toronto and Vancouver, the visible minority population is over twenty percent.

As far as India is concerned, the writers writing in English seem to have decided that the object of their imagination has to be the mother country. One may use the term 'mother country' in the same way as one uses the term 'mother ship'—the original source with which one retains ties at the same time having gained a distance from it.

For these writers whether in Canada, New York or London, the mother country is India. They inhabit inflatable rubber boat on the choppy seas between two continents, which are solid and ossified. But their vision of India is different. This is not the same India that we or for that matter writers who have not ventured beyond the Indian imagination see. In fact, these writers challenge the notion that there is a fixed way of creatively encountering India.

Jhumpa Lahiri writing about disfunctional Indians in America, Amit Chaudhuri describing the travails of 'coming back home,' or Shauna Singh Baldwin narrating the many *discrepancies* that exist between 'home' and 'new home' are as representative of the Indian imagination as any tale hinged around the partition. For writers dipping into this East-West cauldron which deals with the tensions and connections between India and abroad, one can use the term 'diaspora literature.'

Diaspora in the modern world may have different contexts. Expatriation works both as a physical displacement as well as a socio-cultural and psychosomatic identity question. Cultural cross-currents have led to a hybrid culture and a new process of cultural assimilation. A mixed cultural milieu opens up new vistas of communication and dialogue in this cosmopolitan world. As a result, diasporic reciprocation has become one of the recurrent themes in post-colonial world literature.

At the core of diaspora literature is the idea of the nation state. Although fiction is not in any way just an aesthetic extension of political theory, immigrant writers with their focus on India primarily deal with the fiction caused by disparate cultures. The cultural borders perceived by most diaspora writers are, quite understandably, drawn along national lines. In a world without nation states, these writers would have merged with others who deal with cultural confrontations of all kinds. But diaspora literature focuses on (cultural) states that are defined by immigration counters and stamps on one's passport.

For writers dealing with the meeting of disparate cultures occurs on various geographic levels: village-city, city-city, country-country. For the writers of diaspora literature, however, cultural 'rendezvouses' are restricted to those between countries. This is obviously because the authors themselves are dislocated along national lines. Culture clash, the process and resulting guilt of fleeing a restrictive background or tradition, the problem of being displaced from one's own culture and finding oneself in a totally new environment—these are problems for growing numbers of individuals in today's world. In such a situation where the individual is seen as culturally, linguistically or sometimes psychologically estranged, the whole question of individual's identity becomes an unattainable ideal. Writers like Bharati Mukherjee and Jhumpa Lahiri, however, stylistically different they are—write from their own experience of hanging in limbo between two identities: non-Indian and Indian.

The writing of Bharati Mukherjee focuses on the rootlessness caused by diaspora. Physical uprootedness creates within the concerned section of the population a sense of being marginalised and thereby leading a sense of 'otherness' within the geo-political territory to which they have migrated. These immigrants are placed in a situation of both mental and physical diaspora. These writings address important issues of selfhood ethnic and communal identity as well as the nuances and effects of a hybrid culture. The Canadian mosaic of a variety of cultural milieus has led to a unique form of multiculturalism.

Bharati Mukherjee describes her isolation in Canada due to her paradoxical position of being "both too visible and too invisible"[1] in *Days and Nights in Calcutta* while her colour made her too visible, as a writer she was invisible. She recalls, "the media had made me self-conscious about racism, I detect arrogance in the slow-footedness of sales-clerks."[2] After becoming a U.S. citizen in 1988, looking back at her life in Canada (1966-1980), Mukherjee recognises herself as an expatriate there who had clung to her ethnic identity. She traces this position of hers to the ideology of the Canadian mosaic which reinforced the stance of expatriation by encouraging the maintenance of the special characteristics and differences of the native culture: "I was a psychological expatriate though a naturalized Canadian for fifteen years simply because Canada is a country officially hostile to the concept of assimilation. Perceiving myself to be in a comfortable but unwelcoming environment, I struggled to maintain various emblems of my difference."[3]

However, the Canadian policy is vindicated by social psychology. The importance of keeping ethnicity alive is recognised by social scientists who see it as a defence against facelessness and rootlessness.

Not only in the personal and political writings of Mukherjee, but even in her fiction written in Canada, the experience of expatiation is reflected very much. Both in *The Tiger's Daughter* and *Wife*, the protagonists Tara and Dimple are expatriates, geographically as well as in mind and spirit. They share the expatriate characteristic of being ill-at-ease both in the native culture and in the alien one. In these novels, expatriation is not only a major theme but it becomes a metaphor for deeper levels of alienation like existential alienation and self-estrangement. This is revealed in some significant images used in these novels. In *The Tiger's Daughter*, Hotel Catelli Continental described as the "navel of the Universe" (3) becomes an important symbol of a rootless existence, a symbol of Tara's expatriate sensibility. In *Wife* the cage is an important symbol. It stands for a comfortable but restricted existence for isolation and a denial of freedom. It is significant that Dimple kills her husband after watching a TV programme in which a birdcage figured prominently.

In the collection of stories entitled *Darkness* (1985) four were written in Canada, in Montreal and Toronto. They are "The World according to Hsu," "Isolated Incidents," "Hindus" and "Courtly Vision." Mukherjee comments on these stories in her introduction: "The purely Canadian stories in this collection were difficult to write and even more painful to live through. They are uneasy stories about expatriation." (2)

"In the World according to Hsu," Ratna, of Indian origin, and her husband Graeme Clayton, a Canadian Professor of Psychology at McGill University, Montreal are on holiday at an island off the coast of Africa. It is said that he went there to see the Southern Cross and to persuade Ratna to move from French dominant Montreal to English dominant Toronto where the University had offered her the Chair in Personality Development. Ratna prefers Montreal because there she was merely English that is an English-speaking Canadian whereas in Toronto she would not be Canadian not even Indian. She would be labelled a Paki.

The title of the story is derived from an article in *The Scientific American* by Kenneth J. Hsu, read by Graeme during the holiday. The article dealt with a time when the world was a single land mass six million years ago. Then came the collision of continents and separation. The worldview of Hsu thus becomes a metaphor. There is perhaps a longing for the world according to Hsu, a world free from cultural collisions, dilemmas and separation.

While the previous story was mainly from the expatriate's point of view, in the short story "Isolated Incidents," the expatriate is viewed from the point of view of the native Canadian Anne Vane whose job is to file complaints from immigrants on problems concerning Human Rights. Two specific cases of racial discrimination in Toronto are brought to her notice—that of Dr. Supariwala and John Mohan Persawd. Anne Vane's detached view of the cases is mingled with irony. She knows the futility of her work in documenting such cases. Nothing would ultimately come out of it: "Torontonians were proud of their subway, their politeness and of their moral spotlessness. This after all was not New York. Assault on John Mohan Persawd and dozens like him would always be considered isolated incidents not racial." (82-83). The title is ironic. Cases of discrimination towards the visible minority will not be related to racism but will always be ignored as isolated Incidents.

In "Hindus," Mukherjee juxtaposes an expatriate against an immigrant to draw out the contrast. Leela Lahiri reveals an immigrant's fluid identity. She proudly declares, "I am an American citizen" (133) but she is also proud of her Bengali Brahmin Past. Maharajah Patwant Singh of Gotlah is an obvious expatriate with a grievance against India. When Leela and the Maharajah meet after two years, the Maharaja is writing his memories.

While he parades his pain and grievance, Leela celebrates rebirth in a new world.

After analysing the characters in this collection of short stories, we come to conclusion that the theme of expatriation is linked to fragmented, disintegrating alienated characters, while the immigrants are fairly adjusted to the new country and its life style. Canada and the U.S.A. may be seen as objective correlatives of Mukherjee's personal quest from alienation to integration.

Born in London to parents who emigrated from India, Jhumpa Lahiri has been writing since the age of seven. She was raised in Rhode Island, visited India several times and so is able to mirror both worlds. In fact, Calcutta recurs in her stories time and again, a bustling unruly city, so different from the small New England town where she was raised. She says: "I went to Calcutta neither as a tourist nor as a former resident—a valuable position, I think as a writer. I learnt to observe things as an outsider and yet I also knew that as different as Calcutta is from Rhode Island, I belonged there in some fundamental way in the way I didn't seem to belong in the United States."[4]

Jhumpa Lahiri has won the Pulitzer Prize for *Interpreter of Maladies*, a collection of short stories which echoes the cultural displacement of South Asian Immigrants as they try to fit into the jigsaw puzzle of a fast-changing America.

Lahiri herself is an interpreter of maladies, able to touch the pulse point of immigrant angst—the story of people who are caught between two worlds aid belong to neither. As she says, "The older I get, the more aware am I that I have somehow inherited a sense of exile from my parents, even though in many ways—superficial ones largely—I am so much more American than they are. In fact it is still very hard to think of myself as an American."[5]

Lahiri's title story "Interpreter of Maladies" was selected for both the O'Henry Award and the Best American short story. She hit upon the title after a chance encounter with a man who interpreted for a doctor whose patients could not speak English. She says, "when I was cutting the collection together, I knew from the beginning that this had to be the title story, because I think it best expresses thematically, the predicament at the heart of the book—the dilemma, the difficulty and often the impossibility of communicating emotional pain and affliction to others, as well as expressing it to ourselves. In some senses I view my position as a writer, insofar as I attempt to articulate these actions as a sort of interpreter as well."[6]

To conclude I may say that all writers may end up writing diaspora literature because they write about what they experience most forcefully. Or may be the English language itself, not automatically associated with Indianness in which many Indian writers are writing today, carries the seed of Salman Rushdie's inquiries about East versus West, home versus abroad.

NOTES

1. Clark Blaise and Bharati Mukherjee, *Days and Nights in Calcutta* (New York: Doubleday, 1977), p. 169.
2. *Ibid.*
3. Bharati Mukherjee "Immigrant Writing: Give Us Your Maximalists," *The New York Times Book Review*, Aug. 28, 1998.
4. Lavina Melwani, "Interpreting Exile," *The Hindustan Times*, April 23, 2001, p.1.
5. *Ibid.*
6. *Ibid.*

Interpreter of Maladies: A Critical Study

A.K. MUKHERJEE

Jhumpa Lahiri's *Interpreter of Maladies*, a collection of nine stories, a maiden venture, has bagged Pulitzer prize for fiction 2000. It is a great honour for an Indian writer writing in English. This is another milestone after Arundhati Roy's *The God of Small Things*. Indian fiction in English from Raja Rao to Jhumpa Lahiri is a long road—arduous, but exciting and exhilarating. Its expansion is both vertical and horizontal. The present paper makes an attempt to study the nine stories of Jhumpa Lahiri, both in its content and form.

Jhumpa Lahiri is different from other Indian writers writing in English. Most of the Indian fiction writers writing in English are born and brought up in India, although the writers like Anita Desai, Kamala Markandaya, Jhabvala, Vikram Seth, Salman Rushdie are living either in England or America. Lahiri was born in London, of Bengtali parents, grew up in Rhode Island, U.S.A. Naturally, her connection with India may be through her parents and grandparents. So her knowledge of India is bound to be confined to the stories from her grandparents, parents, books and newspapers. India would appear to be sometimes full of wonders, sometimes full of beggars. But the writers who live outside India and confidently write or comment on the economic, social, political and religious scenario may appear very often exaggerated or under-rated. They are liable to lack honesty and authenticity, which a writer should possess. From this standpoint, Jhumpa Lahiri is honest and authentic to her experiences. She writes about the Indians who have settled either in the U.S.A. or England and does not comment on something that she is not well-versed in. The Indians who have settled abroad feel themselves exiled as they are in their consciousness unable to cut off completely their umbilical cords that still bind them in their existential crisis.

Interpreter of Maladies is called "Stories of Bengal, Boston and Beyond." The first story of the book, "A Temporary Matter," relates to the life of Shukumar and Shoba in Boston. The temporary matter is that their electricity would be cut off for an hour for five days. The story is confined to those five days when there will be no electricity for an hour. During those five days, Shukumar and Shoba come closer after the day's busy schedules; in the darkness they play games like telling each one a story from his or her own life. Shukumar welcomed this power cut for an hour as darkness could bring them closer despite differences in their relationship. In the darkness, they could speak their minds to each other. The past, however bitter it might be, looks romantic and beautiful when viewed through the window of the present. But in the morning of the fifth night, the electric company announced that there would be no power cut on that evening as the line had been repaired ahead of its scheduled time. It disappointed Shukumar. But he kept the room dark from eight p.m. and waited for the game. After their dinner, Shoba switched on the light and announced. "I've been looking for an apartment and I've found one." (21) They had enough of enough. Now she needed some time alone. It shocked Shukumar. He thought of telling her the secret he had kept from her. The secret was that she had given birth to a dead male child which he had kept from her as it might have shocked her then. He had promised himself that day that he would never tell Shoba "because he still loved her then." (22) He told her the secret, "our baby was a boy. . . . His skin was more red than brown. He had black hair on his head. He weighed almost five pounds. His fingers were curled shut, just like yours in the night." (22) Shoba, non-plussed, turned the lights off. She came back to the table and sat down, and after a moment Shukumar joined her. The story ends with the words: "they wept together, for the things they now knew." (22)

The story reflects the alienation and loneliness that the emigrants face in a foreign land. The marriage bond, which is still considered sacrosanct m India, is gradually slithering down under the pressure of new needs under a different background. Nevertheless, one needs another's touch in an emotional crisis. That is why Shoba and Shukumar, failing to find any foothold of security, weep.

"When Mr. Pirzada Came to Dine" is the story of Mr. Pirzada, a professor from Bangladesh, doing research in America. He was a regular visitor to an Indian family in Boston. He was worried about the safety of his family in Bangladesh during 1971 war. He had left his wife and seven daughters without anybody to look after them in case of an eventuality. They were left to defend themselves. Naturally Mr. Pirzada looked worried and restless. Every day Lilia, the young daughter of the family, heard her father and Mr. Pirzada talking, discussing progress of the world that they watched on the T.V. Lilia was too young to understand the tension of the grown-ups, especially of Mr. Pirzada. Even she noticed her mother joining them. Lilia was left alone to observe: "most of all I remember the three of them operating during that time as if they were a single person, sharing a single man, a single body, a single silence and a single fear." (41) The story ends with Mr. Pirzada's returning to Bangladesh (Dacca), living in a free country with his wife and seven daughters. But Lilia missed him a lot: "Though I had not seen him for months, it was only then that I felt Mr. Pirzada's absence. It was only then, raising my water glass in his name, that I knew what it meant to miss someone who was so many miles and hours away, just as he had missed his wife." (42)

The title of the story has got romantic undertones although there is nothing romantic in the story. But it is difficult to understand the mind of Lilia who had very little connection with Mr. Pirzada, and Lilia was like one of his daughters left in Bangladesh. One is reminded of Ratan and Mini in Tagore's "The Postmaster" and "The Kabuliwalla." Lilia, although born and brought up in Boston, is unable to get rid of the sentiments which Forster would call, absolutely Indian.

The title story "Interpreter of Maladies" is the story of an emigrant Indian family coming to India, especially to Orissa as tourists. Mr. and Mrs. Das with their three children, Tina, Ronny and Bobby, come to Orissa and visit Puri, Konark and Khandagiri-Udayagiri. Every year they visit their parents who are now living in Asansol. But the interpreter is the tourist guide cum car driver Mr. Kapasi and the story is more concerned about him than the tourists. Mr. Kapasi is an educated man who knows a little bit of French and other foreign languages. From his very young days, he used to act as an interpreter to the foreign tourists and this time he was with an emigrant Indian family from Boston. Mrs. Das came closer to Mr. Kapasi and she appreciated his work as an interpreter which his own wife looked down upon. This brought Mr. Kapasi closer to Mrs. Das and he compared her with his wife. At Konark, they moved together and engaged themselves in seeing erotic sculptures while Mr. Das was busy with the children in taking snaps. At Khandagiri, Mr. Das and the children went to the top of the mountain but Mrs. Das remained in the car. She felt tired. She came to the front seat and sat beside Mr. Kapasi. She told him the secret that Bobby was not Raj's son. She told him her relationship with her husband before and after marriage which very often left her lonely. The third child, Bobby, was not from an English man or an American but from an Indian, a Punjabi friend of Raj who came to stay with them for a week. She told him all this because she wanted an answer, a remedy for her malady. She said, "I was hoping you would help me feel better, says right thing. Suggest some kind of remedy." (65) Mr. Kapasi did not have any remedy with him for her. The only remedy that came to his mind was that she should be honest and tell the secret to Mr. Das. That also he did not suggest. He only asked her, "Is it really pain you feel, Mrs. Das, or is it guilt?" (66) She only looked at him but did not say anything. She opened the car door and went to meet her family. She wanted a readymade answer, a cure for her malady. But the malady is deep rooted and Mr. Kapasi, the interpreter, is no doctor to cure her of the malady. Most of the emigrant Indians suffer from different types of maladies and as Indians they are unable to get rid of their Indian consciousness that they should be honest and true to their married life. The concept of chastity (without understanding) haunts them like a ghost at noon. At the same time they cannot be completely westernized in their thoughts and feelings. This dichotomy is the predicament of the Indians settled abroad.

"A Real Durwan" is the story of Boori Ma, a watch woman, who is ultimately thrown out of the flat because of a theft. The people forget her honesty, her truthfulness. Her only fault was her garrulousness and she always boasted of her rich past and rich parents. The story is set in Bengal and it reminds us of a poem by Tagore "Puratan Bhrutuyu" (The old servant) although Boori Ma was not an idiot.

"Sexy" is the story based on an extra-marital relationship that Laxmi finds nauseating and absurd; Miranda gets herself involved with Dev in London. Emigrant Indians living abroad raise their eyebrows at this but cannot escape from it. The story reaches its climax when the son of Laxmi's cousin, who remains for some time with Miranda, asks her to wear the silver cocktail dress that Miranda had once put on while going with Dev to a restaurant. She had to put on the dress, as Rohin was adamant. When she came out in that dress he told her: "you are sexy." (107) She was taken aback. Dev had used the same word. She asked Rohin what he meant by the word sexy. Rohin reluctantly answered, "It means loving someone you don't know." (107) Rohin further said, "That's what my father did. . . . He sat next to someone he didn't know, someone sexy, and now he loves her instead of my mother." (108) This experience with the boy brought an end to her affair with Dev who was married. Perhaps Miranda came to realise that despite her smartness and beauty, she would not be the real cup of tea for Dev. Love does not mean to be sexy. It rather means being in each other's thoughts. Indians living abroad try to be smarter than the natives although they forget that in basic emotion there is hardly any difference between the East and the West. Even Lawrence never encouraged extramarital relationship in his novels. Sometimes emigrants, especially Indians. behave like upstarts. Although Jhumpa Lahiri is rarely explicit in her opinions or comment, nevertheless, there is always an undertone of irony in her statics.

"Mrs. Sen" is the story of another emigrant in America whose husband is a professor of mathematics in a university. The family is keenly observed by an American boy of eleven years named Eliot who is looked after by Mrs. Sen while his mother goes to work. Mrs. Sen's job is the job of a baby-sitter who has nothing to do at home except buying fish and cooking. Although the boy likes Mrs. Sen, he knows his mother is very critical of Mrs. Sen. She wants Mrs. Sen to go to her house but Mrs. Sen does not know driving. She is learning driving. Eliot observes Mrs. Sen working at home. He is surprised to see the long, big, blade with which Mrs. Sen cuts vegetables and fish and she does not use knife which his mother always uses. She tells Eliot about the Indian marriage where women from neighbouring homes gather to cut vegetables the whole night amidst noise and merrymaking. The American child is gradually exposed to the life of an Indian woman in her kitchen. Eliot feels the warmth in her voice and in her gait that he finds lacking in his mother. What he finds in Mrs. Sen, he does not find in his mother. Every evening after six, he is carried away by his mother in the car. He is appalled by the coldness of his mother to the warm hospitality of Mrs. Sen. The story comes to a climax when Mrs. Sen dashes her car against a telephone pole. Eliot is with her although no one is badly hurt. When Eliot's mother hears this, she stops Eliot from coming to Mrs. Sen anymore. But the poignant part of the story is the intimacy that develops between Mrs. Sen and Eliot. Mrs. Sen has no friends in America. Her husband has no time for her. She tells Eliot how she feels lonely, how her golden dreams of living in a foreign land with her husband vanish like rain in summer. Eliot's mother, an American lady has no time at her disposal to realise the delicate emotion that develops between an American child and an Indian woman who takes time to adapt herself to a foreign country.

"The Blessed House" is the story of Sanjeev and Twinkle; their new house at Connecticut where Sanjeev worked; Twinkle completing her master's thesis at Stanford, a study of an Irish poet whom Sanjeev had never heard of. Sanjeev selected Twinkle and did not agree to marry anybody selected by her parents in

Calcutta. Both were emigrants, although Sanjeev had his parents in India and Twinkle in California. Twinkle's Indian connection was her name that sounded unusual to the ears of Douglas and Nan who came to the new house on the house-warming day. The new house was a blessed one as Twinkle found a statue of Christ and Mother Mary. The switch plates in the bedrooms were decorated with scenes from the Bible. Twinkle as a student of literature wanted to treasure those whereas Sanjeev hated and disapproved of Twinkle's idea. This made him, almost, hate Twinkle as Sanjeev, an executive in a firm, has no time to be bothered by such sentiments. To Twinkle, the house was a blessed house, to Sanjeev, it was a cursed one. Sanjeev felt that the interest for antic monuments in his wife was a temporary matter, just a device to come to the limelight as an Indian woman among the Americans. So the poor husband had nothing to do but "preserve the massive silver face to his ribs, careful not to let the feather hat slip, and followed her." (157)

"The Treatment of Bibi Haldar" is a poignant story that tells us the plight of Bibi Haldar who suffered from a baffling disease which made her family members exasperated, and ultimately she was left alone to suffer. The story is of Bengal. Bibi Haldar was staying with her relations in a flat in Calcutta. She was given a storage room on the roof, "a space in which one could sit but not comfortably stand, featuring an adjoining latrine, curtained entrance, one window without a grille, and shelves made from the panels of the old doors." (159) She recorded inventory for the cosmetics shop that her cousin Haldar owned and managed at the mouth of the courtyard. For her work she was given food, shelter and "sufficient metres of cotton at every October holiday to replenish her wardrobe and act as an inexpensive tailor." (159) Her only obsession in life was to get a husband. Every day she expected a man to come and offer his hand to her, It never materialized. She loved to hear from other women the details of their marriage. She would sigh after seeing their marriage albums. After devouring the details from other women, she would say, "when it happens to me, you will all be present." (160) After futile waiting, she would say, "My face will never be painted with sandalwood paste, who will rub me with turmeric? My name will never be printed with scarlet ink on a card." (160-61) But Mr. and Mrs. Haldar never cared to give any thought to this although Mr. Haldar gave an advertisement after being pestered by the inmates of the flat. Mrs. Haldar, who was in family way, feared Bibi as an evil omen and wanted to get rid of her shadow lest it brought harm to her child. She gave birth to a female child. She froze with fear when her daughter suffered for five days. At last Mr. Haldar winded up his cosmetic shop and left the place with his wife and the daughter. Bibi was left alone with Rs. 300 that Mr. Haldar left with her. But the story takes a turn when the inmates find, after Mr. and Mrs. Haldar's departure, that Bibi Haldar was pregnant. The search for the real culprit ended in futility. She delivered a male child and took care of the child. The story ends with these words, "she was, to the best of her knowledge, cured." (172)

"The Third and Final Continent" is the last story in the collection that moves from London to Boston and gives to the readers a different taste. Although the same emigrant themes—the initial hurdles to settle, to adjust and after sometimes trying to be more native than the natives—the story tells us the strange encounter of a Bengali commerce graduate who moves from Calcutta to London and then to Boston with an old woman of 100 years, Mrs. Croft, in whose house he lodges as a tenant. The old American lady was proud of her own country when America landed on the moon. To her the achievement was "splendid" and she wanted the Bengali gentleman to say the word clearly. She was alone and her daughter Helen made weekend visit to her with provisions for the week. The old lady was very particular about the rent which was to be paid on Friday. She let out her rooms only to bachelors from Harvard or Tech. She belonged to old America who reacted to the long chats by his daughter and the narrator. She did not approve of a woman talking to a bachelor for a long time. It must have sounded unbelievable to Indian ears who come to America with all ideas of an advanced society where, they think, permissiveness is the rule. But Mrs. Croft belongs to the values of old America. The narrator left her home and moved to a new apartment when Mala, his wife, came to him from India. The old lady is dead; the narrator's son goes to college and the child born in America of Indian origin looks askance at the sentimentality of his father. He is born in America to establish an identity of his own; to live as a naturalised citizen of America—an emigrant, although the umbilical cord is still rooted in India and it is difficult to sever it altogether. The story ends with the rumination of the father: "whenever he is discouraged, I tell him that if I can survive on three continents, then there is no obstacle he cannot conquer. While the astronauts, heroes forever, spent mere hours on the moon, I have remained in this new world for nearly thirty years. I know that my achievement is quite ordinary. I am not the only man to seek his fortune far from home, and certainly I am not the last. Still, there are times I am bewildered by each mile I have traveled, each meal I have eaten, each person I have known, each room in which I have slept. As ordinary as it all appears, there are times when it is beyond my imagination." (197-98)

This is the fear and anxiety that remains with an emigrant despite his best efforts to beat the natives in dress, gestures and postures. All the time, there is a feeling of being alienated. It is primarily because he can neither cut off the sweet silken bond that ties him to the land of his origin or his parents. Jhumpa Lahiri is undoubtedly the first emigrant writer who is concerned with their maladies and tries to be an interpreter. Of course, she is quite different from Mr. Kapasi. She probes deep into the maladies but prescribes no cure. She is an artist and the artist's another name is an interpreter. The stories reveal the skill Jhumpa Lahiri has achieved in her maiden venture. There is no chronological or sequential development of stories. She has evolved her own style by changing the mode of narration from past to the present and again reversing it without being nostalgic. Her style is almost cinematic and with the help of montage one gets a glimpse into the meaning of the story. One reading is not enough to understand any of her stories.

Contributors

SHYAM S. AGARWALLA, Dr. R.M. L. College, Ranchi
SUMAN BALA, S.B.S. College, University of Delhi
SATISH BARBUDDHE, B.S.P. College, Paratwada
BRATI BISWAS, Dyal Singh (E) College, University of Delhi
NILA DAS, Kalyani University, West Bengal
SUDHIR DIXIT, Govt. Narmada College, Hoshangabad
RASHMI GAUR, I.I.T., Roorkee
PARMANAND JHA, C.M. College, Darbhanga
PASHUPATI JHA, I.I.T., Roorkee
MADHOO KAMARA, Durga Mahavidyalaya, Raipur
PUSHP LATA, B.I.T.S, Pilani
RUDRA PRASAD MAHTO, B.N.J. College, Sisai
KEYA MAJUMDAR, Women's College, Ranchi
SOMDATTA MANDAL, Vivekanand College, Calcutta
O.P. MATHUR, B.H.U., Varanasi
JYOTI MISHRA, Raipur, Chhatisgarj
ALESSANDRO MONTI, University of Turin, Torino
A.K. MUKHERJEE, Government College, Bhawanipatna
ARUNODAY MUKHERJEE, Ranaghat College, Ranaghat
BHAGABAT NAYAK, Kandarpur College, Kandarpur
INDIRA NITYANANDAM, Navgujarat College, Ahmedabad
SAVITA A. PATIL, K.R.M. Mahila Mahavidyalaya, Nanded
SUNEETA PATNAYAK, D.A.V. College, Chandigarh
KISHAN H. PAWAR, Yeshwant College, Nanded
T. RAVICHANDRAN, I.I.T., Roorkee
V. SAM SAHAYAM, M.S. University, Tirunelveli
JAYDEEP SARANGI, Seva-Bharati Mahavidyalaya, Midnapur
G. DOMINIC SAVIO, American College, Madurai
SUSHILA SINGH, B.H.U., Varanasi